RIGHTS AT WORK

A TWENTIETH CENTURY FUND BOOK

RIGHTS AT WORK

Employment Relations in the Post-Union Era

Richard Edwards

THE BROOKINGS INSTITUTION
Washington, D.C.

About Brookings

The Brookings Institution is a private nonprofit organization devoted to research, education, and publication on important issues of domestic and foreign policy. Its principal purpose is to bring knowledge to bear on current and emerging policy problems. The Institution was founded on December 8, 1927, to merge the activities of the Institute for Government Research, founded in 1916, the Institute of Economics, founded in 1922, and the Robert Brookings Graduate School of Economics, founded in 1924.

The Institution maintains a position of neutrality on issues of public policy. Interpretations or conclusions in Brookings publications should be understood to be solely those of the authors.

410 East 70th Street, New York, N.Y. 10021

Library of Congress Cataloging-in-Publication data

Edwards, Richard.
Rights at work: employment relations in the post-union era
Richard Edwards.
p. cm.
"A Twentieth Century Fund book."
Includes bibliographical references and index.
ISBN 0-8157-2104-8 (alk. paper)
1. Employee rights—United States. I. Title.
HD6971.8.E38 1993
331.01'1'0973—dc20 92-43228
CIP

9 8 7 6 5 4 3 2 1

The paper used in this publication meets the minimum requirements of the American National Standard for Information Sciences—Permanence of paper for Printed Library Materials, ANSI Z39.48-1984

The Twentieth Century Fund is a research foundation undertaking timely analyses of economic, political, and social issues. Not-for-profit and nonpartisan, the Fund was founded in 1919 and endowed by Edward A. Filene.

Foreword

We are in the midst of the greatest alteration in the world of work since industrialization and agricultural mechanization combined to displace the vast majority of farm workers in Western countries. Over the last generation in the United States, the steady decline in percentage of the work force employed in manufacturing and the dramatic increase in competition from overseas have battered employees in one industry after another. No wonder the world of work seems to be changing in an almost bewildering fashion. Intensified by a shaky global economy and technological advances, this evolution in the workplace has heightened the sense of careers at risk and uncertain economic futures.

The way that work is done has changed as a result, raising substantial questions about the relative leverage of labor and thus about the rights of workers versus those of employers. Not surprisingly, these differences have resulted in significant shifts in the way that workers think about their employers and the way employers think about employees.

For past generations, the usual roads to success were hard work, learning a skill and joining a union, or getting a college education. Today, almost a quarter of recent college graduates are accepting jobs that do not require a college education, unions are continuing to lose jobs and members, and middle management is in jeopardy—downsized, rightsized, out of work. New methods of manufacturing, especially the "robotic factory," new concepts such as teamwork and empowerment, and new discoveries about health and environmental risks argue for yet more change. What does the future hold for American workers, particularly those coming into the marketplace and facing the fact that they are the first generation that will probably not do better than their parents did?

The answer to that question is extraordinarily difficult in an era of rapid change, but at a minimim, for the American worker, it involves a mix of legal and public decisionmaking centering on the interpretation of workers' rights. Richard Edwards, dean of the College of Arts and Sciences at the University of Kentucky, examines workplace rights in terms of issues such as recent legal interpretations of rights, legislative initiatives that have expanded rights in a number of areas, and the questions surrounding the noneconomic rights granted by American nonunion companies to their employees and the ambiguities of enforcing such rights.

Edwards's goal is to try to put in perspective the conflict between workers' perceptions that their protections have been declining and employers' beliefs that they have been subject to increasingly stringent restrictions, obligations, and interventions on behalf of employees. The issue is critical because it is unclear where the institutional responsibilities for dealing with these matters lie and whether and to what level we can, as a society, offer protection and remain competitive in a world where the workplace is increasingly international.

This is not the Twentieth Century Fund's first foray into issues affecting America's workers. A few years ago, the Fund sponsored Charles Heckscher's examination of associational unionism in *The New Unionism*, and we have examined issues such as disability, social security, pensions, insurance, and workplace health and safety regulations. We thank Richard Edwards for the light he has shed on this complex and difficult set of issues.

Richard C. Leone, *President*
THE TWENTIETH CENTURY FUND
March 1993

Author's Preface

The question of employees' rights has been an extremely contentious and politically volatile one. Liberals have generally tried to broaden government-guaranteed rights and enhance their enforcement, while conservatives have sought to limit their scope and reduce governmental regulation, preferring to rely on market mechanisms instead. In this book I challenge whether either of these traditional approaches is adequate; more important, I argue that we can find new and more fertile common ground on which to shape future employment relations.

In the past, worker protections have waxed and waned depending upon the balance of power in Washington. During the 1960s, much worker-protection legislation was written into law. During the following quarter-century, with the ambiguous exception of the late 1970s, conservatives were ascendant and federal support of worker protections declined. (Multiple ironies exist here: many worker protections increased during the conservative ascendancy, although they were mostly at the state level; and decreasing federal attention to enforcement may have had little real consequence at the level of the shop floor.)

With the Democrats' victory in 1992, the balance shifted again, and undoubtedly many saw this change as an opportunity for realizing a liberal agenda long delayed. But, as I argue in this book, our present (and likely future) circumstances demand a break with the now outmoded tug-of-war between traditional approaches. The election of President Clinton opened new possibilities for developing a system of workplace relations that can simultaneously ensure the basic rights of workers while fostering international competitiveness. Achieving this "win-win" outcome would contribute greatly to the prospects for sustained economic growth, the creation of high-quality jobs, and the promotion of fairness and dignity for workers.

This book was written as a search for new common ground between employers and their workers on which to shape the future of employment relations, and of workers' rights in particular. If such common ground is to be gained, the federal government must play a central role in moving us toward it; but policymakers must be able to articulate a clear vision of where we are going, or their efforts will simply be interpreted (and supported or opposed) within the rather tired polarities of traditional liberal-versus-conservative discourse. Important new opportunities beckon, and they are too valuable to be lost in outdated controversies.

In writing this book, I was aided by many who made generous and excellent contributions for which I am extremely grateful. The Twentieth Century Fund provided support—both financial and moral—without which this particular book would not have been undertaken nor completed; Nina Massen, John Samples, and Beverly Goldberg were particularly helpful. Nancy Davidson and James R. Schneider at the Brookings Institution and Vincent Ercolano greatly improved the book by providing helpful reviews, insightful criticism, and intelligent editing.

My colleagues at the University of Massachusetts, especially Herbert Gintis, Samuel Bowles, and Michael Podgursky, have offered continuing help by pointing me to literature I had overlooked, exposing weak arguments, and forcing me to confront alternative viewpoints. I was also greatly helped by those who, although formally research assistants, were in fact colleagues and members of the research team: June Lapidus, Lisa Kessler, Kevin Crocker, and Marlies Schoeneberger. I extend my sincere thanks to them. My greatest single debt is to Denny Kalyalya, who simply performed brilliantly in so many ways to help bring this book to completion. Despite all the help, I remain, of course, solely responsible for the argument of the book and for any flaws or deficiencies in it.

Contents

1

Workplace Rights and Wrongs

Events are forcing Americans to think in new ways about the workplace rights of employees. The old ways of establishing and enforcing workers' rights are increasingly ineffective, costly, and even counterproductive. Powerful new forces, especially increasingly intense international competition, the decline of unions, and fundamental changes in labor law, are already reshaping workplace governance in dramatic and surprising ways. Yet out of this evolution may come haphazard new arrangements that serve the interests of neither workers nor employers; nor are the new arrangements likely to further the public interest.

This issue is hardly new. American society has never come to agreement upon the rights its workers should possess in the workplace, and so frequently we revisit the political contention over which rights workers carry with them into their jobs, which ones they lose at the factory (or office or store) gate, and which new rights they acquire at work. These questions continue to bedevil our thinking about work and workers.

Contention over the rules of workplace governance forms but part of the national preoccupation with rights generally. Americans are justly proud of their political and constitutional rights, and perhaps no other feature of our society so defines and unifies us as a people. The right of free speech, for example, is defended by conservatives and liberals alike, the far right and socialists, antiabortionists and pro-choice advocates, fundamentalist Christians and atheists. Indeed, the few who do not accept the canon of free speech—white supremacists, anticommunist fanatics, revolutionary communist groups—stand at the true outer fringes of American society. A similar broad consensus attaches to most of the other great rights enshrined in American tradition.

Public devotion to these rights does not preclude fierce battles over which rights take precedence when they conflict with each other, nor does it prevent disputes over how far these rights extend, or how to apply established rights in new situations. Indeed, because the idea of rights is so widely accepted, claims that can be convincingly stated in terms of rights attain an enhanced legitimacy; and so the language of rights provides the rhetorical context in which most of America's social conflicts are fought.

It is no surprise, then, that many Americans carry a concept of rights with them into the workplace. Because we spend so much time at work and depend upon the income our jobs generate, we are quickly and powerfully affected by the workplace's rules. Because work also serves deeper needs, shaping our identities and satisfying our strivings for status, achievement, and belonging, concepts such as just cause and due process—or more simply put, having rights—seem to most people as applicable to the workplace as elsewhere in society.

In the American panoply of rights, workplace rights are the least defined, the least understood, and the least sanctified by social consensus. It has been difficult to design a system of employee rights that adequately protects individual workers and yet respects the property rights of owners and preserves those managerial prerogatives needed to operate a modern enterprise in a dynamic and competitive economy. As a result, workplace rights constitute a terrain long contested by employers, workers, propagandists, judges, social theorists, politicians, and diverse reformers and reactionaries.

Yet the present contention is not simply a skirmish along the borders of a well-established and accepted system of workers' rights; rather, fundamental issues are at stake. In the demise of the old ways there is not a superior new system inevitably ready to emerge. It is possible that employers will continue to suffer the rigidities and inefficiencies of the traditional system *and* workers will be denied the effective protection that was its chief rationale. To achieve something better, both the business community and the advocates of workers' rights will need to think clearly and without illusions about what is desired and possible. Indeed, much of this book is devoted to clearing our mental landscape of ideological rigidities, outmoded historical attachments, and other chimera that limit vision and prevent real progress.

What is meant by workers' rights, and why are they the focus of contention? I define workers' rights more formally in chapter 2, but consider three recent cases. The first concerns a number of women who worked at American Cyanamid Company's Willow Island, West Virginia, plant. In what became a notorious case, they were forced to choose between losing their jobs and undergoing surgical sterilization.[1]

Willow Island, a paint plant, used what American Cyanamid described as "hundreds" of chemicals that were potentially dangerous to humans; a particular hazard was the high level of ambient lead, known to be harmful to fetuses. American Cyanamid became concerned about the possible problems that might ensue, including, one might surmise, the company's legal liability. In 1978 the company decided to exclude women of "childbearing capacity" from all areas of the plant where such chemicals were used, leaving only a couple of departments open to women presumed to be fertile. Approximately thirty women were employed at the plant, and at the time the new policy was announced, management indicated that only about seven job categories would remain accessible to women of childbearing capacity; women presumed to be fertile and not assigned to those seven categories would be dismissed.

The plant's director of industrial relations, Glen Mercer, held a series of meetings in the plant to inform female employees of the new policy. He announced that the company would consider any woman under the age of fifty to be of childbearing capacity unless she provided proof that she had been surgically sterilized. American Cyanamid refused to exempt workers using contraceptive methods, even insisting that one whose husband had undergone a vasectomy be sterilized if she wished to keep her job. Mercer was accompanied at these meetings by a company doctor and nurse, who explained to the women that the "buttonhole surgery" for sterilization was simple and could be obtained locally. The company's medical insurance would pay for the procedure.

American Cyanamid's female employees faced their painful choice because when the company decided to take its action, they were protected by neither contract language nor statute. The dilemma they faced had simply not been foreseen in either. The Oil, Chemical, and Atomic Workers Union (OCAW), which represented the Willow Island workers, sought to pursue relief for the women under the federal Occupational Safety and Health Act of 1970. The OSH act contains a "general duty clause" requiring each employer to provide to each of his employees employment and a place of employment which are "free from recognized hazards . . . that are causing or likely to cause death or serious physical harm."[2] The OCAW argued that sterilization constitutes "serious physical harm," and that American Cyanamid's policy thus violated the OSH act's general-duty clause.

The OCAW's case against American Cyanamid worked its way through various federal agencies and eventually reached the courts. The workers and their advocates initially prevailed, getting support for their contention from the Labor Department: after a 1979 safety inspection, the Occupational Safety and Health Administration (OSHA) issued a citation and imposed a penalty of $10,000. American Cyanamid successfully appealed, and the case worked its way up through the administrative law courts and the OSHA Review Commission before arriving at the U.S. Court of Appeals for the District of Columbia.

The court of appeals found two points to be significant in undermining the OCAW's case. The first was that Congress in passing the OSH act and the Supreme Court in subsequent interpretation intended "hazard" to mean "physical hazards"; an employment policy (in this case, one requiring proof of reproductive sterility for certain jobs) was not a physical hazard, and therefore the women's situation was not reachable under the OSH act.

The second significant point for the appeals court was that American Cyanamid was not forcing the women to undergo sterilization; rather, it was offering them a choice. The court pointed out that it would have been entirely legal for the company to have closed the department and fired all the employees or to have excluded all women of childbearing age. The court approvingly quoted the OSHA Review Commission's finding that "an employee's decision to undergo sterilization in order to gain or retain employment grows out of economic and social factors which operate primarily outside the workplace. The employer neither controls nor creates these factors."[3] That it gave women the choice of sterilization should not result in the company's being found in violation of the OSH Act. With judges Robert Bork and Antonin Scalia leading the way, the court of appeals in 1984 denied the OCAW's petition for relief.

Because they came years later, these legal maneuverings were but an aftereffect; the lack of rights had already done its damage. By the time American Cyanamid's policy was actually implemented, it applied only to the seven women in the Inorganic Pigments Department. Five chose sterilization; two refused, and were later transferred to lower-paying jobs. One of those sterilized, Lola R., noted, "Mr. Mercer made it perfectly clear that my choice was between sterilization and termination. . . . I would never have considered such sterilization procedure had my job not been on the line." Another, Barbara C., said, "I was afraid of losing my job, pure and simple. I have two children to support."[4] The workers felt they had received little protection from the relevant laws or contracts. Neither did their sacrifice seem successful: in 1980, Cyanamid permanently closed the Inorganic Pigments Department "for economic reasons." The women did win $200,000 in compensation from other lawsuits, based on federal civil-rights statutes.[5]

The issue raised in the American Cyanamid dispute did not go away. In 1991, for example, the U.S. Supreme Court upheld a California court ruling in a similar case involving "fetal protection policies" at a battery plant operated by Johnson Controls, Inc. The California court ruled that such policies resulted in sex discrimination and that women cannot be banned from jobs that potentially involve harm to a fetus. The Supreme Court upheld, but three justices did suggest that a more narrowly tailored version of the Johnson policy would be legal. Questions have since been raised about fetal protection policies at AT&T, Texas Instruments, and elsewhere.[6]

If some workers perceive their rights as being too limited, some employers complain that current job rights can be highly burdensome and too costly, interfering with or blocking their own efforts to become more competitive. Consider the case of Mack Trucks, a large producer of commercial and heavy industrial vehicles. During the 1980s Mack waged a bitter campaign, which sometimes included apparently illegal tactics, to escape such burdens.

Mack has traditionally concentrated its manufacturing facilities in or near Pennsylvania's Lehigh Valley.[7] Company headquarters are in Allentown. Various parts and assembly plants are scattered nearby, in Allentown, Macungie, and Somerset, Pennsylvania; and Hagerstown, Maryland. Mack's employees are represented by the United Auto Workers (UAW).

Under the intense competitive pressures of the early 1980s, pressures that had brought enormous difficulties to other heavy-equipment manufacturers such as Caterpillar, International Harvester (Navistar), and John Deere, Mack Trucks decided to make a dramatic break with its Lehigh Valley traditions. It had already tried "outsourcing"—buying an increasing proportion of its truck components from external, typically nonunion suppliers—and reducing and rearranging work inside. Now it wanted to take a bigger step.

Mack resolved to open a whole new plant, to be operated along the newly fashionable "Japanese" lines, with a new work force. This plant would replace assembly Plant 5-C in Allentown, which would be shut down. In the new plant trucks would be built by work teams, paralleling an experiment at Volvo, rather than on the traditional assembly line. The teams would be composed of equally rated (and paid) "process technicians," eliminating myriad in-plant job definitions and distinctions among workers. Members of lower-level management, as with the Japanese model, would have their offices near the assembly areas. Even upper-level management would work in a large room divided into cubicles. The plant management would be trained to emphasize the open-door approach to problem solving, and managers and workers would share the single cafeteria. And, Mack hoped, the plant would be nonunion.

In short, Mack was going to start over. It would construct and operate what the smart management literature was increasingly urging as the answer to foreign competition. For Mack executives, a crucial part of this new strategy was having "everyone in the plant work together as a team."[8] The only problem with Mack's plans was that the truck manufacturer's contracts with the UAW greatly limited what it could do.

Mack's UAW contract included both a "master" agreement covering all plants and various local or plant-specific contracts. The master contract that ran from 1984 to 1987, in a supplementary document refered to as Letter #15, required the company "not to close any plant or office to which the Mack-UAW Master Agreement applies."[9] Before that contract expired, the company and the union had negotiated a new master contract to run from May 1987 to November 1992. Both contracts contained provisions requiring the company to notify the union if it planned to build new or replacement plants, and the union believed the contract required some process of consultation in planning the new facilities. The contracts also contained tough language granting current Mack workers substantial seniority rights, including rights to job security and preferential recall. Clearly, the contracts conflicted with Mack's hopes for a new, nonunion work force for its new facility.

The first issue for Mack to decide was where to locate the new plant. The company informed the union in October 1985 that it intended to construct a new assembly facility, but indicated that it had not yet chosen a location. In January 1986, Mack announced that it had chosen the small town of Winnsboro in the "right-to-work" state of South Carolina. Although the company declared that it had carefully studied locations in the Lehigh Valley and found them unfeasible, it appears more likely that company executives were determined from the outset to move out of Pennsylvania and, they hoped, out of the UAW's reach.

Mack's announcement shocked the Lehigh Valley, and the company became embroiled in a major public-relations and legal battle once the news spread. Because the Winnsboro plant would replace Plant 5-C, local Lehigh Valley groups, the UAW, workers' families, and others vigorously protested the decision. The dispute drew widespread media attention. Communications from Mack headquarters, perhaps on orders from the company's lawyers and public relations experts, took on an increasingly guarded tone.

The next couple of years saw continuing warfare between the company and the UAW, as Mack tried to make its leap into Japanese-style management successful. Despite what would appear to be (and what arbitrators and judges later agreed was) relatively clear and unambiguous contract language granting incumbent Mack workers priority to the Winnsboro jobs, the company fought desperately to prevent this outcome. It began by denying that the Winnsboro jobs were covered by the master contract, declaring that Winnsboro was a new plant outside UAW jurisdiction. The company also tried to fill the Winnsboro jobs before the Allentown plant closed; if Winnsboro were later declared to be governed by the master contract, and if the UAW insisted on defending the Allentown workers' transfer rights, at least the company would have maneuvered the union into forcing the layoff of Winnsboro residents. With that as its opening move, the union would not find it easy to gain much support in Winnsboro.

The UAW pressed its grievance, and in June 1987 an arbitrator declared that current Mack workers did indeed have rights to the Winnsboro jobs. However, the arbitrator denied the union's request that Winnsboro be added to the Mack-UAW master contract, which in effect would have certified the union as bargaining agent for the yet-unhired Winnsboro workers. But on the main point the union won. The arbitrator directed the company and union to "meet promptly . . . to determine the number of employees to be transferred, the method of canvassing, and the like."[10]

Despite this setback, Mack worked hard to prevent the Lehigh workers from filling the Winnsboro jobs. The company had a clear obligation to offer jobs to current workers first, but Mack pushed ahead to enroll 280 "outside" (new) workers from Winnsboro in a training program and announced that "those who successfully complete the program will be offered employment." The company insisted, despite the arbitrator's finding to the contrary, that it would unilaterally determine the rules, conditions, time limits, and the method of canvassing current workers concerning possible transfer to Winnsboro. It challenged the eligibility of some workers to transfer rights, and attempted to discourage current workers from applying for transfer. For example, it hinted that workers who transferred would lose their seniority. It attempted to dissuade those who did transfer from signing union cards: "We hope that we can convince you of what millions of employees at other major manufacturers have already discovered; that unions are part of the past, not the future."[11]

Mack executives found themselves increasingly embroiled in litigation. Federal district judge Edward Cahn returned the case for a "determination of the manner, procedures, and time limits within which Mack will offer to its employees the first opportunity for employment at the Winnsboro facility." A new arbitrator reaffirmed the previous arbitrator's award, reiterating that the prior decision "clearly establishes the priority rights of employees in the Allentown, Macungie, Hagerstown, and Somerset plants to jobs at Winnsboro, over the hiring of 'outsiders.'" On other points, including the company canvass of current workers and the "short time limits" allowed for workers to exercise their transfer rights, the new arbitrator likewise found for the union.[12]

Despite losing in court and in arbitration, the Mack managers stuck to their strategy, pressing ahead with plans to hire a second class of outsiders, roughly 250 more workers. Winnsboro opened with a mix of old and new workers, and after two years in operation, the plant employed about 900 workers, 398 of whom were transferees from Pennsylvania. The Winnsboro plant remained without a union until 1989, when the UAW won a representation election. Thus, Mack entered the 1990s with a unionized plant in Winnsboro. In October 1990 Mack Trucks was acquired by Renault. After a rocky start, production at the new plant became increasingly cost effective, although the plant was not operating at full capacity.[13]

Why was Mack Trucks willing to engage in such a long and bitter battle, which apparently included some illegal tactics, to prevent Lehigh Valley workers from transferring to Winnsboro? Mack's actions might appear especially puzzling because the powerful UAW is well known for its advocacy of "cooperative" labor-management relationships. In general, it has been a pioneer among unions in trying out new approaches, with its Saturn and NUMMI agreements with General Motors being widely noted examples.[14]

Clearly, Mack found the conditions under which it operated in the Lehigh Valley to be burdensome and counterproductive to its efforts to become more competitive. Although the company was unwilling to state publicly its reasons for the move, the Winnsboro plant's general manager, Don Lindgren, articulated the company's position in a letter to transferees: "Given the nature of the [Winnsboro] plant, its layout and organizational structure, it is essential that everyone in the plant work together as a team. . . . Because of the confrontational attitude of the UAW toward Mack in recent years, we believe that the union would harm our ability to form the kind of team that we need to operate efficiently and effectively in

Winnsboro."[15] Mack expected to gain great benefits by escaping Lehigh and the kinds of protections that its workers traditionally had enjoyed.

A different aspect of the contention over workers' rights is evident in the dispute that Randy Morriss and Debra White had with their employer, the Coleman Company, of Wichita, Kansas.[16] Coleman, a manufacturer of camp stoves and other recreational and outing products, had employed Morriss as a production supervisor and White as an executive secretary. Morriss had received consistently favorable job evaluations and salary increases, and was promoted first to department manager and then to manufacturing engineer. White, hired in 1977 and subsequently promoted to executive secretary, was described by her supervisor as the best secretary he had ever had; she also received consistently favorable job evaluations. Yet both were peremptorily fired in November 1984.

All parties seem to agree on the facts of the dispute. Coleman allows its managers to purchase surplus company cars, and Debra White's supervisor, Ralph Call, was entitled to buy one. However, the next available car was in Greenville, South Carolina, and Call apparently did not want to make the trip. White described the situation to her friend Morriss, who indicated a willingness to retrieve the car. Morriss and Call quickly came to an agreement.

Call first told White to make an airline reservation for Morriss for the next Tuesday morning. However, Morriss had a Tuesday night class at Wichita State University, so Call and Morriss agreed that Morriss could leave on Wednesday instead. Call also agreed to Morriss's request for an extra travel day.

On Tuesday White and Morriss discussed the upcoming trip, and White decided she would like to come along. After Wednesday the plant would be shut down for inventory anyway; if she simply used a vacation day on Wednesday, as she was entitled to do, neither of them would miss any additional days of work. She and Morriss flew out of Wichita on Wednesday morning, White paying her own way. Both considered the trip a purely private affair.

Back at the office, however, suspicions arose that something was amiss. One of Call's subordinates, Robert Sloan, the plant manager for Coleman's "downtown" factory, had instructed the company's director of security to investigate, and he reported back that Morriss and White had left Wichita together. Call then launched his own investigation: he called Debra White's mother, who told him she did not know where her daughter was. With no further information, Call made his decision: when Morriss and White returned with his car to Wichita, he would fire them both.

As he himself admitted, Call was a tough man to work for, and he had very strong religious beliefs. At the time of their trip, White was unmarried and Morriss was separated from his wife. Although Sloan later indicated that, in his judgment, it would not have been grounds for dismissal if Morriss had taken his wife or a male employee without clearing it with his boss, he did not apply this standard to Morriss and White. When they returned from their trip, Call fired them, apparently because he did not think that a married man and an unmarried woman had any business traveling together to another city. Morriss and White then appealed directly to Sheldon Coleman, Jr., but since Coleman was new on the job, he refused to overrule Call.

Normally, Call's decision would have ended the matter. After all, most employees serve "at will," which means that they can be fired for "good cause or for no cause, or even for bad cause."[17] Morriss and White, according to the company, were at-will employees, and whatever the merits of their case, the company had the unfettered right to fire them. (Call later declared that he had terminated them for "dishonesty," "breach of trust," and "for increasing the company's insurance liability," but it was not clear that anyone believed him. In any event, the company never tried to argue that Morriss and White were fired for good cause, only that, because they were at-will employees, the cause did not matter.)

But Morriss and Call refused to accept the decision, and took the Coleman Company to the Sedgwick (Kansas) district court. The court, following many years of case-law precedent, simply dismissed their case—at-will employees had no right to have a dismissal reviewed. But the court of appeals, more attuned to changing legal fashions, reversed that decision. The Kansas Supreme Court, in *Morriss* v. *Coleman Company*, upheld the appeals court, enunciating in the process a whole new doctrine: "There was a legitimate issue of fact whether there was an implied contract by Coleman to treat its employees fairly and in good faith and that an employee would not be terminated except for just cause."[18] That is, Morriss and White would get their day in court, and the Coleman Company would have to prove it had not acted in bad faith. Ultimately, Coleman settled the case for $15,000; the low settlement reflected the fact that Morriss and White, being excellent employees, had quickly found other well-paying jobs, and so the damages they could collect were greatly limited. Nonetheless their case meant that Kansas, as I discuss later in this book, had joined the growing legal revolution that is rewriting most states' labor laws.

Given the increasing costs and uncertainties surrounding workers' rights, employers as well as workers now have a real stake in developing and implementing a better system. How much the current chaos of workplace rights costs American industry and ultimately the public is probably unknowable, but the amount must be substantial. A well-designed alternative system of workers' rights would also impose some costs on employers, but net gains are likely to be available to all of the participants—employers, workers, and the public. In the case of workers' rights, the zero-sum analysis—if you win, I lose—may be wrong.

The uncertainty surrounding workplace rights derives in part from a venerable but continuing and profound dispute between two conceptions of rights. Each conception exalts some social values, identifies what it sees as the most fundamental threats to those values, and argues for rights that are intended to protect against those threats. Naturally, each conception argues that the rights thus established ought to be respected as society's most fundamental rights and that they should govern in any clash with other, less basic rights.

One view, which derives from nineteenth-century liberalism, makes liberty preeminent. Its adherents see government restrictions on what individuals can do as the chief threat to liberty and argue therefore that people must have rights to protect themselves against overweening government actions or regulations. This view advances rights as a brake on state actions, and it makes predominant a commitment to property rights and freedom of contract. It would permit only the most minimal governmental guarantees to workers in their relations with employers. Workers would then be free to achieve (or have the burden of achieving) any additional rights, protections, or benefits through voluntary market contracting.[19]

The second conception, deriving from twentieth-century (or at least post–New Deal) liberalism, also values liberty, but places a second value, equality, alongside it. While agreeing that government restrictions are a potential danger to liberty, advocates of twentieth-century liberalism view the debilitating or degrading consequences that individuals may suffer in the ordinary operation of a market economy as a threat to equality. (Twentieth-century liberalism usually interprets equality in the restricted sense of eliminating the most debasing circumstances.) Rights must be established to protect individuals from the worst market-economy consequences. With respect to work, this view would constrain private employment contracts when necessary, either by injecting into the employment relationship some rights enjoyed by individuals elsewhere in civic society or by creating specific new rights required to achieve what are deemed to be minimally acceptable social outcomes. Because equality as well as liberty must be protected, a somewhat diminished defense of liberty is necessarily the price that must be paid for the increased protection of equality. Whereas nineteenth-century liberalism defends against state actions, twentieth-century liberalism also requires some state actions, creating a positive obligation for the government to intervene.[20]

Historically, workplace rights have come to be defined as some sort of combination of or compromise between the two competing liberal visions. I term this legal and social compromise a *rights regime*, meaning to include both the actual substance of rights that are commonly or customarily available to workers and the institutions and doctrines that uphold, enforce, and give logic to those rights. The particular compromises struck, although sometimes workable, were never thoroughly coherent nor, it turns out, were they capable of achieving enduring social support. The actual rights that workers could exercise have thus waxed and waned, depending on where the compromise was struck and on the relative strengths of employers and workers.

One rights regime, heavily overbalanced in favor of nineteenth-century liberalism, predominated for the first several decades of the twentieth century. It premised employment on a strict at-will doctrine, arguing (in the words of an oft-quoted passage from *Payne* v. *Western & Atlantic Railroad*) that "men must be left, without interference to buy and sell where they please, and to discharge or retain employees at will for good cause or for no cause, or even for bad cause without thereby being guilty of an unlawful act *per se*. It is a right which an employee may exercise in the same way, to the same extent, for the same cause or want of cause as the employer."[21] This regime provided few rights to workers, on the following logic: an employer could dismiss an employee at any time without committing an illegal act; whenever an employee claimed some right, the employer could fire the worker, at which point the "right" that was claimed would be a nullity. Therefore, any arrangements between employer and worker were merely elements of their employment relationship, which either party was free to continue abiding by or to terminate. Clearly, the most important institution articulating and enforcing this regime was the courts, which were zealous in defense of the at-will doctrine.

A second rights regime, weighted more heavily toward twentieth-century liberalism, persisted for most of the postwar period—from, roughly, the late 1940s through the late 1970s. In the postwar regime, the mechanism of collective bargaining was substituted for the unimpeded sway of the at-will rule, and unions were granted explicit legal recognition. Union-employer bargaining occurred under a set of rules established in law and extensively supervised by the National Labor Relations Board (NLRB). Statutory provision of rights, as in minimum-wage requirements and antidiscrimination legislation, further restricted the operation of the at-will doctrine. In place of courts, the primary institutions defining and enforcing workers' rights were unions, statutes, and regulatory bodies. The system of industrial governance that emerged incorporated unions as junior partners in the joint management of workplaces. Underlying this arrangement was a trade-off that provided benefits to both employers and workers: managements were given a relatively free hand to run their businesses, including, in particular, control over the introduction of new production technology and product pricing. In return the unions won for labor a share in the productivity bonus via higher wages and some protection from arbitrary treatment, primarily through seniority provisions and grievance rights. This was the classical period of modern industrial relations.

As I argue later, the classical age is over. The demise of the postwar rights regime is in part a consequence of the tremendous industrial restructuring forced on American employers by the international integration of economic life. The world's developed economies, especially those of the European Community, North America, and East Asia, have increasingly become linked in a single marketplace, and American firms have found their individual product and service markets subjected to intense international competition. As a result, these employers have been faced with growing pressures to produce better products, cut costs, bring new products and services to market quickly, adopt new management strategies, introduce innovative production technologies, and in diverse other ways become more competitive. Understandably, they have not ignored how they organize their work forces and what rights at the job workers have.

In the new international competition, American employers have changed some of their long-standing labor priorities. Work-force stability has become less important than the capacity to adapt (although the two are not intrinsically in conflict); long-term commitments have become less attractive, and short-term labor flexibility more important; labor costs, especially fringe benefits, have come under increased scrutiny; and practices that hinder how quickly and effectively employers can redeploy their labor forces have come to be seen as much greater obstacles than previously. As employers have attempted to implement their new priorities, they have run into traditional workplace practices—that welter of customs, federal and state statutory protections, collectively bargained privileges, administrative regulations, company rules, and workers' expectations that have served to regulate relations between employers and workers.

Employers have responded to these pressures in diverse ways. Some have tried to reduce the quality of the jobs they offer. More important, employers offering low-quality jobs have expanded their operations, while employers offering the traditional high-quality (industrial, unionized) jobs have contracted their payrolls. The result is more jobs with lower wages, reduced benefits, more part-time work and temporary workers, more subcontracting, and intensified work schedules. Not surprisingly, this period has seen a growing employer animus toward unions, with more employer attempts to defeat union organizing drives and to decertify unions. Some nonunionized employers have also jumped into the act, seeking to sweep away customary labor protections. Thus, along with the efforts to cut wages and benefits has come an attack on many traditional workers' rights.

Yet the pressure of international competition has also pushed in the opposite direction: it has increased many employers' need for highly motivated, loyal, hardworking employees. The drive to produce better products, for example, and especially the urgency to reduce product defects (one recently popular management philosophy is called "zero defects") relies on workers who care about the quality of the products they make and who identify their own fortunes with that of their company. Efforts to upgrade, adapt, innovate, and improve company operations (another highly touted new management idea is *kaizen*, "continual upgrading") depend on enlisting the continuing enthusiastic support of the firm's work force in implementing and carrying through the changes. When employers repeatedly introduce new technologies and new processes, they increase the demand for workers with strong skills, and perhaps even more, for workers who can readily learn new skills.

Thus employers have tried to adjust to the new international economy by transforming how they do business—either by attempting to cut away those traditional protections that American workers have come to expect, or by striving to develop innovative forms of work-force management that will more fully engage workers and release more of their productive energies for dedication to the company's goals. Either way, employers have inevitably called into question the postwar regime's body of traditional worker protections.

Growing international competition is not the only force at work; the decline of American unions certainly has also contributed to the demise of the postwar system. As I explore in detail later in this book, unions have been transformed from one of the major institutional players in the American economy to a much more marginal broker enrolling only a small minority of American workers. This decline has knocked out an important support of the postwar system.

Changes in public policy effected during the Reagan and Bush administrations have also hastened the decay of the postwar regime. During these years the federal government turned from being supporter, mediator, and regulator of the system, with an avowed goal of making it work, to being basically out of sympathy with it. Through the appointment of hostile regulators, interpretations of labor law generally unfavorable to unions and the system, and other measures, the two Republican administrations and many Democratic sympathizers signaled their unwillingness to sustain that regime. More broadly, the political triumphs of the modern conservative movement created (or reflected) a generally hostile public attitude toward unions, regulation, and the institutional relationships on which the postwar rights regime had been based.

Still other and perhaps more surprising forces are acting on the postwar regime. Even during the generally antilabor Reagan and Bush administrations, federal legislation extended new workplace rights to employees, among them mandatory early notification of plant closings, greater rights for workers with disabilities, and increased protections for older workers. The Clinton administration quickly achieved passage of family leave legislation, and it may look favorably on bills to mandate comparable-worth pay, child-care benefits, enhanced antidiscrimination enforcement, reform of federal labor-relations legislation, and other labor protections. Much more has occurred at the state level. State legislatures during the 1980s and early 1990s pitched in with greatly expanded state-level protections for workers; these ranged from the Massachusetts right-to-know law concerning toxic materials in the workplace, to Montana's remedy-for-wrongful-discharge statute, to South Carolina's legislation protecting those who file for worker's compensation from retaliation, to an Iowa law granting dismissed employees the right to continue and convert their group health insurance, to Florida's Whistle-Blower's Act of 1986. Perhaps in response to the dismal prospects for expanded federal-level job protections, state legislatures during this period enacted a vast array of new legislation.[22]

Despite the substantial changes brought by legislative initiatives, even more dramatic change has come from another source: the courts of the fifty states. State judges have stepped into the middle of the growing dispute over workers' rights to launch a far-reaching challenge to traditional work-rights legal doctrine. They have been confronted with the fundamental issue in its starkest terms: should workers be left to the unrestricted perils of the labor market, as nineteenth-century liberalism's contract theory would have it? In 1985, the New Jersey Supreme Court, considering a suit against the giant Hoffman–La Roche pharmaceuticals firm, asked this basic question: "Is [traditional contract doctrine] adequate for the realities of such a workplace?"[23] Its answer, and that of most other state courts during the 1980s, turned traditional labor law on its head: the court voiced a resounding no. In consequence, judges have begun a drastic rewriting of the most basic legal doctrines governing workers' rights, modifying those doctrines in ways that are much more favorable to employees. Indeed, the changes they are introducing could prove to be of more significance to workers than all the recent legislation.

These events do not mean that somehow, behind the backs of the politicians and pundits who declared that the 1980s signaled a return to the "free" labor market, workers'-rights advocates have snatched victories from the jaws of defeat. The social process has been far more complex than that. Workers' protections generally have been diminished in recent decades. However, employers have had imposed upon them a growing body of restrictions, interventions, intrusions, and obligations. The result is what economists call a "deadweight loss"; that is, both sides lose.

The various currents and crosscurrents do mean, however, that further dramatic change in how American society regulates employment relations is almost inevitable. During the 1990s the basic rights that people carry with them into their workplaces will be reformulated. The demise of the postwar rights regime, the deeply transformative impact of intensifying international competition, the withering of unions, the eagerness of state legislatures to enact new legislative protections, and above all state judges' sweeping revisions of basic labor law combine to produce a volatile mix.

That workplace rights are again a matter of significant political dispute might surprise some. After all, with the precipitous decline of Big Labor and the triumph of a free-market ideology during the Reagan and Bush administrations, many assumed that such disputes were now history. They were wrong. The issue of fair treatment of employees during work did not go away, and the central questions face America again: What rights should workers possess on the job? Which institutions will define and enforce workers' rights? What role should public policy play?

To these questions most employers' groups and workers' advocates give answers that mainly look backward. On one side, conservative commentators, some business groups, and the academic right wing have applauded the demise of the postwar compromise on workers' rights and called for the elimination of all restrictions on voluntary contract. Because they see a market system as both efficient and fair, they would have America return to an era when workers had few or no mandated rights.[24] On the other side, union groups and other workers' advocates, although largely defeated or intimidated by the unfavorable political tides of the recent past, have responded with appeals to revive the old system. They would have us reinvigorate workers' rights through the mechanisms of union organizing and collective bargaining and of statutory, especially federal, mandates of specific rights.[25] In effect, one side urges a reconstruction of the rights regime of nineteenth-century liberalism, built upon a strict at-will doctrine, while the other argues for trying to nail twentieth-century liberalism's postwar rights regime back together. As is shown in this book, neither seems to be a promising or feasible line of future development.[26]

Thus we desperately need some new thinking in this area, some creative and innovative approaches that will lead us out of the old ideological trenches and permit us to discover a new common ground. Do the larger changes in the world bring new opportunities for workers' rights along with the new problems and constraints? If so, where do those opportunities lie?[27] Can these opportunities be exploited for the better protection of workers and for greater economic competitiveness?

My proposals for how to find a new common ground are presented in chapters 8 and 9. My suggestions are based on a primary theme: we must make explicit and enforceable the extensive body of employee rights already unilaterally extended to workers by their employers; that is, we must extend in a rational and systematic way what state judges, in their inevitably uneven and hodgepodge way, have begun. Employers have built up a substantial common-law corpus of workers' prerogatives, protections, claims, and promises of fair dealing. Tailored to the specific needs of individual workplaces, these diverse rights have many flaws, among them their uncertain legal status and the consequent reliance on cumbersome and costly litigation to resolve industrial disputes arising from them. But despite their problems, these rights offer a solid and realistic basis upon which to construct a new workers' rights regime.

Before these new possibilities can be appreciated, however, some ideological commitments and historical attachments that inhibit progress toward new common ground must be cleared away. On the side of employers, and even more so the public-policy establishment, a major barrier to progress is adherence to a rigid if selective free-market doctrine. In chapter 3 I challenge this economic logic on its own terms, arguing that there are ample reasons in theory to favor the establishment of workers' rights. On the side of workers'-rights advocates, the main obstacle to progress is an inordinate attachment to the traditional ways of achieving workers' rights—collective bargaining and statutory grant. In chapters 4 and 5 I assess the real potential of these traditional mechanisms to serve as the central institutions in a new rights regime; for different reasons, each is found lacking.

Next I consider employer-granted workers' rights, that is, employers' promises of fair treatment and other worker protections or benefits made by nonunion employers during the process of labor-market competition and bargaining. Employers presumably make these promises to recruit, retain, and motivate their workers. In chapter 6 I survey existing employers' promises, and in chapter 7 review state courts' extensive and ongoing revision of the legal interpretation of employment contracts and employers' promises.

Having provided this background, I next consider new possibilities for social compromise on workers' rights. In chapter 8 I argue that employers as well as workers have a significant stake in the construction of an effective new system of workers' rights. Such a system must avoid the increasing intrusion of courts in the regulation of workplace relations and provide a more satisfactory basis for attracting, motivating, and retaining employees who are highly productive, hardworking, and committed to an enterprise's success. A new vision of workers' rights is needed.

Finally, in chapter 9 I propose some specific public-policy strategies that could form the basis of a new workers'-rights regime. These strategies incorporate some simple requirements:

—Information on each enterprise's workers' rights should be publicly available and regularly provided to each job applicant.

—Employer promises that are intended as rights should be identified and enforceable.

—There should be a public system other than the civil courts to mediate and arbitrate disputes over workplace rights, a system that fosters quick, simple, inexpensive, and legitimate resolution.

—Minimal levels of rights should be mandated through a mechanism that eschews the "one-size-fits-all" approach of statutory rights and explicitly incorporates sufficient flexibility to permit different combinations of rights for the highly differentiated workplaces of the American economy. I propose that these strategies be implemented through some simple rules governing employee handbooks.

Notes to Chapter 1

1. Information on the American Cyanamid case is taken from *Oil, Chemical, and Atomic Workers* v. *American Cyanamid Company*, 741 F.2d 444 (1984); and the briefs filed in this case: Brief for Petitioners (OCAW); Brief for Respondent, American Cyanamid Company; Reply Brief for Petitioners (OCAW); Brief of *Amicus Curiae*, Washington Legal Foundation; and Brief of *Amicus Curiae*, Coalition for the Reproductive Rights of Workers.

2. OSH act, P.L. 91-596 (1970), section (5)(a)(1). See also "Protecting the Baby, Work in Pregnancy Poses Legal Frontier," *New York Times*, August 2, 1988, p. A1.

3. *Oil, Chemical, and Atomic Workers* v. *American Cyanamid*, 741 F.2d 444 (1984), p. 447.

4. Brief for Petitioners, p. 8(n).

5. *New York Times*, "Protecting the Baby."

6. *Wall Street Journal*, "California Court Rejects Fetal-Protection Policy," May 21, 1990, p. B-5; "AT&T Is Urging Transfer for Some Pregnant Women," January 14, 1987, p. 2. *New York Times*, "Justices Hear Arguments in Fetal-Protection Case," October 11, 1990, p. A10; "Protecting the Baby, Work in Pregnancy Poses Legal Frontier," August 2, 1988, p. A1; and "Court Voids Limits to Women in Jobs on Basis of Fetus," March 21, 1991, p. A1.

7. Information on the Mack case comes from various documents made available to me, including letters from United Auto Workers vice-president Bill Casstevens to Mack employees who belonged to the UAW; letters from Local 677, UAW; letters from Mack Trucks, Inc., to employees; arbitrator Arthur Stark's award of June 19, 1987; arbitrator Eric Schmertz's award of August 30, 1987; Judge Edward Cahn's order of October 9, 1987; appendix D of the UAW-Mack master contract; the UAW report of 1987 negotiations; "UAW, Mack Trucks Battle for South Carolina Plant" (Springfield, Mass., *Sunday Republican*, November 22, 1987); as well as personal interviews with company officials, UAW leaders, local journalists, and community leaders.

8. Letter from Mack plant general manager Don Lindgren to employees, July 27, 1987.

9. Quoted in Arthur Stark's arbitration award of June 19, 1987.

10. Arthur Stark's arbitration award, June 19, 1987.

11. Quotes from Bill Casstevens letter, July 11, 1987; and Don Lindgren letter, July 27, 1987. Mack, once it was forced to comply with the

contracts it had signed, gave its workers the briefest time possible to decide whether or not to transfer. In some cases it appeared that workers had just twenty-four hours to make up their minds. One woman compared the company's ultimatum to "holding a gun to my husband's and my head. . . . They wouldn't even give us an extra two weeks to make the move." Casper (Wyo.) *Star-Tribune*, July 27, 1987.

12. From order by Judge Edward Cahn, October 9, 1987; and award by Eric Schmertz, August 30, 1987.

13. Personal interview; Kerry Hannon, "On the Road Again," *Forbes*, May 16, 1988, pp. 37–38. The Winnsboro election was held in April 1989 and agreements were ratified on February 14, 1990; information provided by the UAW.

14. The Saturn agreement governs labor-management relations at the Tennessee plant where General Motors produces the Saturn automobile; NUMMI is the GM-Toyota joint venture (New United Motor Manufacturing, Inc.) in California that assembles the Chevrolet Nova. In both cases the employer worked out highly innovative labor arrangements with the UAW. For an excellent analysis of the NUMMI innovations, see Clair Brown and Michael Reich (1989).

15. Don Lindgren letter, July 27, 1987.

16. All information and quotations on this case are taken from *Morriss* v. *Coleman Company, Inc.*, 738 P.2d 841 (Kan. 1987).

17. *Payne* v. *Western & Atlantic Railroad*, 81 Tenn. 507 (1884) at 518–19. This case represented an early and much-cited use of "Wood's Rule," which established the modern understanding of at-will employment; see H. G. Wood (1887, 1877), #134, at 272.

18. *Morriss* v. *Coleman*, 738 P.2d 841 (Kan. 1987) at 849.

19. The classic articulation of economic liberalism is provided by Adam Smith [1776] (1937); that of liberty as a preeminent value is given by Alexis de Tocqueville (1841). A modern restatement, itself a classic, is made by Milton Friedman (1962); this viewpoint can also be found in most modern economics textbooks. Joseph A. Schumpeter (1954, p. 394) defined economic liberalism concisely as "the theory that the best way of promoting economic development and general welfare is to remove fetters from the private-enterprise economy and to leave it alone." A useful discussion of economic liberalism is provided by Robert Alan Dahl (1985), chaps. 1 and 2.

20. For articulations of twentieth-century liberalism, see John Kenneth Galbraith (1958); John Maurice Clark (1939); and Robert Dahl (1985), chaps. 2 and 3. More recent statements include Arthur Okun (1975). The classic works espousing application of this perspective to workers' rights and labor organization belong to the "industrial relations" school. For example, see John Dunlop (1958). Recent statements are Samuel Bowles, David Gordon, and Thomas Weisskopf (1983, 1990); Robert Alan Dahl (1985), chaps. 4 and 5; Ira C. Magaziner and Robert B. Reich (1982); and Robert B. Reich (1991).

21. *Payne* v. *Western & Atlantic Railroad*, 81 Tenn. 507 (1884) at 518–19, as quoted in Richard Epstein (1984), pp. 947–48.

22. For a state-by-state summary of the extensive legislation enacted in 1990 alone, see Richard Nelson (1991); see also Richard Nelson (1986).

23. *Woolley* v. *Hoffman–La Roche, Inc.*, 491 A.2d 1257 (N.J. 1985) at 1260.

24. See, for example, Howard Jensen (n.d.); Morgan O. Reynolds (1982); and Joseph D. Reid (1983). For editorial opinion, see *Wall Street Journal*, "Mandated Labor Costs," February 16, 1988, p. 36. The 1988 Republican party platform, although vague as such documents characteristically are, states: "work place benefits should be freely negotiated by employee-employer bargaining. We oppose government requirements that shrink workers' paychecks by diverting money away from wages to pay for federal requirements. These hidden taxes add to labor costs without paying those who labor. That is the liberals' way of replacing collective bargaining with congressional edicts about what's good for employees" (p. 9). Under the section, "The Rights of Workers" (p. 35), the platform reaffirms the right of workers to join unions, but its main emphasis is on support of "right-to-work" laws, opposition to compulsory dues for partisan purposes, amendment of the Hobbs Act "so that union officials . . . are once again subject to the law's prohibition against extortion and violence in labor disputes," and measures "to provide greater protection from labor violence for workers who choose to work during strikes." The 1992 Republican platform includes one brief paragraph on labor which emphasizes reducing labor regulation (p. 29).

25. AFL-CIO (1985); and Executive Council Statement on the Employment-At-Will Doctrine, February 20, 1987, Bal Harbor, Florida; Sar Levitan, Peter Carlson, and Isaac Shapiro (1986), especially chap. 11.

26. Another response is the call for "labor-management cooperation." See, for example, John Simmons and William Mares (1983), and Stephen Schlossberg and Steven Fetter (1987). This third response is more difficult to assess because the advocates of cooperation have been reluctant to move beyond descriptions of cooperative processes and individual success stories. In particular, what cooperation might mean for workers' rights remains obscure. One effort to shed some light is provided in *Vanderbilt Law Review* (1988); for a contrary, unionist view, see Mike Parker and Jane Slaughter (1988).

27. For a discussion of one set of new opportunities for labor, see Richard Edwards and Paolo Garonna (1991).

2

Defining Workers' Rights

The rights of workers have long been subject to dispute. In the fourth century B.C., Plato argued that those "occupied in the handicraft arts" be excluded from citizenship, because citizens needed to "secure and preserve the public order of the state," and because this task was itself "an art which requires much study." His oligarchic views were disputed by Greek democrats who urged that all free men should be citizens on an equal footing. Plato also believed that "hardly any human being is capable of pursuing two professions or two arts rightly," and so he proposed that "no one who is a smith shall also be a carpenter, and if he be a carpenter, he shall not superintend the smith's art rather than his own."[1] Many more recent disputes have turned on just such rules.

The rights of American workers have been debated since the birth of the nation. In 1791, for example, house carpenters in Philadelphia struck for a ten-hour workday. In 1805 a case that was to set legal precedent for a century was decided; eight Philadelphia shoemakers who had joined forces to improve their working conditions were convicted of having formed "a combination and conspiracy to raise wages." In 1894 Nebraska workers who had achieved the enactment of legislation granting them overtime pay when the workday ran beyond eight hours saw their right evaporate in an adverse state supreme court decision. In the 1930s most hourly workers won the right to a minimum wage and overtime pay after forty hours' work during a week. In the 1960s the courts and Congress granted workers protection from racial and sexual discrimination. In the 1980 *Yeshiva* decision, private-college professors lost their right to federal protection of unionization activities, a loss identical to that suffered by industrial foremen in the late 1940s, and like it traceable to the 1947 Taft-Hartley Act's curtailment of workers' rights. In 1988 some workers won the right to sixty days' advance notice in the event of a factory closing or mass layoff.[2]

Although these struggles and countless others have encompassed rich, multifaceted conflicts of material interests and divergent cultures, what is striking about them is what they have in common: the pervasive, almost universal appropriation of the language of rights. In 1844, for example, the Lynn, Massachusetts, shoemakers, in a struggle with the newly emergent shoe merchant–capitalists, signed a "declaration of independence" proclaiming that "our employers have robbed us of certain rights which they will, in our opinion, never voluntarily restore."[3] Throughout this long history, workers' rights have been evoked in opposition to employers' rights, property rights have been counterposed to civil rights, and some personal rights have clashed with other personal rights. As Samuel Bowles and Herbert Gintis have noted, the "lingua franca of politics is the discourse of rights."[4]

But what exactly is meant by *rights*? And what are *workers' rights*? In this chapter these terms are defined.

Rights and Workers' Rights

Perhaps because it has been appropriated for so many purposes, the concept of rights has been applied in widely different ways. In ordinary lawyers' language, rights are frequently taken to mean any claims that can be enforced in a court of law; thus, a worker who has earned her wage but has not been paid is said to have a "right" to it. For most economists, rights are only created by law; a gain from voluntary market exchange (such as a wage) would not usually be called a right. As is shown in this chapter, neither of these notions is adequate for an analysis of workplace rights; a more incisive definition is required.

In general, by *rights* I mean legitimate and enforceable claims or privileges that individuals obtain through membership in a group and that entitle or protect those individuals in some specific way from the prevailing system of governance.

Rights are an individual's legitimate and enforceable claims to some desired treatment, situation, or resource. Legal scholar Neil MacCormick puts the point this way: "Rights always and necessarily concern human goods, that is, concern what it is, at least in normal circumstances, good for a person to have. When positive laws establish rights, for example expressly by legislation, what they do is secure individuals (or members of a particular defined set of individuals) in the enjoyment of some good or other."[5] Thus rights may be thought of as one way that societies distribute "goods" (broadly construed), like other methods such as market exchanges, elections, gifts, and government programs providing services or subsidies. To be legitimate, the claims (rights) must derive from recognized or accepted authority.[6]

An individual comes to possess rights because of membership in the group or category for whom such rights are defined; nothing further, such as a promise or performance on the part of the individual, is needed to establish access to or eligibility for the right. (Why or how rights are provided to the group is a different matter, taken up later.) Consider, for example, the right to vote. Individuals possess this right by virtue of being nonfelon citizens of majority age (that is, by being members of the adult nonfelon citizenry); they do not earn the right to vote by promising to do something or by doing that thing. Rights derive from a predefined status—membership in the relevant group.[7]

Sometimes the definition of the group possessing a right changes, but this does not alter the basic point that an individual's access to rights comes via group membership. For example, the group that is defined as having First Amendment rights or a right to protection from discrimination has been enlarged to include not only U.S. citizens but all who are legally within the jurisdiction of the United States. One of the more interesting recent developments regarding rights is the virtual collapse (except for voting) of the legal distinction between citizenship and other legal residency.[8] The group has been expanded, but the link between rights and group membership remains.

Rights may be limited or denied altogether to certain groups or categories of members, but such limits do not prevent the claims or privileges from functioning as rights for others. For example, minor citizens may not claim full access to citizens' rights: they cannot vote, nor can they claim a right to privacy from their parents or guardians, yet voting and privacy are rights possessed by adult citizens. Of course, exclusions accepted in one age (for example, those denying suffrage to blacks or women) may be abolished at a later time.

The final element in my definition of rights—that rights entitle or protect individuals in some specific way from the established system of governance—means that rights are exercised in opposition to or as limitations upon the ordinary exercise of legitimate power. For example, the Constitution establishes Congress's prerogative to make laws and provide for their enforcement. Americans' Fifth Amendment rights, however, prevent the government from establishing procedures, like those of Tudor England's notorious Star Chamber court, that compel self-incrimination; thus, rights limit in a specific way what otherwise is established as the legitimate system of governance. Legal philosopher Ronald Dworkin puts it this way: "Individual rights are political trumps held by individuals. Individuals have rights when, for some reason, a collective goal is not a sufficient justification for denying them what they wish, as individuals, to have or to do, or not a sufficient justification for imposing some loss or injury upon them."[9]

Rights may take the form either of positive claims by individuals or of limitations (or duties imposed) on the actions of the state or others. As an individual's claim or entitlement, a right grants to an individual certain benefits regardless of whether the relevant governing body wants to provide those benefits. For example, courts in many jurisdictions have ruled that schoolchildren in poor communities have a right to equal education; local or state agencies have thus been ordered to expend additional funds toward that objective.[10] As a limitation, a right prevents an action that a governing body might otherwise choose to take (or requires an action that it otherwise would not choose to take). For instance, the First Amendment, by prohibiting the establishment of a state religion, prevents local school authorities from requiring students to pray. In either form, rights provide a means by which the individual can require an outcome favored by that individual over the outcome that would otherwise result from the prevailing system of governance or the ordinary administration of that governance.

Ronald Dworkin provides a useful distinction between what he terms "background rights" and "institutional rights." Background rights are those "rights that provide a justification for political decisions by society in the abstract." Different political theories naturally will argue for different constellations of background rights, but examples might include rights to liberty, fairness, or property, or the right of a person to the property of another if that person needs it more. By contrast, institutional rights are rights created by or deriving from a specific institutional context and that "provide a justification for a decision by some particular and specified political institution".[11] Examples of institutional rights include those contained in the Bill of Rights, the 1964 Civil Rights Act, and various state statutes; alternatively, as Dworkin argues, because institutional rights are associated with many kinds of institutions, one could also say that "a chess player has a 'chess' right to be awarded a point in a tournament if he checkmates an opponent."[12]

Dworkin's distinction is simply one way of posing the deeper question of the source or ultimate authority from which people's most basic or profound rights derive. Political theories, and with them ways of constructing identity and defining interests, turn on whether the fundamental source of individual rights is presumed to be natural law, a constitution based on some notion of the consent of the governed, a Rawlsian hypothetical social contract, or some other construct.[13] Dworkin's distinction is useful for my analysis because it helps locate workplace rights as institutional rights; to the extent that background rights impinge upon the analysis, I argue, they do so in understandable ways mediated by the institutional context. I return to this point later in this chapter.

The definition of *workers' rights* follows from this general concept of rights as legitimated claims or privileges (goods) that an employee possesses as a result of being an employee and that the employee may exercise as protection from the established workplace governance. As with civic rights, both membership and the limitation of power are inherent in the meaning of workplace rights. Being a worker is defined by the existence of an employment relationship;

all those who are employed constitute a group—employees—and workers' rights are those rights that derive from a person's status as an employee (or from membership in the group of employees). Thus, for example, all Americans, whether employees or not, can claim a right to worship as they please, but only employees can claim a right to a minimum wage. Absent an employment relationship, the right to a minimum wage has no meaning. Unemployed persons, retirees, foreign tourists, and self-employed individuals cannot exercise this right.

Compared to a citizen's constitutional or statutory rights, workers' rights have one unusual feature: the worker may be fired and thereby lose work rights (that is, his or her membership). If rights derive from group membership, expulsion from the group results in a loss of rights. Whereas citizens rarely face the loss of their citizenship (and hence loss of their civic or constitutional rights), workers frequently lose or leave employment and certainly the threat of dismissal is frequently present and credible. Indeed, an employer may dismiss or lay off a worker precisely to deny the worker her rights. Because of this limitation, how effectively a worker can exercise his rights will usually depend upon such diverse factors as the tightness of labor markets, the presence or absence of unions, employers' commitment to workers' rights, the degree of governmental resolve to protect workers' rights, and employers' options for organizing production elsewhere.

Workers' rights must be distinguished from another category of employee's claims or privileges, one that may be termed *quid pro quo benefits*. Quid pro quo benefits are rewards or claims that depend upon and are received in return for some promise or performance; they are *earned* benefits. By contrast, rights can be claimed merely as a consequence of membership in the group. The most important quid pro quo benefit is an employee's wage or salary (at least that part greater than the legal minimum wage); other quid pro quo benefits include other benefits and compensation that an individual worker may negotiate in his or her contract. Quid pro quo benefits are by nature differentially available to individuals, depending upon the *quo*—upon what promise has been made or performance provided.

The distinction between rights and quid pro quo benefits is sometimes blurred in lawyers' everyday language about rights, but it remains fundamental. In the example cited earlier (in which a worker earns but is denied a wage and claims it as a right), the worker does have a right, but it is not the wage. If her employment constitutes a valid contract, she has a right in the ordinary civil law to have it enforced; the gain she receives from exercising her right, that is, the wage itself, remains a quid pro quo benefit. Of course, one could define workers' rights as encompassing *any* enforceable claims of workers; rights would then include an individual's contractual benefits as well as, for example, tort claims stemming from the negligence of fellow workers and other matters that can be gained in court. But such a definition would be overreaching and self-defeating: the term *rights* would cease to have a distinct meaning of its own. Hence the narrower definition I have adopted.

Note that workers' rights are, for the individual worker, supracontractual and in this sense nonnegotiable. This is simply the obverse of noting that rights are conferred by virtue of group membership (in the group of "employees"). In the case just cited, the worker has a right to have a valid contract enforced; this right is not something she obtained through negotiation or could give up through negotiation (although she could make another contract agreeing not to exercise her right, or she could choose not to exercise her right). An individual worker can make extra deals for additional rewards, that is, for added quid pro quo benefits. For example, when IBM hires a systems engineer, that engineer receives a salary, certain pension or stock-option perquisites, and other benefits. All of these emoluments clearly derive from employment, but we do not consider the worker's claim to them as rights, because they are determined by the two parties (IBM and the engineer) establishing the employment relationship. The engineer does have the right, if employed, to receive a wage at least equal to the legal minimum, but he has no right to any particular wage above this minimum. The actual wage is a matter of bargaining. By contrast, the right to a safe workplace and the right to engage in activities aimed at forming a union are not negotiable; they are guaranteed by law. (Whether they are achieved in practice is another matter.) Workers' rights thus reflect those workers' claims or privileges that are acknowledged or accepted as properly available to all workers in the relevant group. For the individual worker they are supracontractual.

Immediately one can see a problem, because the sharp conceptual distinction I have drawn between rights and benefits becomes murky in the real world of the workplace. A claim may appear in some guises or with respect to certain aspects as a right, and in others as a benefit. Employers and workers frequently dispute whether a particular claim or privilege is or is not a right; indeed, the court dockets are filled with suits and countersuits aimed at enforcing or defining or denying putative rights. Over time, what society accepts as workers' rights changes, because inevitably there is a "historical and moral" or socially determined component to the demarcation of rights from other types of claims.

Do the practical difficulties in locating and marking the boundary between workers' rights and their other claims (or nonrights) vitiate the usefulness of my definition of worker rights? Several points may be noted. First, the issue of defining the boundary between rights and nonrights arises equally in the case of political and constitutional rights, where there is extensive debate over whether "goods" such as privacy, health care, and access to abortion are rights; yet no one would suggest dismissing the concept of rights from the civic sphere. Applying an appropriate and useful definition of workplace rights, although it differs in content from that underlying civic rights, creates no novel logical difficulties. Second, ongoing contention over the identification of specific rights, whether in civic life or the workplace, does not imply that the definition of rights is faulty, only that its implementation is contentious.

Finally, whereas the practical difficulty of identifying the boundary between rights and nonrights and the shifting of that boundary from time to time might suggest the unimportance of the border, in fact it indicates the opposite: employers and workers struggle to change the boundary because it means so much. The practical consequence that follows when a particular claim is placed on one side or the other of this conceptual line is great. Indeed, for broader political rights, it is precisely the clear conceptual distinction between rights and nonrights and the problematical but consequential nature of its implementation that leads to discussion of rights being the "lingua franca of politics"; the language of rights serves the same function in the struggle over workplace rights.

Types of Workplace Rights

Workplace rights serve to provide workers with desired outcomes (or protect them from unwanted outcomes) where contrary outcomes would result from the ordinary administration of workplace governance. They are "trumps" that an individual worker can use against the authority of the foreman or general manager or the employing enterprise itself. As will be shown, workers' rights may issue from sources external to the employer (e.g., from a constitution or statute). They may emanate from agreements entered into by the employer (for example, union contracts), or they may derive from the employer itself, as an established part of "company policy."

The system of governance in the workplace is different from that in civic society, and its authority is derived from different moral assumptions and power bases, yet rights have a similar operational meaning in both. What distinguishes workplace rights is that they are shaped and constrained by the specific context of the employment relationship, and this difference often proves crucial for how rights are administered in practice and in what circumstances the possessors of those rights may reasonably depend upon them. My approach is not to ignore this critical difference; for example, I do not presume that by using the language of rights for both civic society and the workplace I can thereby assume that there is an equivalence in reality. Neither am I interested in drawing upon the rhetorical force of the rights language to score political points about the workplace. Rather, I want to analyze workplace rights as specific institutional rights by direct scrutiny of their functioning in the workplace.

Understood as institutional rights, workers' rights may be categorized according to their source: law, union contracts, or employers' promises.[14] The first group, what I refer to as *statutory rights*, consists of workers' rights that are established through the mechanism of law. The Fair Labor Standards Act, for example, grants most production-level workers the right to receive "time and a half" for work beyond forty hours a week. The Civil Rights Act of 1964 grants workers (and job applicants) the right to workplace treatment free of discrimination based on race, color, religion, sex, or national origin. The Massachusetts "right-to-know" law gives workers in that state the right to be notified if certain specified hazardous substances are present in the workplace. Statutory law has been a favored method of establishing rights for workers because it provides a powerful way to make claims universal (at least for the relevant group) and enforceable. The right to a minimum wage, for example, or the right to a safe workplace, can be established in a statute and its obligations impinge on all those covered by the law.

Collective bargaining has provided a second source of workers' rights, rights which I term *collective contract rights*. Workers have used collective bargaining to achieve many of their most significant rights, including seniority preferences, grievance mechanisms, job-security provisions, rights to retraining, job bidding and the posting of rights, job assignment rights, and standards for evaluation. Not all union-negotiated claims are rights; unions bargain for such quid pro quo benefits as good wages, incentive pay, and bonuses. Bargained rights have effect only for those workers covered by the contract, but such rights have much the same legal and practical effect for covered workers as do statutory rights for all workers.

A third source of workers' rights is employer grants or promises of rights; these *enterprise rights*, as I label them, consist of those claims or privileges that employers unilaterally grant or promise to their workers. Such rights may be established, for example, by the highest-level executives to protect workers against the actions of mid-level managers, or established by the firm as a collective entity to protect workers from the actions of any manager, even a high-level one. Typically enterprise rights are available to nonunion, private-sector employees, such as nonunion workers in large firms, workers in many nonprofit organizations, and nonunion supervisory and technical personnel employed by unionized firms.

Examples of enterprise rights include the right to petition beyond one's immediate supervisor, the right to be free from physical intimidation, the right to a grievance or complaint system, the right to have express standards for evaluation, the right to some due process in discipline, the right to a "just-cause" standard for dismissal, the right to have one's job clearly defined with specified job tasks, the right to freedom from having to bribe one's supervisor or suffer from nepotism or undue favoritism, the right of nonunion craft workers to follow craft rules such as those governing the tasks that plumbers or carpenters will perform, and the right to have one's say when subjected to discipline or dismissal.[15]

Enterprise rights derive from the explicit rules and promises of specific enterprises; they are not simply what is indicated by the looser term *customs and practices*, which may be taken to refer to the patterns of work and interaction that develop informally within a workplace. Such patterns are frequently a powerful element in the organization of the workplace, and in some cases they clearly provide important protections and benefits to workers. Informal rules among workers to limit production function in this way. However, customs and practices are not rights as that term is used here, because they do not derive from recognized or legitimated authority. My distinction, then, is between those workers' claims that come through the mechanism of legitimated authority and function as rights and diverse other workers' claims that spring from other sources, such as bargaining in markets or customs and practices.[16] To make this distinction, I restrict the term *enterprise rights* to those claims explicitly granted by employers.

Although enterprise rights are defined as distinct from customs and practices, it is nonetheless true that enterprise rights are significantly shaped by the evolution of customs and practices. That is, which rights employers decide to grant and when and to whom they grant them depend on the general cultural expectations that have developed for workplace governance. Certain customs and practices have become so entrenched in particular workplaces or so generalized in society that employers are forced to institute them. An example is the opportunity for a worker to have his say (on such matters as discipline) to someone higher than his immediate supervisor; this custom spread with the demise early in this century of the production system based on autocratic foremen. In consequence, most employers feel obligated to promise their employees some rights of complaint or approval. In many cases, an employer grant may simply formalize a preexisting practice. Other enterprise rights originate with management.

Enterprise rights are more clearly defined in and are conceptually more relevant to larger enterprises than tiny ones, and so throughout this book I presume that the discussion of firm-specific rights applies only to firms above a certain threshold size. I arbitrarily set the threshold at twenty employees. Even in the smallest companies some rights are necessary and appropriate, for instance, statutory protections from toxic materials, sweatshop hours and wages, and physical intimidation. One could also argue that some of the most abused and disenfranchised workers toil or have toiled in small companies. But the concept of rights presumes a more or less formal and established system of governance against which rights can protect, and small firms almost always lack that. Small firms have a personalized, idiosyncratic, changeable, and ultimately informal and nonsystematic form of workplace control; the formalism of rights has little place, either descriptively or normatively, as an antidote to a small employer's overbearing and abusive behavior.[17] Therefore, the analysis of enterprise rights in the following chapters is not intended to apply to very small firms.

Enterprise rights is the most problematic category of workers' rights, because such rights are the least defined, are the most weakly rooted in law, and are specific to each enterprise. Their saliency in the full array of workers' rights varies across time and space. Unlike statutory and collective contract rights, enterprise rights have a legally ambiguous status involving "implicit contracts" and "implied promises," concepts that judges sometimes choose to recognize but at other times seemingly ignore.

Despite their limitations, enterprise rights constitute a crucial part of those rights that American workers effectively exercise in practice. In many ways they are the most interesting and significant of workers' rights. The importance of such rights becomes apparent if one compares the petition and appeal rights of a nonunionized Ford worker of the 1920s to those of a similarly nonunionized Polaroid worker at present. For the faintest dissent, the Ford worker was subject to immediate discipline, often extending to physical intimidation or dismissal, with no appeal possible and no due-process rights of any kind. By contrast, the Polaroid worker enjoys substantial rights—relief from any overt retaliation, job-performance standards provided in established personnel guides, and the right to several levels of administrative appeal. These rights, mandated by company policy and reinforced by custom and company practice, exist because both workers' and employers' standards of acceptable treatment have changed. Yet the Polaroid worker's rights are not contained in any collective-bargaining contract, and at least until several years ago would not have been enforceable in court.[18] The striking difference between these two situations is sometimes glibly dismissed as simply "sophisticated" management or even "management manipulation"; in fact, the modern worker's advantage reflects a legacy available to many of today's workers, employees who are not now and may never have been unionized and yet who benefit from this result of the struggle for workers' rights.

My interpretation of rights contrasts with a common view among economists that rights derive exclusively and directly from law and that all claims traceable to the market should be seen as negotiated benefits. Yet workers' claims established through law are not inevitably rights nor, as I argue, is law the only mechanism used to establish workers' rights. Law may establish quid pro quo benefits that are simply provided through the public sector; such is the case when a government agency pays wages to its employees or offers vocational training on a fee basis. More to the point, workers' rights may also derive from sources other than law, including collective bargaining and employer grants. The collective contract rights and enterprise rights that individual workers exercise fit the usual definition of rights, as outlined earlier. In some contexts, they may be as efficacious or more efficacious than statutory rights, and they have a real historical existence in the daily lives of workers. This more historical and organic definition of rights, applied in subsequent chapters, will prove more useful than simply identifying rights with the protections provided through law.

I now return to Ronald Dworkin's distinction between background rights and institutional rights. Earlier in this chapter I claimed that workplace rights are institutional rights and that to the extent that background rights impinge upon my analysis, they do so through understandable and identifiable institutional mediation. There are at least two possible objections to this claim. First, some workplace rights could themselves be claimed as background rights. For example, one could postulate that workers have a fundamental or background right to a safe workplace or to employment itself (recall that in Dworkin's schema background rights "provide a justification for political decisions by society in the abstract.")[19] Postulating that some specific right of workers is a background right is clearly possible, and one could develop a political theory that does so.[20] That, however, is not the argument I make; in the analysis that follows, I treat all workplace rights as institutional rights, that is, as concrete legal rights that derive from specific sources (law, collective contracts, and enterprise rules and promises) in particular institutions.

A second and more telling objection can be stated as follows: assume workplace rights are stipulated to be institutional rights; how these institutional rights are identified, understood, interpreted, and adjudicated depends on background rights. This position would directly (and perhaps mechanically) apply Dworkin's "rights thesis" on how judges decide "hard cases" to workers' rights issues; in Dworkin's words, "the rights thesis, in its descriptive aspect, holds that judicial decisions in hard cases are characteristically generated by principle not policy."[21] Thus, in application to the workplace, hard cases involving workers' rights would also be decided by "principle, not policy."

But the stated objection is not the only possible way to apply Dworkin's thesis, and in this case, I maintain, it is not the most appropriate application. As Neil MacCormick properly suggests in correcting a strict Dworkinian interpretation, background rights (or Dworkin's "principles" which justify decisions about rights) must come from a process in which "to some extent we find them, and to some extent we make them."[22] For workplace rights, both the finding and the making are heavily shaped by the institutional context and, at least in the immediate sense, other authority than (Dworkinian) principle or background rights tends to prevail. In particular, hard cases (where by definition ordinary precedents do not suffice) are usually decided by appeal to the large body of established nonworkplace law and precedent (for example, ordinary contract law) rather than by appeal to background rights. Judges have relied on this nonworkplace law to provide the rules of construction, standards, and precedents that have informed their decisions. Thus, in deciding "hard" workers'-rights cases, appeals to background rights have been less important.[23]

Even so, one cannot entirely dismiss background rights from the analysis. At certain key points in recent jurisprudence, judges have called upon larger concepts of justice to redefine the law. For example, with respect to one of the most dramatic recent changes—the use of contract law to redefine the at-will doctrine—the imperatives of basic fairness clearly seem to have influenced judges' decisions. So, too, background rights form part of the normative argument for workers' rights. Thus Dworkin's distinction remains useful in the case of workplace rights, although his rights thesis has less descriptive power and less normative immediacy than when applied to general political rights.

The approach I adopt, then, is to view workplace rights as favored outcomes or "goods" that are normatively secured to employees and for which eligibility is established by the employees' employment relationship. Rights equip individuals with the power to achieve a desired outcome, thereby trumping or forestalling another outcome that otherwise would have resulted from the ordinary or prevailing system of workplace governance. These rights are intrinsically institutional in form and derivation, although society's understanding of them is shaped by notions of background rights. Workplace rights may be justified or rooted in both reasons of principle and reasons of policy.[24]

Workers' rights, like other institutional rights, are mutable, historically contingent, and uneven across industries, occupations, time, and place. They may be in conflict with one another, with the employer's rights to property, and with other rights (for example, consumers' rights) guaranteed in society. The exercise of workers' rights therefore is constrained by the exercise of other (and others') rights. While all rights are conditioned by their context, workers' rights are especially so: because they are rooted in a fragile employment relationship, they are more peculiarly subject to situational vagaries than the other rights with which Americans are familiar. Nonetheless, workers enjoy a wide range of rights deriving from a variety of sources.

Notes to Chapter 2

1. Plato (1952), pp. 740–41. See also Mortimer J. Adler (1952), chap. 44, especially p. 927.

2. Philip Foner (1947), chap. 5 and p. 78; *Low* v. *Rees Printing Co.,* 41 Neb. 127, 59 N.W. 362 (1894); *National Labor Relations Board* v. *Yeshiva University,* 444 U.S. 672 (1980); U.S. Code (1988), Worker Adjustment and Retraining Notification Act, 102 Stat. 890, P.L. 100-379 (August 4, 1988).

3. From *The Awl,* August 14, 1844, as quoted in Norman Ware (1924), p. 42.

4. Samuel Bowles and Herbert Gintis (1986), p. 32.

5. Neil MacCormick (1982), p. 143. Ronald Dworkin (1977), in a curious omission for a book focused on rights, never gives a precise definition of rights, but he does note that "a political right is an individuated political aim. An individual has a right to some opportunity or resource or liberty if it counts in favor of a political decision that the decision is likely to advance or protect the state of affairs in which he enjoys the right, even when no other political aim is served and some political aim is disserved thereby,

and counts against that decision that it will retard or endanger that state of affairs, even when some other political aim is thereby served" (p. 91). He contrasts a "right" in this sense with a "goal," which he describes as a "nonindividuated political aim."

6. What ultimately constitutes "accepted authority" is, of course, the subject of persistent debate. For reasons that will become apparent, that is, because I interpret workplace rights as institutional rights rather than background rights, I need not enter this debate in order to analyze workers' rights. See the sources cited in note 13, this chapter.

7. In many discussions of political rights, membership is ignored because universality is assumed; for example, Ronald Dworkin (1977, p. 94, n. 1) says, "I shall assume, in this essay, that all political rights are universal." In such analyses, the "group" is simply humanity. In discussing abstract rights such as property or liberty, one can perhaps ignore membership, although such a device works less well historically (for example, women's rights to own property or slaves' rights to liberty or property). But universality is clearly not the general case for rights; membership is relevant, and especially for discussing workplace rights.

8. William Rogers Brubaker (1989).

9. Ronald Dworkin (1977, p. xi).

10. "23 States Face Suits on School Funds," *New York Times,* September 2, 1992, p. A13. At the federal level, the leading Supreme Court decision goes the other way; see *San Antonio Ind. School Dist.* v. *Rodriguez*, 411 U.S. 1 (1973).

11. Ronald Dworkin (1977), p. 93.

12. Ronald Dworkin (1977), p. 101.

13. John Rawls (1971); see also Neil MacCormick (1982), chap. 5. To give a flavor of the recent debate, H. L. A. Hart (1961) distinguishes between "primary" and "secondary" rules, the latter being those that specify how and by whom primary rules (which grant rights) may be established, changed, or extinguished; for Hart, then, what is at issue is how a community's fundamental secondary rule, or what he terms a "rule of recognition," comes into being. Dworkin (1977, pp. 22, 84–97), by contrast, makes the claims of morality central in his distinction between a "principle" ("a standard that is to be observed, not because it will advance or secure an economic, political, or social situation deemed desirable, but because it is a requirement of justice or fairness or some other dimension of morality") and a "policy" (a "standard that sets out a goal to be reached, generally an improvement in some economic, political, or social feature of the community"); political rights derive from judges involved in "hard cases" who confirm or deny concrete rights in decisions generated by principle, not policy.

14. It may be thought that the U.S. Constitution would also be a significant source of workers' rights, but it seems generally agreed among legal scholars that employees have few constitutional (as opposed to statutory) rights; of course, constitutional rights primarily protect against government actions. There is, for example, no constitutional right to strike (William

Gould, 1986b, p. 101); private-sector workers have limited free-speech rights (Staughton Lynd, 1978; Carolina Alliance for Fair Employment, 1987), and public-sector workers' free-speech rights, although more extensive, are also limited (William Gould, 1986b, pp. 172–73). A 1983 case (*Novosel* v. *Nationwide Insurance Co.,* 721 F.2d 894), in which an employee successfully sued for wrongful discharge resulting from his refusal to join his employer's effort to lobby the state legislature, has somewhat extended free-speech rights of private-sector workers.

15. Ronald Berenbeim (1980); Richard Edwards (1979), chap. 8.

16. The term *legitimate authority* should not be interpreted as lending any moral superiority to its rights over workers' claims deriving from other sources (for example, from their market bargaining or from customs and practices); the term is used only for purposes of making a technical distinction between the different categories of workers' claims. It is easy to imagine the reverse: a worker's claim to a decent livelihood, bargained through and enforced by the market, may be more important to justice than a (legitimated) right to bid on job vacancies. My point is simply that these are different social mechanisms for distributing what Neil MacCormick terms "goods."

17. Richard Edwards (1979), chap. 2; J. K. Galbraith (1973), chaps. 6–8. As is noted in chapter 9 of this book, workers employed in establishments with fewer than twenty employees constituted about 26 percent of the employed labor force in 1988; because enterprises may have more than one establishment, this is probably a relatively high estimate of the percentage of workers in enterprises with fewer than twenty employees.

18. Peter B. Doeringer and Michael J. Piore (1971); Herbert Gutman (1973); David Montgomery (1979); see my book, *Contested Terrain* (1979), re the Polaroid-Ford comparison. See also David W. Ewing (1989), pp. 299–308.

19. Ronald Dworkin (1977), p. 93. Dworkin's thesis is intended to be both descriptive and normative: "I propose . . . the thesis that judicial decisions in civil cases, even in hard cases . . . characteristically are and should be generated by principle not policy" (Dworkin, 1977, p. 84). My interest in this thesis is mainly in its descriptive aspect; I argue, for example, that policy (in the sense articulated by Dworkin) provides an important justification for workers' rights.

20. See, for example, Samuel Bowles and Herbert Gintis (1986) or National Conference of Catholic Bishops (1986), both of which might be interpreted in this way.

21. Ronald Dworkin (1977), pp. 96–97.

22. Neil MacCormick (1982), p. 137.

23. This last point may draw objections on grounds that judges in "hard" workers'-rights cases *cite* nonworkplace precedents to justify their rulings but actually *use* background rights to reach their decisions. This explanation, although possible, requires a degree of judicial misdirection or lack of self-consciousness that makes it implausible. In any event, testing

such a thesis seemingly would require psychological inquiry, personal interviews of judges, analysis of judges' private notes and diaries, or other investigation beyond the scope of this study.

24. My approach departs from Dworkin's normative argument by considering both principle and policy as potential acceptable justifications for rights. For example, underlying my discussion in chapter 3 of the right to fair treatment are the notion of fairness as a principle (background right) and the idea that fair treatment in the workplace, like the distribution of minimal levels of food and water, furthers an important social goal. As description, Dworkin's thesis is open to serious question, as he himself (1977, p. 96) appears to recognize: "Different arguments of principle and policy can often be made in support of the same political decision [i.e., right]." Dworkin's concern (p. 96) that anchoring rights in policy rather than exclusively in principle may make them more vulnerable is based on an empirical and possibly false assumption; if this assumption is applied to workplace rights (which Dworkin does not do), I believe it is at least misdirected.

3

The Economic Rationale for Workers' Rights

Why, as a matter of principle or public policy, should employees have special rights at all? Shouldn't society simply leave the matter to be resolved in the marketplace, letting individual workers contract for the conditions of their own employment? And if workers are to have special rights, which rights should they be?

Ultimately, the rights that workers possess are determined by a historical process, and in later chapters I explore how these questions have been resolved in practice—how market forces, political action, jurisprudence, and institutional mobilization and decay have produced a temporally shifting array of workers' rights. This later analysis will be important to understanding where American society is now and the opportunities that lie ahead.

In this chapter, workers' rights are examined in the context of economic theory. Conventional, or neoclassical, economic theory argues that markets are the most appropriate and most effective mechanism for regulating employment and other economic relationships; any departure from market processes (such as the statutory establishment of workers' rights) in deciding social outcomes is assumed to be suboptimal unless the contrary can be proven. Neoclassical theory would argue for only the most minimal worker protections, such as the ban on slavery.[1] This perspective dominates the public debate, so that workers' rights advocates frequently find themselves on the defensive, arguing in effect, "Yes, but . . . ." Without either accepting or attempting to refute neoclassical economics' larger theoretical orientation, I wish to show that sufficient reasons exist to justify supporting a regime of workers' rights. In effect, I seek to affirm on economic grounds the legitimate place of workers' rights in public policy.

Although I pose the questions here in an academic way, as if society could consider them de novo, one should remember that courts and legislatures are daily grappling with the same issues. In so doing, they (the courts especially) must attempt to find some larger justification or logic for their actions. Conventional economics has largely discredited a positive view of workers' rights, but as I hope to show, another economics is possible.

Why Special Rights for Workers?

Because answering the question, Why special rights for workers?, will be important to the rest of the book's argument, I develop it at some length. However, the essence of my answer can be stated briefly: some social relationships or outcomes are so vital to the welfare of society and may be so inadequately determined by the market that society has rightly refused to leave their determination solely to the market. The fair treatment of employees during work meets these tests and justifies special protections.

Society has established rights as a method of distributing minimal levels of certain "goods" (broadly construed), that is, of mandating outcomes for a wide variety of social relationships or circumstances. (Such goods are sometimes termed "merit goods" in economic analysis.) In doing so, it has acted to ban some outcomes that are both possible in the market and so detrimental to society or individuals that intervention is warranted. The standards accepted as minimal and the efficacy of efforts to meet those standards have varied over time, but these practical considerations do not alter the fundamental point. Examples of generally accepted interventions include fixing the distribution of votes; ensuring provision of food, water, and health care; and regulating the conditions of employment. Based on the belief that ballot-selling in any form erodes the principles and legitimacy of democratic institutions, the vending of votes is prohibited entirely. Society permits markets to organize most of the provision and allocation of food, water, and health care, but precludes the market's harshest possible outcomes—for example, total deprivation for an individual who is unable to purchase these goods. Moreover, society has long insisted on taking some direct actions (for instance, stocking foodstuffs against famine, protecting public water supplies, supplying public-health nurses) to ensure that at least minimal standards of supply and distribution are met.

For the conditions of employment, both American history and present opinions are more mixed. At base, there is virtual unanimity on the proposition that at least some of the conditions of employment clearly present circumstances of such vital social importance that society cannot be indifferent to all possible market outcomes. For example, slavery, physical abuse by an employer, and racial and gender discrimination, even if entered into under a voluntary contract, are outlawed, and few would decry these interventions.

Beyond these minimal interventions, consensus breaks down. The viewpoint I adopt is that public policy must foster acceptable working conditions while accommodating other economic and social needs.[2] What drives and justifies public intervention in employment conditions, I argue below, are some peculiar structural features of the labor market that prevent this market from producing socially optimal types and levels of workers' rights. In brief, this market is characterized by long-term relationships in which, for job-seekers, the conditions for market contracting are distorted by asymmetries of information, inequality in bargaining status, and a lack of contract enforceability; for job-holders, the opportunities for recontracting are limited because of a weak "exit" threat due to the high personal cost of worker mobility; and bargaining by individual workers for their rights is not optimal because of public goods and economies of scale characteristics of workers' rights.

Together, these various elements produce a situation in which there is a systematic undervaluation and underproduction of workers' rights; that is, these circumstances make the labor market, in the absence of legal safeguards, an inadequate mechanism for dealing with workers' rights. (Subsequent chapters show that collective bargaining and legislation, for different reasons, are not very effective either.) In the face of these obstacles, appropriate and effective public intervention in setting employment conditions, of which workers' rights is one form, could contribute to outcomes more favorable to individuals and to society.

The Conservative Neoclassical View

This answer, especially when focused on the conditions of employment, is by no means universally accepted. Indeed, conservative and even much liberal thinking on the labor market argues against any public intervention. The contrary argument is most fully developed within the conservative strain in neoclassical economics.[3] Although the theory often takes highly mathematical form, the argument itself is simple: competitive markets produce optimal social outcomes, and because labor markets are competitive, labor markets left to themselves will produce optimal outcomes. No state intervention is needed or would be helpful.

This noninterventionist logic is expanded as follows.[4] Workers are free to choose for whom they work, just as employers are free to choose whom they hire. If workers value the benefits that would be obtained through workers' rights, then in the absence of rights granted by legal fiat, workers will be attracted to employers who, other things being equal, offer such benefits. Employers, in competing for workers, will have an incentive to make such offers. If such benefits are costly to the firm, employers who offer rightslike benefits will discover that they can compensate for their costs by offering a lower wage to attract such workers, and workers who desire such benefits will be ready (and forced by competition) to accept lower wages in compensation for getting rightslike benefits.

Each worker will be able to choose the optimal mix of a wage and rightslike benefits, where (costly) benefits produce a corresponding reduction in the wage, with the exact amount of the reduction to be determined through the market process. Because benefits are costly to employers, they will have an incentive to provide or "produce" them as efficiently as possible—for example, by letting them impose as little disruption or cost on the production process as possible. Because workers must "pay" for rightslike benefits with a lower wage, they will choose only those benefits and only as much of them as are "worth" the lowering of the wage. Hence employers will produce benefits efficiently, they will produce as much as workers will "buy," and such benefits will not, from a social perspective, be overproduced. No state intervention is needed: through the market itself, workers get the benefits they desire, and the socially optimal level of rights-like benefits is efficiently produced.

A particular form of this argument is especially compelling. Could one not expect that market competition would establish the optimal provision of workers' rights through the following process? Suppose that there are many employers competing to hire workers; suppose further that workers desire both wages and workers' rights, though each worker in a somewhat different combination, some valuing wages more highly than workers' rights, others the reverse, and workers also differing among themselves as to the mix of various rights they desire. Then each firm will offer a distinct combination of wages and workers' rights, and workers will simply sort themselves among employers so as to realize the combination closest to their own desires. If the number of firms is very large, one could imagine that every worker will find some firm that offers a combination very close to that worker's optimal combination. If in the aggregate what workers want and what employers offer does not fit, those employers who are offering the most desired combinations will face large (excess) labor supplies whereas those employers offering the "wrong" combinations will see meager or dwindling labor supplies. This pressure will force the latter group of employers to change its offerings to include more of those most desired by workers, and workers will be forced by competition for jobs to accommodate their desires to what employers are willing to offer. Thus, workers will be able to find in the marketplace the mix they want, subject only to normal economic constraints.[5]

This is a powerful argument. It challenges not just the merits of some specific right of workers, but rather the admissibility of virtually all workers' rights. Of course, the argument is an application of the general neoclassical theory used by market advocates against most forms of state intervention. It would admit the need for state intervention only under certain, but narrowly limited, restrictions—essentially those conditions in which a market can be expected to fail and a government intervention can be expected to improve the situation. If labor markets are not competitive or if important externalities exist, then it is possible that state intervention (for example, a state guarantee of workers' rights) could help offset the market failure; absent such features, however, state interference is said to be unwarranted.[6]

Are there, in labor markets, structural elements of market failure sufficient to justify, even on neoclassical terms, government intervention? Apart from a few notable exceptions, a general lack of competition cannot be claimed; there are many people looking for jobs and many employers offering jobs. Indeed, it is exactly the often fierce competition in labor markets that has given rise to the unions' long-held goal of taking wages and employment out of competition. There are, however, several other elements of labor-market structure and functioning, *especially as they specifically relate to workers' rights*, that raise serious questions about whether the market (without legal guarantees) will produce optimal outcomes.

The balance of this chapter proceeds as follows. First I consider features of the market in which job-seekers operate, to argue that asymmetries of information, inequality in bargaining status, and lack of contract enforceability—all with respect to workers' rights, but not necessarily with respect to other elements of the employment contract—establish a market context in which it cannot be presumed that the market will produce the optimal level and mix of workers' rights. Job-seekers may be new entrants to the labor market, unemployed persons, or currently employed workers seeking new employment; for each, however, the contract for the employment being sought may be thought of as an initial contract with a new employer. Next, I consider workers continuing with their current employers and the opportunities for them to recontract; I argue that typically the high personal cost of mobility and other aspects of job choice result in a reduced efficacy of "exit" and, again especially for workers' rights, in limited opportunities for effective recontracting. Finally, I consider the nature and supply of workers' rights to argue that their public-goods and economies-of-scale characteristics make them inappropriate "goods" for individual market-bargaining.[7]

Market Distortions Facing Job-Seekers

Can market mechanisms be relied upon to determine socially optimal levels and mixes of workers' rights? The answer depends, in the first instance, on whether the circumstances facing job-seekers and employers create the conditions for efficient market competition. Three peculiar structural features of the labor market suggest that they do not: asymmetric information, structural inequality among bargaining agents, and lack of contract enforceability.

Asymmetric Information

The labor market, absent legal guarantees, cannot be assumed to provide the optimal determination of workers' rights because workers lack the information about rights that is essential to efficient market competition.

It is axiomatic that unless market actors have adequate information, there cannot be a full competitive process with its resulting presumed benefits to society. What constitutes "adequate" is in some dispute. The pure neoclassical model requires an assumption of "perfect knowledge" on the part of all actors in order to derive its strict conclusions on efficiency. Although one may doubt if real market actors ever have the perfect information required by the theoretical models, nonetheless it seems reasonable that for many markets (for example, the stock market or many consumer markets) there is a level of knowledge approaching full information.

Recognizing how severe (and, in many cases, unrealistic) the conventional assumptions about information are, economists have begun exploring the consequences for competitive theory of partial or imperfect information.[8] In general, if information is costly, one can assume that market actors will pay for more information until the added value of additional information no longer exceeds the cost of it. Thus, information may in some cases be treated simply as another productive resource, and no exceptional difficulties for competitive market efficiency ensue.

More severe problems occur, however, when the basic structure or nature of the exchange situation produces asymmetric or "private" information. Asymmetrically incomplete information violates the conditions for normal market competition and can be presumed to result in market failure. Economist Ronald Coase attempted to get around this problem by arguing that even where competitive markets do not exist, people will nonetheless achieve efficient (Pareto-optimal) outcomes by direct negotiation, internalizing all externalities as it were, so long as transactions costs do not prevent such an outcome. But more recent theoretical modeling of "noncooperative bargaining" and "private information" makes such a broad claim unlikely to be valid except in a tautological sense.[9]

The main conclusion derived from these models "is that bargaining is typically inefficient when, as is likely, each bargainer knows something relevant that the other does not."[10] Results from many contexts—such as labor markets, credit markets, and the medical services markets—reinforce the conclusion that asymmetric or incomplete information opens the door to strategic and opportunistic behavior on the part of some actors, and that such behavior is almost invariably inconsistent with the conclusion that the market necessarily produces socially optimal outcomes.[11]

Asymmetric information has thus been shown to result in efficiency distortions and market failure. William Samuelson, for example, analyzed property rights and bargaining in the presence of "private information" and found that negotiation will not lead to fully efficient outcomes.[12] Bruce Greenwald demonstrated that adverse selection (resulting from informational asymmetries) in the labor market "may seriously impair a worker's freedom to change jobs."[13] Given this inefficiency, the introduction of legal constraints can increase market efficiency, at least in some and perhaps in many contexts.[14]

With respect to workers' rights, structural barriers in the market prevent workers from obtaining certain information, depriving them of adequate knowledge and causing market failure.[15] What are these barriers? Workers have, or in principle have access to, substantial information about certain types of workers' rights: for both statutory rights and collective contract rights, the rights that workers possess are public information and easily obtained. As I argue later, even here—especially with regard to some statutory rights, where legislation and court decisions make the interpretation of such rights extremely complex—there may be economies of scale in the bargaining process resulting from the high and fixed costs of understanding the complex workplace circumstances regulated by these rights. If workers were forced to rely on individual bargaining to gain these rights for their own employment contracts, the costliness of the information likely would preclude effective bargaining by individuals.

Far more serious, however, is the asymmetry of information concerning enterprise rights—precisely those rights for which workers lack statutory or collective-bargaining support. As I argue later, the proprietary nature of corporate employment systems has resulted in a situation in which job seekers generally cannot obtain reliable information on enterprise rights, and therefore cannot compare such rights across different employers. This is not simply a problem of the intrinsic or "real" cost of the information being high (as it is, for example, with statutory rights), but rather in addition one of legal and other institutional barriers that prevent access to it. Without information, job-seekers or employees cannot bargain effectively, and so there is a presumption of market failure.

Structural Inequality among Bargaining Agents

Efficient market determination of workers' rights is also inhibited by the fundamental structural inequality that typically exists between an individual job-seeker and the employer.

Consider the actors in a labor market. Competition does not require that bargaining agents be equal in size, scope, or economic power, but it does presume a sufficient degree of equality between employer and employee to enable all market actors to register their demands and supplies free of coercion or intimidation. But this degree of equality typically does not hold between employers and workers. The stories that economists tell for illustration usually involve an individual entrepreneur or a small firm (what some have termed "lemonade-stand capitalism") with whom the seller of labor may stand on relatively equal footing; but the reality for most workers is that they are hired by large enterprises.

The discrepancy between employer and worker results in the two sides having very different stakes in the outcome of individual bargaining. For all but the very smallest employers, it makes little difference which worker is hired or fired or leaves; that is, the employer's stake in any particular employee is typically slight. But for the individual employee, obtaining, losing, or leaving a job is a matter of great personal consequence, increasingly so as the worker grows older. This inequality was well expressed by a judge in the 1957 case *McClelland* v. *Northern Ireland General Health Services Board:* "As a matter of practical common sense, the situations of the employer . . . and that of one of its servants [that is, employees] are very different. The loss or damage to the [employer] occasioned by the departure of one of its servants would, save in very exceptional circumstances, be negligible. To a servant . . . the security of employment . . . is of immense value."[16]

The asymmetry in the bargaining powers of an employer and the individual worker was exactly what led to the legalization of labor unions; in the words of the 1932 Norris-LaGuardia Act, which provided the basis of the modern legal recognition of unions, "The individual unorganized worker is commonly helpless to exercise actual liberty of contract and to protect his freedom of labor, and thereby to obtain acceptable terms and conditions of employment."[17] The idea in Norris-LaGuardia and the more recent labor legislation that flowed from it was that market contracts could not be fairly negotiated between the individual worker and his or her (large) employer; instead, the bargaining should be between, on one side, an employer, who has a group of jobs to offer and a large stake in the conditions attached to them collectively; and on the other side, a union, representing a group of workers with a similarly large stake in the outcome. In an economy with many firms and many unions, the conditions required for free competitive markets would prevail. Instead of destroying competition by creating the conditions of bilateral duopoly, as is commonly asserted, unions were seen as providing a necessary means of achieving effective competition in the labor market.[18]

Not all workers are the same, and some individual workers clearly have substantial market power. Those workers with rare and valuable skills, or who have crucial knowledge of the particular enterprise's operations, or who in some other way have created specific circumstances inducing the employer to have a significant stake in them may have substantial bargaining power vis-à-vis their employers, especially in the short run. Such workers may be well placed to work out employment contracts to their advantage. But for the general case such special circumstances cannot be presumed.

The courts on many occasions have recognized that key aspects of their decisions touching on industrial relations rely on an assumption of a sufficient degree of equality between the two parties to the employment contract. Without such a presumption, the ensuing transaction arguably fails the test of being a valid contract. Supreme Court Justice Felix Frankfurter stated the general legal principle as follows: "The courts generally refuse to lend themselves to the enforcement of a 'bargain' in which one party has unjustly taken advantage of the economic necessities of the other."[19] Courts therefore have worried about how to fashion a legal doctrine that redresses what they acknowledge as a serious imbalance of power between the individual worker and his or her employer.[20] They found a solution in the legal recognition of unions. The highly conservative Supreme Court of 1921, for example, declared that unions "were organized out of the necessities of the situation. A single employee was helpless in dealing with an employer. . . . Union was essential to give laborers opportunity to deal on equality with their employer."[21] In the courts' thinking, the right to join or form a union extends this redress, in principle at least, to all workers, including those who choose not to exercise their right to unionize.

Thus courts, in particular the U.S. Supreme Court, have been especially careful—some complain that they have been creative—in legitimizing and defending the enforceability of collective contracts against more conservative conspiracy or restraint-of-trade arguments. The courts took this tack because to do otherwise would be to reopen the legally troublesome issue of the inequality between the makers of labor contracts. Although this legalism served for most of the twentieth century, today there are so few workers represented by unions that the courts, and especially state courts in whose jurisdiction such matters primarily rest, have increasingly felt compelled to move to other legal reasoning to redress the bargaining imbalance.

For the persistent conservative neoclassical economist, however, the evidence provided to this point is not persuasive: instead, there is appeal to the impersonal working of market forces. Although each individual worker may stand relatively powerless before a potential employer, the weight of large numbers of such powerless individuals, when summed, is said to be great. Hence, the final effect is still to create a balance that establishes market competition. Even gross inequality in bargaining status is therefore seen as no threat to the presumed benefits of markets.

This argument is usually saved by the division of knowledge into academic disciplines, for few social scientists know the rules of labor law; but it is less compelling when placed within the real-world institutional context. As is shown later in this book, the impersonal working of market forces produces labor contracts that, for the most part, workers have found to be not legally enforceable: it is precisely the criterion of whether or not the contract has been *personally bargained* (or bargained by a union, in those cases where there is a certified collective bargaining agent) that judges use to determine if the contract is enforceable as a contract or simply constitutes an employer gratuity that is unenforceable at law. For example, with respect to job security, one observer, after reviewing the extensive legal experience on this matter, stated flatly: "The primary reason courts refused to overcome the employment at will doctrine based on principles of breach of contract was that employers and employees failed to bargain for or negotiate about job security."[22] That is, unless the individual worker can provide evidence showing that he personally bargained over this issue, courts have traditionally assumed that the employers retain their employment-at-will rights to fire their employees at any time for any cause or no cause. Thus, the conservative neoclassical economist concedes the lack of direct bargaining, because this concession is thought to be trivial and irrelevant; yet it is this very omission that is taken by judges to be crucial and that renders the contract provisions unenforceable.[23]

Lack of Contract Enforceability

The market process may fail to provide the optimal mix and level of workers' rights because, in the nature of the transaction, workers cannot be assured that they will be able to obtain enforcement of the contracts they make.

Market processes cannot be expected to achieve efficient outcomes if market bargains or contracts are routinely unenforceable. Much economic analysis simply presumes that contracts are enforceable; alternatively, some analysis (for example, of bond defaults, warranties, and insurance) considers the possibility of occasional contract failure as an insurance problem. However, what happens when lack of contract enforceability is not a relatively rare disruption of otherwise normal contract relations, but rather a routine and pervasive element of the transaction itself? An extensive literature has developed in exploration of this problem, which Samuel Bowles and Herbert Gintis have termed "contested exchange."[24] At a minimum, virtually all observers agree that the problem of contract enforceability has proven much more complex than initially recognized and itself a possible cause of market failure.

For workers, the problem of contract enforceability, like that of asymmetric information, changes in character with respect to different elements of the wage bargain. With respect to the wage itself, for example, contract enforceability may not be a significant problem; unless workers are paid, they are unlikely to continue working. Although many wage disputes come before administrative boards and the courts, the law is fairly clear because the wage bargain itself is straightforward, and certainly the means for enforcement are well known.[25] With respect to statutory rights and collective contract rights, the processes for enforcement are also well established. The actual enforcement mechanisms (for example, litigation to recover back wages or assert workplace-safety rights) may be beyond the means of individual workers; in such cases, while contract enforcement in principle is no issue, in practice it is one.

Once again, however, the situation is more difficult with respect to enterprise rights—precisely those rights that have developed out of the market as prescribed by the conservative neoclassical approach. As noted earlier, courts have traditionally refused to recognize as valid any contract in which the employer promises a right that was not personally bargained for by the worker, and as I note below, significant public-goods and economies-of-scale characteristics of workers' rights largely prevent employers from engaging in bargaining with individual workers (other than unusual workers in unusually high demand). Combined, these features mean that most job-seekers and job-holders are precluded from obtaining enforceable contracts concerning enterprise rights.

In recognition of situations in which contract enforceability may be a problem, some economists have begun exploring the role of informal or implicit mechanisms to ensure contract enforcement, using such notions as "implicit contracts," enforcement by "reputational effect," and repeat-purchase and "self-enforcing" contracts.[26] Such informal (or nonlegal) mechanisms may bring pressures that impinge on workers or employers or both, and it seems that in certain cases such pressures indeed have impact; for example, the usefulness to consumers of product warranties seems at least partly based on the discipline imposed by informal mechanisms. Nonetheless, the efficacy of such mechanisms to enforce what would otherwise be legally unenforceable contracts (rather than as a supplementary pressure for otherwise enforceable contracts) is open to serious question.

The question with respect to work rights is whether reliance on informal mechanisms to constrain employer behavior is adequate. There are several reasons to believe that such mechanisms are likely to be faulty.[27] The possibility of damage to an employer's reputation would seem to constrain employer behavior most effectively when the abrogation of an implicit contract occurs near the time other implicit contracts are being made (for example, when other workers are being hired), when the fact of the abrogation will become widely known, and when the abrogation concerns the central element or elements of the contract. Such conditions may hold, for instance, with respect to layoffs when the employer has promised continuing employment, and it is here that the reputational argument has been most frequently made.[28] With respect to most workers' rights, however, all three of these conditions are missing or greatly attenuated. The abrogation of an individual employee's workplace rights, for example, need not involve any change in the package of rights promised to other workers; the abrogation may not become known, especially if the employee continues in her employment with the firm, and an employee may decide that unless it threatens to end the employment relationship itself, the abrogation is not worth fighting.

Thus, reputational threat is most likely to be effective for such decisive and highly visible matters as hiring and firing; it seems much less likely to be effective with respect to particular elements in the conditions of continuing employment. Even so, recent American industrial history contains many cases of major employers dismissing long-term employees, thereby breaking what many had perceived to be the principal implicit promises of these firms.[29] Such actions simply serve as reminders that contract enforcement through informal mechanisms, though possibly effective in some cases, does not fully replace legal enforcement.

One implication of the endogenous-enforcement interpretation of contracts is that anything that increases workers' rights on the job will improve their bargaining situation, that is, increase their capacity to extract "rents" from their employers. Such an increase may or may not be judged desirable, because either the "original," pre-rights outcome or the new, with-rights outcome might be considered socially superior. From a pure efficiency perspective, however, if it were intended that workers' rights were to be introduced to remedy enforceability problems without altering relative bargaining strengths, some mechanism would be required to attenuate this distributional side effect.

In regard to workers' enterprise rights, the problem of enforceability is substantial. A market process devoid of legal guarantees cannot be presumed to arrive at optimal results when the basic contract to be bargained lacks legal enforcement and has only weak mechanisms of informal enforcement.

Limited Effectiveness of Recontracting

Structural problems that distort job-seekers' initial market bargains would be less salient if employment could be seen as a process of frequent or continuous recontracting. In effect, any omission or distortion in a worker's initial employment contract with an employer could be recouped in subsequent recontracting. Unfortunately, the circumstances facing incumbent workers do not suggest such relief.

It was to analyze situations involving long-term relationships that Albert Hirschman proposed his distinction between "exit" and "voice" responses in economic relations.[30] In a labor market, for example, a worker can signal his preferences by choosing to leave (exit) the relationship with one employer and move to another job offering a different package of worker benefits. Or, the worker can signal his preferences by staying with the original employer and using persuasion, politics, or other means (voice) to change conditions at the current workplace. It was Hirschman's insight that while neoclassical competition relies on the exit mechanism, there are many situations in life that favor recourse to the voice option.

Reduced Efficacy of 'Exit'

For most workers, employment is a relationship more suited to voice than exit; in part, voice is favored because exit is too costly. Consider the situation of an employed worker. Competition based on exit (in the labor market or in any other transaction) is most effective where the costs attendant upon making market choices and registering preferences are slight, where choices are frequently repeated so that learning can occur, and where the effects of this transaction are straightforward or separable from other consequences. It is least persuasive where the costs of registering choice are great, choices occur infrequently, and their effects are encumbered by other, large, and perhaps uncertain consequences.

To illustrate: if I choose McDonald's hamburgers over Burger King's chicken, I vote my market preference in a way that sends a clear signal to producers about my tastes, yet the act of signaling costs me little and these costs are easily understandable (I deprive myself of the chicken). If I make a bad choice, the consequences are not severe. Also, I am likely to be confronted with this decision frequently, so I can learn from my mistakes and even from my correct choices.

Negotiating job conditions represents the opposite set of circumstances. For incumbent workers, the costs of job mobility are typically very high. For example, if a worker has developed some skills ("specific human capital") that are usable only with the current firm, mobility means abandoning these skills. If the worker's benefits (health insurance, retirement pay) are tied to the current employer, mobility implies leaving behind these benefits. If the worker has specialized skills for which there are limited local markets, leaving the present job may require a geographic move as well. In order to use exit to signal a preference for more job rights by changing jobs, this worker must undertake an action that is likely to disrupt and put at risk (as well as reduce) her income and may inconvenience her personal life, dislocate her family, cause her to leave her community, and cost her her workday friends and colleagues. For exactly such reasons, people do not switch jobs frequently, and so they typically have little experience to draw upon.[31] Here, a market signal is extremely costly, has uncertain implications, and brings extensive and unrelated consequences. Registering one's choice is costly, and making a mistaken choice especially so.

The consequence of this combination of circumstances is that exit or the threat of exit by workers has greatly reduced efficacy. Of course, for any particular worker, changing jobs may be worthwhile if his present job rights are meager and the prospects of rights in alternative jobs are great; also, those employees with skills that are in high demand or who are otherwise favorably situated may have multiple opportunities for mobility. For workers as a whole, changing jobs may not be so costly if aggregate unemployment is very low, so that alternative employment is easy to secure; unfortunately, as a large scholarly literature has shown, such favorable circumstances are typically self-eliminating.[32] In general, the labor market, especially with respect to its determination of workers' rights, provides a poor context in which to rely on competition via the exit option.

Weak Voice

In such circumstances one might ask: would not voice provide a less costly, more straightforward way than exit to register job preferences? One of the circumstances favoring the voice option over exit is the high cost and complexity of registering one's preferences by exit. As Hirschman (thinking about consumer choices) noted, "Voice is likely to be an active mechanism primarily with respect to the more substantial purchases. . . . When the consumer has been dissatisfied with an inexpensive, nondurable good, he will most probably go over to a different variety without making a fuss."[33] That is, in the situation of choosing a McDonald's hamburger over Burger King chicken, exit is indeed uncomplicated and almost costless and serves as an appropriate signaling mechanism. But exit is less satisfactory when it is highly costly, as it is in the labor market: "[Consider] when an organization is able to exact a *high price for exit* . . . such a price can range from loss of life-long associations to . . . deprivation of livelihood. . . . If an organization has the ability to exact a high price for exit, it thereby acquires a powerful defense against one of the member's most potent weapons: the threat of exit. Obviously, if exit is followed by severe sanctions the very idea of exit is going to be repressed and the threat will not be uttered for fear that the sanction will apply to the threat as well as to the act itself."[34]

Moreover, voice has certain real advantages over exit. Most significantly, it can convey a more complex message: "The information [that voice] supplies is rich and detailed compared to the bareness and blankness of silent exit."[35] Exit rarely provides insights into which rights workers prefer, whereas voice may be full of relevant information. In the labor market, because of the grave consequences for a worker attendant upon changing his job, workers seem to need other ways to register their tastes than by simply exiting.

Given these circumstances, it is not surprising that there should have emerged mechanisms, such as unionization and statute, by which to strengthen the voice option for workers. James Medoff has shown that one of the most powerful reasons that workers are interested in unions is a desire for increased voice. As Medoff and Richard Freeman have argued, enhanced voice offers one of the two "faces" of unionism (the other being monopoly power), and it is perhaps the aspect of unionism that contributes to the apparently higher productivity of unionized workers.[36] Nonetheless, as I argue in the next two chapters, voice opportunities that appear through unionization and statute are ineffective and not likely to offer attractive strategies for enhancing workers' voice.

More to the point here, voice opportunities available through individual recontracting in a market process are also weak. This is so for two reasons. First, the reduced efficacy of exit for workers means that the threat of exit is also weak; but for the individual worker, the threat of exit is one of the most potent means of obtaining effective voice, and so individual workers have a weakened position from which to recontract with their current employers. Again, individual differences exist; some workers, those who have scarce skills or are otherwise in high demand, may be in strong bargaining positions and thus have strong voice opportunities. What is relevant here, however, is not individual differences but rather the systematic weakness of voice resulting from the very nature of the labor exchange; the reasons that make exit a weak feature of labor markets also make voice, in the absence of legal safeguards, weak. Second, as is shown later, workers' rights are inappropriate goods to leave for individual bargaining because of their public-goods and economies-of-scale characteristics.

Thus, recontracting, although in principle able to redress the distortions produced by market failures facing job-seekers, in actuality suffers from its own intrinsic weaknesses. The inadequate provision of voice to continuing workers constitutes one of the most significant rationales for legal guarantees.

Inappropriateness of Individual Bargaining

Reliance on markets to determine the proper level and mix of workers' rights assumes that the "good" being traded is appropriate for individual market exchange. In the case of workers' rights, this assumption is likely to be invalid.

Public Goods

The labor market may fail to provide an optimal mix and level of workers' rights because workers' rights possess significant elements of public goods.

A *good* is any product, service, or other thing that is desired. Economists distinguish between two types of goods, *private goods* (the kind of goods society is most familiar with) and *public goods*. The consumption or use of a private good only or primarily affects the individual who consumes or uses it; other persons receive little or no benefit. By contrast, when a public good is available for one person to consume or use, it is also available (or at least accrues significant benefits) to everyone else; that is, if it is provided to one, it is provided to all. Sometimes this characteristic is called "nonrival" consumption.[37] Food you consume is a private good; others get no benefit from it. Malaria control is a public good; if the swamp is drained to kill the mosquitoes that could infect you, they cannot infect others either, and so others necessarily benefit from your "consumption" of malaria control.

Workers' rights tend to have significant inherent public-good aspects, that is, one worker's possession or use of a claim or privilege results in the benefit or protection being made available to other workers. For example, an individual worker's claim to a workplace free of contaminants typically cannot be honored for one worker without simultaneously benefiting all other employees in the workplace. Another example is the right to seniority-based protection in determining layoffs: one worker cannot exercise seniority rights without triggering other workers' (at least implicit) recourse to seniority also, because seniority order can only be defined with reference to other workers. In economists' terms, a safe workplace and the seniority system are public rather than private goods, "public" here meaning that one person's use of a good necessarily implies others' use of or access to it as well.

Individualizing the benefit from a public good may be technically infeasible, prohibitively costly, or simply not possible because it would be too great a violation of a norm—workers', employers', or society's sense of justice. Some workers' rights have a public-goods character because their claims are culturally acknowledged or mandated as properly universal benefits, "universal," at least, for the affected group. For example, protection against racial discrimination is not left to employers to bargain over with their workers, to be offered to some workers and withheld from others; provision of this benefit on a quid pro quo basis, with different workers receiving different amounts of discrimination protection depending on their bargaining power, would deeply offend social values. What distinguishes a claim to protection against discrimination, say, from a claim to a certain wage level, is that differential protection against racial discrimination (as a public principle) so offends prevailing cultural norms that it is precluded, whereas providing differential wages to workers does not so offend.[38] For this third group of workers' rights as well as those whose public-good characteristics derive from technical or economic factors, providing the claim for one implies creating it for all.

Collective contract rights and enterprise rights have the character of "local" public goods; the benefits from enterprise rights extend to others nearby but not to all workers in the society. The benefits may extend to other workers in the same firm or at least the same labor-force category within the firm, or they may extend more broadly.[39]

When workers achieve or are provided with claims or privileges that have significant public-good aspects, those claims tend to become defined as rights. They become rights because it is impossible or highly costly to provide them differentially within the affected work force on a quid pro quo basis. Each worker in a workplace cannot "earn" a different level of workplace safety or relief from racial discrimination by good or poor job performance. Rights are thus granted where the claim that is made intrinsically (whether because of technical, economic, or cultural factors) confers a benefit on similar or nearby workers.

The logic of this argument may be presented somewhat more formally. The employment relationship involves three elements: labor time or services, wages, and workers' rights. Let *wages* here stand for all forms of quid pro quo compensation (salary, bonuses, pension, health benefits, and so forth). Let *workers' rights* incorporate all the claims or protections that workers have as supracontractual rights, including for example the set of understandings on how workers will be treated on the job. The employment relationship, then, involves an exchange of wages for labor time in the context of (or on the assumption of) a set of workers' rights. Although recent research has focused on a reexamination of the concept of labor time, effort, and the intensity of work, my concern here is primarily with the other two elements.[40]

To highlight the significant differences, I assume throughout the following discussion that the amount of wages paid to each worker is fixed; similarly, I assume that the level or degree of worker protection granted via workers' rights is constant and remains at this specified level; only the form or manner in which the (constant amount of) wages and the (constant level of) protection are provided can vary.

Workers' rights differ from wages in that wages are a private good whereas workers' rights contain important aspects of a public good. Although one could construct scenarios in which other people in the firm (say, other workers) benefit from the wage paid to one worker, the benefits normally and overwhelmingly accrue to the recipient of the wage.[41] The wage is one of those goods traded in markets for which the simple, private-good market analysis seems quite appropriate.

Workers' rights, however, possess significant public-good aspects, as noted above. As for other public goods, economic theory offers two lessons about workers' rights. First, if workers' rights are provided to some workers, others cannot be excluded from them and so the supplier cannot charge for them; second, the private market fails to achieve the best outcome, because it will result in the provision of too little of workers' rights. The first lesson—that users of a public good cannot be excluded from it—explains why public-goods-type workers' claims tend to become rights.[42] Translated for the workplace, this lesson implies that the employer cannot bargain with individual workers over any workers' rights already granted to other workers, because an individual worker will, ipso facto, obtain those rights anyway. Nothing can be extracted in a quid pro quo contract. Hence claims that have significant public-goods aspects cannot be effectively bargained over, and tend, if provided, to be provided as rights.

A less than optimal amount of workers' rights will be provided, however, because the second lesson is that the private market is a faulty mechanism for determining how much of a public good should be provided.[43] On one side, each worker may reasonably hope to be a "free rider" on rights granted to other workers, saving her individual bargaining power for strictly private contract benefits. After all, that worker knows that she will necessarily have access to whatever public-good benefits are provided.[44] Thus workers ("demanders" of rights) will not reveal their true preferences nor demand as much workers' rights as they really want, because they can gain such rights via other employees' bargaining. If they all unite (unionize), the incentive not to reveal their true demands for workers' rights vanishes. But absent such collusion, the system of individual workers bargaining in the market for individual contracts will produce a less than optimal supply of workers' rights. On the other side, the supplier of a public good cannot "charge" individuals for using it, because there is no mechanism for excluding nonpayers from it—if a public good is provided, by definition all in the relevant group receive it. Hence, absent some collective mechanism to pay for providing the public good, the supplier has no incentive to provide it.

The public-goods characteristics of workers' rights renders the market an inefficient mechanism for determining the level and mix of workers' rights. Or, to put it differently, workers' rights are an inappropriate "good" to leave to individual market contracting.

Economies of Scale

The labor market may also fail to provide the right mix and level of workers' rights because of economies of scale in the supplying of workers' claims. Suppose that the cost of providing a separate, individualized claim for each worker is substantial. Suppose further that if the employer establishes a common or standardized claim, the cost per worker of providing that claim to many workers is substantially less. These circumstances produce an economic incentive to convert the claim from a quid pro quo benefit to a workers' right. Where significant economies of scale in the creation, provision, administration, and enforcement of workers' claims exist, there is an economic incentive to offer identical claims to many workers;

that is, such claims will tend, other things being equal, to become rights.

Consider again the differences between wages and workers' rights. Wages are straightforward: the cost to the employer for each worker is independent of the scale of employment. (I continue the assumption that the amount of wages and level of workers' rights are fixed.)[45] If, for example, all workers in a firm receive the same wage, the employer's cost *per worker* is the same regardless of whether the firm employs ten or a hundred or a thousand workers. If each worker receives a different wage, depending on, say, seniority or productivity or educational level, the administrative cost of paying differentiated wages is trivial and the cost to the firm of paying the wage received by any particular worker remains independent of or unaffected by the firm's scale.

With workers' rights, however, the employer's cost structure is more complicated (as are the costs borne by workers). For one thing, the administrative cost attached to each set of rights is likely to be significant and some substantial portion of it is likely to be fixed. Let all those costs of developing, negotiating, implementing, monitoring, administering, enforcing, and otherwise operating a set of workers' rights be labeled the "transactions" costs. As with wages, the level or amount of workers' rights provided to each employee is assumed to be constant. Consider then how the employer's per-worker cost of providing this constant level of rights varies when there is a change in the number of workers to which each set of rights applies.

One case—in which an employer must provide a separate and distinct rights package for each worker—would occur, for instance, if each employee had his own contract which, while providing my assumed constant level of rights, included variations in the specific conditions or terms of those rights. Here, the transactions costs per worker incurred by the employer are likely to be substantial. Separate regulations will need to be developed for each worker, individual rather than standardized contracts will need to be drawn up, and negotiation to reach agreement with each worker will be required. Also, administration and enforcement of rights will be different for each worker and consequently require greatly expanded supervision and managerial input. The administrative apparatus needed to implement the rights gained by one worker may be different from those needed for others. All these factors would tend to add significant costs.

Consider now what happens when the firm extends the coverage of the same rights package to more and more of its workers. In this case, the transactions costs it incurs per worker are likely to decline dramatically. The procedures and contracts become standardized because they govern many workers, each grievance or complaint officer can serve many more workers, and development costs are spread over many workers. The lowest transaction cost could be expected when a single standardized package of workers' protections is extended to the firm's entire work force. These considerations suggest that there are major economies of scale at the firm or plant level to be realized in providing workers' claims in the form of a supracontractual package applicable to all, that is, in the form of enterprise rights.

On the other side of the bargaining, one sees that workers also experience economies of scale in gaining information when workers' rights are extended in a standard package to larger numbers of workers. To be able to bargain effectively, any worker or worker's agent must have detailed knowledge of the various areas of workers' rights. The cost for any individual worker to gain this knowledge in order to negotiate a successful employment contract would be enormous. Clearly, a group of workers would be able to obtain information at much lower average costs if they combined forces and divided up the tasks, one learning about due-process provisions, another about workplace safety, and so on, or more likely, if collectively they hired an agent who specialized in bargaining. The same can be said for the costs of monitoring and enforcing rights. The larger the group, at least within some reasonable range such as the firm's work force, the lower the average cost per worker of gaining and exercising work rights.

Employers themselves, where sufficiently large, can capture these economies of scale by unilateral action. That is, each employer can decide to offer only one set of rights to its work force (or one to each major group thereof). Indeed, this is just what employers do when they promulgate enterprise rights, a point confirmed in the market outcomes themselves. Almost every employer, unless it must bargain with a union, will negotiate with an individual worker over pay; asking the boss for a raise is a time-honored and thoroughly legitimate endeavor. By contrast, few employers are willing to bargain with an individual worker over such issues as workplace safety or the stages of a progressive disciplinary procedure or the right to a neutral arbitrator in case of a dispute with the worker's supervisor. Here as elsewhere, there is not uniformity: special deals will always be made for exceptionally valuable or scarce personnel. But in most cases, individual workers are not welcomed to negotiate on these topics. Because workers' rights have significant local public-goods aspects and the per-worker cost to the employer of providing a constant level of protection declines, employers have a strong incentive to provide a standard package of rights for all their workers, or at least for all their workers within each major group of employees. In consequence, employers routinely offer just one standard rights package to each major group of workers. But as has been already suggested and will become clear in a subsequent chapter, the problem with this method of granting rights from the worker's perspective is the spotty and often completely lacking enforceability of the rights that employers promise.

Thus workers are not likely to be able to bargain individually for enterprise rights because of economies of scale in their provision. And when employers offer them as promises outside the bargaining, workers cannot get them enforced. For this reason as well as ones discussed earlier, workers' rights are inappropriate "goods" to leave for individual market contracting. Moreover, employers may not realize the return (in enhanced morale, productivity, or labor-force quality) that they hope to obtain from extending benefits, and workers may be driven to look for other avenues of approach to the rights question.

Other Externalities

Bargaining by individuals for workers' rights may also be inappropriate because of the existence of other workers'-rights externalities. Various observers have pointed out that there exist several other sources of market failure in regard to the determination of workers' rights, looking in particular at externalities that are present. For example, Philippe Aghion and Benjamin Hermalin have argued that legal interventions can enhance labor-market efficiency in situations where adverse selection precludes efficient bargaining over employment rights.[46] David Levine has explored how various externalities (especially those associated with just-cause firing policies in the face of adverse selection) result in an inefficient supply of workers' rights.[47] Papers by Gilbert Skillman, Gregory Dow, Samuel Bowles and Herbert Gintis, and others raise further concerns about the efficiency of market processes when the "commodity" being traded is labor, when capital markets (especially as related to workers) are imperfect, and in other situations.[48] All of these results complement the arguments cited above for why markets cannot be presumed to produce the optimal level and mix of workers' rights.

Some readers may wonder why I have omitted from discussion the argument that is often made first and most passionately in behalf of workers' rights—that of equity or justice for workers. The state should guarantee workers' rights, the argument goes, because without such guarantees workers will be exploited or deprived of the job conditions they deserve; or, to state the point in economists' terms, social welfare can be improved by altering the market-determined distribution of economic outcomes (including workers' rights) in favor of workers. I have excluded this argument not because I think it is irrelevant or wrong, but rather because it is, within the confines of contemporary economic theory, considered to be a political rather than an economic argument; that is, this argument would have to be made by appealing to what one considers to be a just distribution of economic outcomes, about which citizens can disagree but economists have nothing of substance to say. As indicated above, I believe that even on the terrain of contemporary economic theory there are valid reasons for rejecting exclusive reliance on the market mechanism to determine workers' rights. To the extent that equity or justice arguments point to the same result, they only reinforce my conclusion.

To what conclusion do all these arguments lead? Simply this: there are strong reasons for doubting that bargaining by individual workers in the market will produce the optimal level and mix of workers' rights. Too little of workers' rights will be produced and the mix, given the poor signaling mechanisms, may be wrong. Other mechanisms may be needed to remediate the market failures.

The crucial tension, however, is not the market *versus* workers' rights, but rather the market within one set of legal constraints *versus* the market within a different set of legal constraints. It is true that guaranteeing extensive workers' rights would limit what employers and workers can stipulate in their employment contracts. Making a contract under the constraints of a given set of workers' rights typically will produce a different outcome from that derived from bargaining without such rights. But markets always operate within some legal and institutional environment that limits and shapes how they function. In this sense, workers' rights are no different from laws that grant joint-stock companies limited liability or laws that prohibit pollution. Thus the "free market" is not the real issue; rather the question is, which legal and institutional framework best promotes the market outcomes desired by society?

For instance, suppose an employer and a worker freely negotiate a contract that permits the employer to whip the worker if the worker fails to sustain a given production pace. Such a contract, although freely entered into, would be unenforceable in law because it violates basic statutes against assault. Few today would complain of this restriction on voluntary contract. All workers' rights are, in principle, no different from the ban on corporal punishment. Rights can therefore be thought of as one mechanism that society uses to distribute goods (broadly construed) *via* the shaping of market decisions. Rights are not so much a substitute for market transactions as they are a means of governing or influencing the outcome of market processes.

To say that markets always operate within a legal and institutional environment is not to say that any particular environment or proposed environment is socially virtuous. Rather, each environment must be scrutinized to see if it produces desirable outcomes. The purpose of public policy is to establish an institutional context that fosters the best outcomes.

Rethinking Workers' Rights

I have argued in this chapter that there are good reasons in economic theory for supporting a regime of workers' rights. In the labor market, job-seekers face asymmetries of information, inequality in bargaining status, and a lack of contract enforceability with respect to workers' rights; these features result in market failures such that it cannot be presumed that the market will produce the optimal level and mix of workers' rights. Workers continuing with their current employers confront highly limited opportunities for recontracting, especially for workers' rights, because of high personal costs of mobility and other aspects of job choice that result in a reduced efficacy of exit and weak voice. Finally, the public-goods and economies-of-scale characteristics of workers' rights make them inappropriate "goods" for individual market bargaining.

This discussion serves to clear the theoretical landscape so that evaluation of workers' rights can turn on the real and practical consequences of alternate rights regimes, as it should, rather than be prematurely limited by theoretical prejudice. The case that other arrangements would do better than markets (without guarantees) has not yet been made; but now it becomes an open question.

My approach to workers' rights also suggests the need to move beyond conceiving of workers' rights as single-dimensional, a zero-sum game in which workers win by having more rights and employers lose by having fewer management prerogatives. That dimension is undeniably present. But there are others as well. First, as already alluded to, workers' rights are likely to be correlated with increased employee morale, commitment to the enterprise's success, and productivity. Thus, the employer may gain more in enhanced worker performance than it loses by yielding rights; indeed, this is exactly the conclusion employers have come to in their decision to grant enterprise rights.

Second, given the balance between workers and employers, how do workers' rights affect market outcomes? Desirable market outcomes presumably may be achieved in a variety of ways, and there may be a variety of market outcomes that are deemed desirable. If so, there is a need to understand *what kinds* of rights push market outcomes in desirable directions. A given level of worker protection may generally be achieved by diverse means. For example, workers may achieve enhanced job security by means of seniority rights, by extensive layoff-notice requirements, by rights to retraining, or by guarantees of substantial severance pay. Each right offers the worker some protection or assistance against unemployment: seniority, by increasing the probability that the worker will keep the current job; the layoff notice, by granting the worker more time to find other employment before becoming unemployed; retraining, by enhancing the worker's ability to obtain a replacement job; and severance pay, by supporting the worker while she explores new opportunities. In principle, each right could be set at such a level as to generate the *same* degree of worker protection. These rights then would become alternate ways of achieving an identical level of worker protection, yet they may have very different effects on productive efficiency. A given set of rights may involve very different costs, depending on whether it is applied or implemented at a national level or a plant level. It is for this reason that I have described market failure in terms of the *mix* as well as the *level* of workers' rights.

In the next several chapters I turn to a review of the sources of present-day workers' rights. I examine the three main contemporary sources of workers' rights—collective bargaining, statutory provision, and unilateral employer grant. My review focuses on this tension: How can rights provide adequate protections for workers and yet not impose such high costs as to damage employers' competitiveness? Although the reasons differ in each case, I submit that all three contemporary sources of rights do poorly on this test, and so they offer little promise as the basis for a future rights regime. However, there are other and more promising approaches, which I consider in the final chapters.

Notes to Chapter 3

1. As Lawrence H. Summers (1989, p. 178) notes, "Analysis of competitive equilibrium militates against mandating employer benefits, just as it militates against other government interventions." (Summers's own paper, however, explores the potential benefits of interventions.) Even the ban on (noninherited) slavery would be opposed by some extreme libertarians such as Robert Nozick (1974), and T. Bergstrom (1971) has shown how slavery can be Pareto-efficient. Peter J. Hammond (1990, p. 7; see also J. L. Coles and Peter J. Hammond, 1986) notes that "perfectly competitive markets are quite capable of producing Pareto-efficient allocations in which some consumers have insufficient resources to survive."

2. One could either posit a market in workers' rights (with firms as suppliers and workers as buyers) or make workers' rights an element in the labor market (where workers offer work in exchange for wages and working conditions including workers' rights, and firms offer wages and working conditions for labor). I have adopted the latter convention, because I am considering one transaction with multiple elements. For example, it is not possible for a worker to "buy" workers' rights without simultaneously selling

her labor. Again by convention, I refer to the labor market (singular), although in empirical application one might wish to distinguish markets separated by region, type of labor, and so forth.

3. The conservative strain is sometimes called the "new classical" or "neo-Walrasian" economics; for ease of exposition, I will refer to it simply as *conservative neoclassical*. This characterization would not fit much of the work of other neoclassical economists, for example, that of Robert Solow, Joseph Stiglitz, Martin Weitzman, Kenneth Arrow, and George Akerlof. *Public intervention* for purposes of my discussion means either laws establishing rights, laws permitting unions to bargain for rights, or court recognition and enforcement of quasi rights. A typical statement opposing intervention is made by the conservative neoclassicist Edward P. Lazear (1988, p. 39), speaking of job security rules: "The government's role should be limited to enforcement of explicit employment contracts between workers and firms. Any benefit that can be achieved by a government-dictated job security rule can be duplicated by a privately contracted one. Neither contract costs nor enforceability problems present a compelling argument against this view." See also the statement by Lawrence H. Summers in note 1 above. For other arguments against public intervention, see Morgan O. Reynolds (1987) and Tibor R. Machan (1987).

4. See, for instance, the papers in Sherwin Rosen (1981), Gregg J. Duncan and Frank P. Stafford (1980), Ronald G. Ehrenberg (1986), Ronald G. Ehrenberg and Paul L. Schumann (1982, 1984), Ronald G. Ehrenberg and Robert S. Smith (1985), Edward P. Lazear (1988), and Lawrence H. Summers (1989).

5. This is the argument made, but with reference to the provision of public goods by local governments, by Charles Tiebout (1956) in his classic article. The argument in the text simply replaces "local governments" with "employers" and considers the specific local public good of workers' rights. Joseph Stiglitz (1977, p. 331), after a thorough review of the local public goods model, concludes: "Tiebout's argument that the local provision of public goods resolves the problem of revealing preferences for public goods is clearly incorrect. For true public goods, without strong congestion effects, efficient size groupings will entail sufficient diversity within the community for the problem of preference revelation to remain." For other criticisms of the Tiebout model, see James M. Buchanan and Charles J. Goetz (1972), and Matthew Edel and Elliott Sclar (1974).

6. For a critical and insightful review of questions facing current "welfare" theory or the theory of "public economics," see Peter J. Hammond (1990).

7. I do not here treat another basis for rejecting the free-market argument when applied to labor markets: labor markets do not clear, and hence the optimality conclusions do not hold. For an overview from a leading neoclassical economist, focusing on why the labor market is not smoothly self-clearing, see Robert M. Solow (1980). The nonclearing nature of this market has been demonstrated at the microlevel by recent work (labeled labor-extraction, contingent-labor, or efficiency-wage models) on the theory

of the firm; see Samuel Bowles (1985). At the macrolevel, the dynamics of investment behavior produce a corresponding mechanism for preventing labor-market clearing; see Samuel Bowles and Richard Edwards (1985).

Note also that there is a distributional (or equity) aspect to the argument as well. Workers may be able collectively to achieve benefits for themselves that they cannot attain through individual market-contracting alone. The neoclassical argument is predicated on the assumption of a "correct" initial distribution of endowments, or a postmarket redistribution, or agnosticism on distributional matters. But if state intervention is the method by which a democratic society chooses to impose a preferred new distribution or redistribution, the neoclassicist cannot object. See Peter J. Hammond (1990).

8. Kenneth J. Arrow (1973) provided the seminal statement of modern concern with the institutional implications of market situations in which the buyer lacks knowledge about product quality or is seriously disadvantaged in this respect to the seller. His main example is the medical market, but he notes (p. 307) that "very much the same considerations apply to the quality of working conditions. The firm is frequently in a better position to know the consequences (the health hazards, for example) involved in working conditions than the worker is, and the considerations . . . in the case of sale of goods have a direct parallel in the analysis of working conditions in the relation of a firm to its workers."

9. Standard treatments of imperfect information are provided in Jean-Jacques Laffont (1990) and Louis Phlips (1988). See also Edward C. Prescott and Robert M. Townsend (1984). Coase's argument is stated in Ronald Coase (1960). Extensions of the "Coase Theorem" are discussed in Guido Calabresi (1968). Duncan Kennedy (1981) provides a thorough critique. Peter J. Hammond (1990) provides an acerbic and useful review of the general topic, with specific comments on Coase (p. 7). See also William Samuelson (1985). For a review of noncooperative-bargaining models, see John Sutton (1986).

10. Joseph Farrell (1987), p. 115.

11. Within the labor market, such results have been reported for "adverse selection" by Bruce C. Greenwald (1986), for example. J. Luis Guasch and Andrew Weiss (1981) analyze a model of self-selection in which a hiring firm can choose to impose a test fee on job applicants. W. Bentley MacLeod and James M. Malcomson (1988) consider "private information" in a model that combines adverse selection and moral hazard. Beth Allen and Costas Azariadis (1988, pp. 104, 108) explore "what happens if all publicly available signals are weakly correlated with the relevant private observation or, in extreme cases, completely orthogonal to it," and conclude that "*if the added budget constraints* [imposed by informational requirements] *become tightly binding on sufficiently many people, then there are grounds for welfare-improving intervention by an uninformed government.* Well-informed governments, of course, may be able to cure [even] relatively small distortions as well." See also the extensive literatures cited in each paper and the review by Joseph Farrell (1987). Jean-Jacques Laffont (1990, chaps. 10 and 11) provides a general neoclassical treatment of these issues.

12. William Samuelson (1985).

13. Bruce C. Greenwald (1986, p. 325).

14. Philippe Aghion and Benjamin Hermalin (1990).

15. See, for example, Kenneth Arrow (1973), pp. 303–18. Others who note information as a market failure include Lawrence H. Summers (1989) and Olivia S. Mitchell (1990).

16. *McClelland* v. *N.I. General Health Services Board,* 1 W.L.R. 594, 612 (1957).

17. U.S. Statutes at Large, Norris-LaGuardia Act, vol. 47, pt. I, p. 70.

18. This was recognized, for example, in *American Shipbuilding Co.* v. *NLRB,* 380 U.S. 300, 317 (1965). The Supreme Court stated that the National Labor Relations Act "protect[s] employee organization in countervailance to the employers' bargaining power, and . . . establish[es] a system of collective bargaining whereby the newly coequal adversaries might resolve their disputes."

19. *United States* v. *Bethlehem Steel Corporation,* 315 U.S. 289, 326 (1942); although not in an employment context, this premise was used, for example, by a New Jersey court in *Henningsen* v. *Bloomfield Motors, Inc.,* 32 N.J. 358 (1960) at 389, 161 A.2d 69 (1960) at 86.

20. Instances of this concern in case law are manifested in *American Steel Foundries* v. *Tri-City Trades Council et al.,* 257 U.S. 184 (1921) at 209; and *Woolley* v. *Hoffman-LaRoche, Inc.,* 99 N.J. 284, 491 A.2d 1257, *modified,* 101 N.J. 10, 499 A.2d 515 (1985), in which the New Jersey Supreme Court found that limitations on employment at will were necessary because of the superior bargaining position of the employer. See also *McClelland* v. *Northern Ireland General Health Services Board,* 1 W.L.R. 594, 612 (1957), already quoted in this chapter (note 16). For concern in legal scholarship, see Lawrence E. Blades (1967), who notes the inequality of bargaining power except for exceptionally well-placed employees. Susan Marrinan (1984) considers the connection between unequal bargaining power and the at-will rule. See *Harvard Law Review* (1980), which considers the justification for judicial intervention in the superior bargaining power of the employer. The 1932 Norris-LaGuardia Act established this idea in legislation; see quote in this chapter at note 17.

In some cases, legislation and the courts have exempted certain categories of workers, presumably because they were not thought to be in unacceptably unequal bargaining positions or simply because of political compromises. Thus, for example, agricultural workers and domestic employees were exempted from the Fair Labor Standards Act. Regardless of the reason, such exceptions do not vitiate the judges' concern in the cases covered.

21. *American Steel Foundries* v. *Tri-City Central Trades Council et al.,* 257 U.S. 184 (1921), 209. The full quotation is:

> Labor unions are recognized by the Clayton Act as legal when instituted for mutual help and lawfully carrying out their legitimate objects. They have long been thus recognized by the courts. They were organized out of the necessities of the situation. A single employee was helpless in dealing with an employer. He was dependent ordinar-

> ily on his daily wage for the maintenance of himself and family. If the employer refused to pay him the wages that he thought fair, he was nevertheless unable to leave the employ and to resist arbitrary and unfair treatment. Union was essential to give laborers opportunity to deal on equality with their employer. They united to exert influence upon him and to leave him in a body in order by this inconvenience to induce him to make better terms with them. They were witholding their labor of economic value to make him pay what they thought it was worth. The right to combine for such a lawful purpose has in many years not been denied by any court. The strike became a lawful instrument in a lawful economic struggle or competition between employer and employees as to the share or division between them of the joint product of labor and capital. To render this combination at all effective, employees must make their combination extend beyond one shop.

See chapter 7 below, and Kelly McWilliams (1986), for a discussion of some of the new rights being created by judges.

22. Kelly McWilliams (1986), p. 347.

23. Duncan Kennedy (1982) criticizes the "unequal bargaining power" explanation on both legal and political grounds, arguing in part that by focusing on unequal bargaining, this argument implicitly concedes that if the bargaining strengths were not unequal, the outcomes would be socially acceptable, a concession Kennedy is unwilling to make.

24. Samuel Bowles and Herbert Gintis (1990, 1993).

25. Even here, the extensive new literature on shirking, agency, efficiency wages, and what Samuel Bowles and Herbert Gintis (1993) call an "enforcement rent" suggests that market allocations are not as simple as the conservative neoclassical approach would indicate.

26. For an early review of implicit contracts, see Sherwin Rosen (1981); Rosen (p. 1144) notes that the literature "reveals considerable controversy and strongly held differences of opinion on the meaning of the term and its implications." See also the discussion in Donald O. Parsons (1986, pp. 800–02). For one discussion of reputation, see W. Bentley MacLeod and James M. Malcomson (1988). An analysis using repeat-purchase is given in Benjamin Klein and Keith B. Leffler (1981). Jonathan Thomas and Tim Worrall (1988) consider self-enforcing contracts for wages. See also Jean-Jacques Laffont (1990), chaps. 10 and 11. The view that implicit contracts are made effectively enforceable by the bad reputation that an employer would acquire if it abrogated or violated them requires extremely strong and implausible assumptions concerning factors such as workers' access to information and the comparative ability of workers and managers to control and disseminate information. This seems not to have deterred development of the theory.

27. Dan A. Black and Mark A. Loewenstein (1991, p. 64) note, "Analyses of implicit contracts typically appeal to adverse reputation effects as providing employers with an incentive to honor their agreements, although

this argument is almost never spelled out in much detail. Upon reflection, there are several reasons for doubting the effectiveness of reputation as an enforcement mechanism." Black and Loewenstein point to differing understandings of the nature of the contract, difficulty in detecting violations, the distinction between current workers (whose contracts may be violated) and future workers (whom the firm hopes to hire and who are the ones who can punish violations), and the lag between investment in reputation and its actual creation (and hence its usefulness as a disciplining device). For a general review of implicit contracts, see Sherwin Rosen (1981).

28. For example, a firm that lays off workers to whom it has made an implicit promise of continuing employment may need to hire new workers (for example, because it needs new kinds of workers); they will be harder to attract if the firm's reputation is damaged. Laid-off workers, because they no longer have any connection to the firm, are likely to have few reasons to shrink from publicizing the firm's abrogation. Because the abrogation involves the central element in the agreement (that is, continuation of the employment relationship itself), the damage to the firm's reputation is likely to be greater.

29. For example, "Digital Breaks Its No-Layoff Tradition," thereby ending a thirty-three-year implicit promise to its workers; *Boston Globe*, January 10, 1991, p. 51; "Texas Instruments Lays Off 725," *Boston Globe,* January 18, 1991, p. 67. Similar stories have been written about IBM, Polaroid, Xerox, General Motors, and many other corporations.

30. Albert Hirschman (1970).

31. Robert E. Hall (1982, p. 716) estimates that "the typical worker today is holding a job which has lasted or will last about eight years. Over a quarter of all workers are holding jobs which will last twenty years or more. Sixty percent hold jobs which will last five years or more." For workers who only change jobs every eight years, there is little opportunity to learn from but great loss in making a mistake. See also James Rebitzer (1987).

32. See, for example, Samuel Bowles, David M. Gordon, and Thomas E. Weisskopf (1990, especially chap. 5). See also Samuel Bowles (1985), Carl Shapiro and Joseph Stiglitz (1984), Juliet B. Schor and Samuel Bowles (1987), Samuel Bowles, David M. Gordon, and Thomas E. Weisskopf (1989), Juliet B. Schor (1991), and Samuel Bowles and Richard Edwards (1985, 1992).

33. Albert Hirschman (1970), pp. 40–41.

34. Albert Hirschman (1970), pp. 96–97.

35. Albert Hirschman (1981), p. 220.

36. James L. Medoff (1987); Richard Freeman and James Medoff (1984). A 1988 Louis Harris poll found that office workers overwhelmingly desired, but few currently enjoyed, "a free exchange of information among employees and departments" and "a participatory management style at all levels of decision-making." *New York Times*, June 14, 1988, p. A25.

37. See John G. Head (1974), chaps. 3 and 8; Allan Feldman (1980), chap. 6; and Richard A. Musgrave and Peggy B. Musgrave (1973), chap. 3.

Paul Samuelson in his classic statement (1954) noted that for a private good, X, the total consumed is indicated by: $X = X' + X'' + \ldots + X^n$, where X' is the consumption of the first person, and so forth, whereas for a public good, Y, the total is: $Y = Y' = Y'' = \ldots = Y^n$. This would be the case for a *pure* public good, not the local public good discussed later.

38. There are two externalities involving racial discrimination. First, citizens are offended if a firm discriminates; it is in response to this externality that racial discrimination is prohibited (see Duncan Kennedy, 1981). Second, one worker cannot be promised nondiscrimination if a second worker in the enterprise faces discrimination; this externality involves a workplace public good.

39. A local public good, Z, would thus have some characteristic like $Z = Z' + Z'' + \ldots + Z^n$ and $Z_a = Z_b = \ldots = Z_z = 0$, where Zs with superscripts refer to the consumption of workers in the plant and Zs with subscripts refer to the consumption of other workers. Alternatively, Z' might differ from Z'' but both be positive; in the example given in the text, if I live further from the swamp than you do, we may both get benefits but your benefit is greater than mine. John Head (1974, pp. 84–86) uses the term "club good" when the numbers receiving benefits is small.

40. The work referred to is that of "labor extraction" or "efficiency wage" models of the firm; among many, see Samuel Bowles (1985), and George A. Akerlof and Janet L. Yellen (1986). See also Richard Edwards (1979). In conventional neoclassical theory, "labor" usually refers to labor time with an implicit constant level of effort assumed.

41. Wages would be a public good, for example, if workers were altruistic, so that Employee *A* derived pleasure from Employee *B*'s pay raise. Alternatively, if Employee *A*'s chances for a raise were increased by Employee *B*'s receipt of a raise, *A* would derive a benefit from *B*'s raise.

42. See Richard A. Musgrave and Peggy B. Musgrave (1973, chap. 3) for a discussion of "market failure due to nonexcludability" and "market failure due to nonrival consumption."

43. John Head (1974, p. 79), thinking about the markets that would be required to produce the optimal output of a public good, notes: "Perfect competition is simply not capable of generating marginal prices which discriminate between different consumers of a given product."

44. Knut Wicksell (1958, p. 82) writes, "If the individual is to spend his money for private and public uses so that his satisfaction is maximized, he will obviously pay nothing whatsoever for public purposes. . . . Whether he pays much or little will affect the scope of public services so slightly, that for all practical purposes he himself will not notice it at all."

45. All that is required here is that the total compensation received by each worker be constant; its division between wages and other compensation is immaterial. The question then is whether the employer's cost of providing a constant level of compensation is itself constant or not.

46. Philippe Aghion and Benjamin Hermalin (1990).

47. David I. Levine (1991; see also 1989 and 1992).

48. See the papers in Samuel Bowles, Herbert Gintis, and Bo Gustafsson (1993).

4

The Shrinking Realm of Collective Bargaining

The postwar regime of workers' rights was based on two intertwined and mutually reinforcing sets of arrangements: collective bargaining and the statutory provision of rights. In this chapter and the one that follows, I argue that the enfeebling of collective bargaining and an excessive reliance on statutory provision caused the system to collapse. More important, if a durable new system of workers' rights is to be devised, a new means of support must be found.

Collective bargaining was—and, where it still exists, is—a subtle blend of legal requirement and voluntary contract, of local flexibility and general impact, and of public policy and private accommodation. Nonetheless, I argue that collective bargaining no longer provides a useful framework for a generalized system of workers' rights. Put simply, this is because unions today represent far too few workers to serve as the centerpiece for workers' rights. In the private sector, union members now account for only about one out of every eight workers. The overwhelming majority of workers do not have or do not choose to have unions to represent them.

A more complete answer, however, requires an understanding of how collective bargaining functioned as one of the two principal supports for workers' rights in the postwar era.

Workers' Rights under the NLRA

The essence of the system set up by the 1935 National Labor Relations Act was simple: government would guarantee the right of workers to form unions and bargain collectively with their employers. Fostering such worker organization was declared to be national policy: it was through unions that the inherent imbalance in bargaining strengths between individual workers and their employers was to be redressed. The employer and employees would then be left alone, under the NLRA, to work out the particular conditions of employment, subject to relatively few restrictions.

Thus, under the NLRA, public power would be used to compel and facilitate bargaining, but not to dictate the result. This system was not an act of noblesse oblige toward the workers: as has been shown, an explicit rectification of unequal bargaining strengths was needed to provide a rationale for the employment-at-will doctrine. Legitimizing the unions permitted courts, when viewing individual employment contracts, to abandon their usual reluctance "to lend themselves to the enforcement of a 'bargain' in which one party has unjustly taken advantage of the economic necessities of the other."[1]

In the careful balancing of the NLRA, public power compels employer and workers (if workers choose) to engage in a process whose outcome is open in several respects. Both parties are required to bargain "in good faith," but the terms of the contract are not prescribed. The balance among the various bargained items is left largely unfettered by the law. Even the question of whether or not the bargaining results in agreement is left open. Such use of public power may be termed *stimulative* and *permissive*: stimulative in the sense that it requires some positive action on the part of those governed by the law; permissive because it does not prescribe the outcome.

For roughly three decades, from about 1945 to the mid-1970s, collective bargaining served as the principal source of workers' rights. For most workers, however, its impact was indirect. When the NLRA was passed, it was widely expected that virtually all of the major branches of industry and commerce would be more or less rapidly unionized. Collective bargaining would therefore become the usual or predominant form of industrial relations and would directly produce rights for most workers. This expectation was not realized.

Union membership as a proportion of the total work force peaked at 25.4 percent in 1954.

Despite their minority status, the unions exercised a powerful influence on the working conditions of almost all workers. Where direct representation did not exist, workers gained rights in two indirect ways: through emulation and through statutory generalization. Emulation occurred as employers, faced with the threat of a unionization drive, preemptively and unilaterally granted rights similar to those enjoyed by union workers. Such employers could then argue to their workers that a union was unnecessary because the workers had already attained all the benefits that a union would bring. This pressure on employers has been termed the union "threat effect."

More generally, workers in nonunion plants, even if unable to organize a union or credibly threaten to do so, nonetheless came to expect and demand unionlike rights, and in many cases their employers felt forced to grant such rights. (Although the focus here is on workers' rights, it should be noted that this pressure worked powerfully on competitive wage rates as well.) The example of highly profitable and unionized operations may also have persuaded some employers of the real benefits to themselves, in the form of higher productivity and worker commitment, to be derived from a rule-structured work process. However transmitted, the model of successful and unionized plants meant that the influence of collective bargaining extended far beyond its direct reach; workers in nonunionized as well as unionized industries gained rights through the collective-bargaining process.

The process of emulation contributed to, for instance, a widespread acceptance of the idea that a worker should be able to appeal to authorities higher than his immediate supervisor. One of the first rights won by unions for their members typically was a recognized grievance procedure. The grievance machinery gives workers "voice" in the workplace. But today virtually all large nonunion employers and many smaller nonunion employers offer some grievance procedure to their workers as well.[2] In nonunion workplaces these rights are usually referred to as "the open-door policy," that is, the practice of plant managers and other supervisors of keeping their doors open to workers who want to express grievances. Employer-established appeals procedures lack many of the features of equal treatment and independence that characterize union grievance systems; in the latter case workers can rely on the union to present their grievances and protect them from retaliation, and final appeal to an outside and reasonably independent arbitrator usually is also possible. Nonetheless, one should not undervalue the importance, even in restricted form, of the appeal rights gained by nonunion workers. Similarly, unions won other rights for nonunion workers through emulation: the right to paid vacation time, important seniority prerogatives, medical benefits, and break time during work are all products of this process.

Emulation, by its very nature, results in uneven extension of rights to the nonunion work force. Some nonunion employers emulate union gains, others do not. Among those who do, some follow the union-won rights closely, others do so only partially, or reshape or distort union-gained rights for their own purposes. Thus, while the effects of emulation and the union threat have been powerful, they have been felt very unevenly.

The second indirect method by which collectively bargained rights became available to nonunion workers, statutory generalization, developed in this way: unions, through collective bargaining, would achieve a certain benefit or prerogative for their members in the organized industries. As experience with the benefit or right became widespread, workers and their representatives would press for enactment of a law making the benefit or right available to all workers. A right gained through collective bargaining for a limited group of workers thus became a kind of bridgehead within which to organize a broader political coalition, including workers in the nonunion industries, union-sector employers wishing to see the costs of the new gain imposed on their nonunionized competitors, and the organized-labor movement and its political allies. By securing even a little terrain, collective bargaining opened the way for new legislative gains.

Nearly all the rights that later became statute-based were in some sense explored by unions and initially won in collective bargaining; statutory generalization, at the state or national level, provided the means to extend these rights to the nonunion work force. This paradigm was followed in the cases of hours restrictions, the minimum wage, and overtime pay, for example, and for antidiscrimination and equal-pay rights. Health and safety rights reflected strong union influence, not only in the immediate sense of labor's lobbying in behalf of laws but more fundamentally in the unions' persistent raising of occupational safety concerns. The national Occupational Safety and Health Act (OSH act) grew directly out of union campaigns around "black-lung" and "brown-lung" diseases. Although some unionized industries (underground coal mining and construction were notorious examples) remained highly dangerous, the discrepancy between substantial safety consciousness in unionized industries (such as auto-making and steel) and management's callousness toward worker injuries and deaths in many nonunion industries (such as textiles and construction) fueled demands for government intervention to halt the industrial carnage.

Statutory generalization was also important in the area of pensions. Employer-provided private pension plans had first multiplied as union-won pension benefits, and then rapidly proliferated as nonunion employers came to use them as part of their union-avoidance strategy. Most of the unions did not gain control over pension administration, but they nonetheless constituted a strong countervailing presence that monitored employer management of the plans. For nonunionized employees, however, no such external supervisory body existed; even for unionized workers bankruptcy, merger, acquisition, or buyout always placed their pension benefits at risk. The growth and problems of private pension plans eventually generated the public support of regulation that led to passage of the Employee Retirement Income Security Act (ERISA) in 1974.

Even where the strategy of statutory provision failed, its logic was apparent. The most crucial case was medical care. As early as the years preceding World War II, the United Mine Workers had established hospitals to serve workers. Collectively bargained health benefits appeared throughout the union sector soon after the war. The natural extension of this benefit was national health care, first proposed by President Harry S. Truman in his 1948 State of the Union address. But Truman's initiative died, and when the issue was revived in the mid-1960s, only the limited medicare program was enacted. The defeat of national health care showed one of the political limits of the strategy of statutory provision.[3]

In all these cases, statutory generalization brought to the nonunion labor force rights initially won privately by unions.[4] Thus the political process provided a second means of transmitting gains from collective bargaining to nonunion workers.

Together, indirect mechanisms produced impressive results. American workers as a group gained important new rights throughout the postwar period and especially in the 1960s and early 1970s. Those rights rooted in federal legislation are considered in the next chapter. In addition, many workers gained other rights: explicit pay scales and task-defined jobs, relief from nepotism and favoritism, grievance and appeal rights, paid vacation, health benefits, and in many instances, job posting, bidding, and seniority rights. The growth of these rights coincided with and contributed to the change in the prevailing ideology of corporate management. The new theories (the human-relations model; Douglas McGregor's theory Y; and organizational behavior models) rejected old-fashioned Taylorism in favor of a more humanistic management approach. Frederick Taylor's philosophy of "scientific management" worked when workers had no rights and no realistic expectations of rights; in the postwar period, such a brute style no longer appeared as effective. Most large nonunion employers moved to construct an alternate system of "bureaucratic control" that defined rights for nonunionized workers, albeit for management ends and within a highly restricted framework.[5] Thus the results of collective bargaining, understood broadly, were impressive gains for workers during the postwar period.

The irony was that even as unions were having a wide impact, they failed to expand the share of the labor force they represented; in fact, the union sector was shrinking. Understandably, the unions chose to trumpet their victories and downplay the significance of their own losses.[6] Unfortunately for the unions, however, even the indirect mechanisms of union influence depended ultimately on the size of the unions' presence in the labor force. Eventually the indirect mechanisms would be eroded by the union decline, as was apparent by the 1980s. Despite its impressive results historically, by the 1990s collective bargaining no longer appeared capable of serving as the central institution of workplace rights.

This last point needs to be stated precisely so as to avoid the exaggeration that weakens rather than strengthens an argument. The question at issue here is whether or not collective bargaining shows sufficient promise for the work force at large to make it the centerpiece of a strategy to revitalize workers' rights. The answer to this question is surely no, unless conditions change drastically. My negative prognosis, however, does not deny the continuing importance of unions. For the foreseeable future, millions of workers in the union sector will depend upon collective bargaining as the central mechanism for advancing their interests. Moreover, in certain segments (for example, the public sector, where there is less employer opposition; and nonmobile service industries such as hotels, food retailing, and hospitals, where the level of unionization is relatively low), unionization may spread, thereby introducing new workers to collective bargaining. Nor can one entirely rule out a dramatic upsurge in unionization such as occurred in the 1930s, especially if the economy should suffer some catastrophe comparable to the Great Depression. Given these qualifications, however, my conclusion nonetheless is that collective bargaining does not seem capable of serving as the central institutional device for a new regime of workplace rights.

The Union Decline

The most obvious reason collective bargaining is no longer so central is the recent decline in unions' strength and reach. Unions once enjoyed great industrial strength, and in the political arena they were part of the central power triad of business, labor, and the public interest, what Europeans call the "social partners." Now, in both the industrial and political arenas, the unions have been reduced to special-interest status, one among many players with continuing but limited influence.

The unions' recent decline has been qualitative and moral as well as numerical. During the first years of numerical decline, from the mid-1950s to the mid-1960s, the unions maintained their institutional and organizational presence reasonably well, despite share losses; for these years, share loss was not necessarily a good index of the unions' general strength. But certainly since the mid-1970s, the unions' quantitative decline has mirrored and reinforced their qualitative losses, which include the decay of their institutional infrastructure, a weakening of their cultural links to working-class communities, the disappearance of their organizational presence in many industries, a marked decline in the power of their ideology to attract adherents and to motivate commitment, the erosion of their political influence, and a decrease in their members' militance. The qualitative dimensions of the union decline need to be kept in mind even as one focuses on the numerical losses.

My proposition here—that collective bargaining cannot serve as the mainstay of a new system of workers' rights—runs counter to much conventional wisdom, especially that accepted by advocates of workers' rights. Because unions have for so long served as the principal device for defending and advancing workers' interests, because collective bargaining was such a central feature of the postwar workers'-rights regime, and because unions retain such a strong if nostalgic hold on the loyalties of workers'-rights advocates, the arithmetic of the union decline must be better understood before my proposition will be accepted with any confidence.[7]

The extent of the unions' decline can be measured by an index of their private-sector share (or density), that is, the percentage of all private employees whose jobs are covered by union contracts.[8] Unions now represent less than 12 percent of the private-sector nonagricultural labor force, less than a third of the peak union share achieved during 1952–54 (see figure 4-1).[9]

Public-sector unions have done much better; indeed, they have provided almost the only area of growth for the union movement. Public-sector unions and employee associations increased their share during the 1970s and 1980s from about one-quarter to nearly 40 percent of the public-sector labor force. But in several ways this good news for unions is less heartening for workers: for one thing, the public sector employs only about 15 percent of the total labor force, so quantitatively, private-sector developments dwarf those in the public sector. Moreover, public-sector workers to a far greater extent derive workplace rights from civil-service regulations, and so public-sector collective contract rights are less likely to provide a model for emulation in other workplaces. The at-will doctrine, for example, is highly attenuated in the public sector, and elaborate, explicit, and typically formalized procedures govern promotion, assignment to pay steps and benefits levels, discipline, job training, layoffs, and job assignment. It is in the private sector, where few of these rights or procedures exist by law, that collective bargaining has been crucial in delivering rights to workers.

Figure 4-1. Changes in Union Share, 1945–90[a]

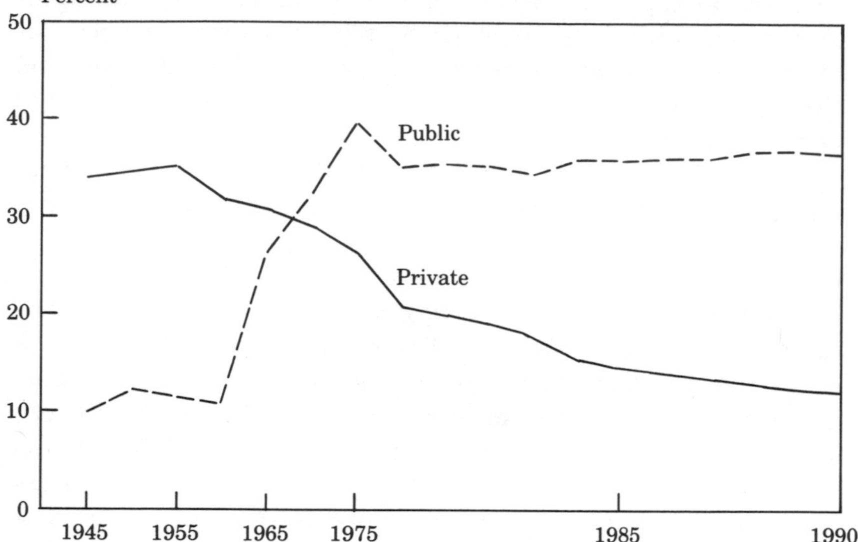

Sources: Troy and Sheflin (1985); Bureau of Labor Statistics, *Employment and Earnings* (January issues, 1985–92).

a. *Private* is union members as a percentage of all private, nonagricultural wage and salary workers. *Public* is union members as a percentage of total public-sector employment. The increase in public unionization between 1960 and 1970 reflects in part the recategorization of employee associations as unions.

Because unions historically have had their center of gravity in the private sector, growth in public-sector unions and decline in the private sector promise not only to change the composition of union membership but also to alter more fundamentally the unions' orientation and operations. For the purposes of this book, however, what is relevant is that private-sector unionism is in a prolonged state of decline. Richard Freeman, one of the closest scholars of unionism, calls this "the effective de-unionization of most of the U.S. labor force."[10]

The arithmetic of unionism's declining fortunes is highly revealing. Because the labor force grows between 1.5 and 2 percent each year, overall union membership must grow by an equivalent percent as well, or the union share will decline; if union membership drops, the unions' share will decline even faster. Union membership may fail to keep up with labor-force growth either because union membership in already organized enterprises fails to grow fast enough, or because efforts to organize new enterprises fail to bring in enough new members, or both. In practice there is always some attrition from the already-organized membership because of plant shutdowns, the natural demise of some union industries, and the fact that the workers at new plants are almost always initially nonunion. Unions therefore cannot maintain their share without substantial new organizing.

The evidence on the attrition rate in the already-organized enterprises is not very satisfactory, because reliable data are scarce and notoriously tardy. One estimate suggests that unions would lose roughly 3 percent of their share each year in the absence of new organizing.[11] The attrition rate may have increased recently, but by how much is not clear. William Dickens and Jonathan Leonard calculate that the "automatic" loss of union members (not share) appears to have increased during the 1970s (the latest period they studied), but the rates of attrition were not markedly different from those suffered during the decade 1955–64. Richard Freeman, using admittedly crude calculations, estimated the "net depreciation or appreciation of union density," considering both changes in employment in unionized establishments and the rate of growth of total employment; he found that the net depreciation rate increased from 3.4 percent in the 1960s to 4.7 percent in the 1970s to 6.1 percent in the period 1980–85. Other evidence, more indirect, reinforces these findings.[12]

These relationships can be illustrated as follows (using rounded numbers for ease of presentation). The total number of employees in the nonagricultural private-sector labor force in 1990 was about 91 million. Of these, about 10.2 million were union members, and so the union share was between 11 and 12 percent. Assume that private payrolls grow 2 percent per year; to keep up with the growth in the private labor force, every year unions need to attract 204,000 (2 percent of 10.2 million) new members from among private-sector workers. Assume further that the natural attrition rate among union membership is 3 percent of the union share per year; to replace members lost through attrition, unions need to attract 306,000 (3 percent of 10.2 million) new members. Considering both factors together, unions would need to organize about 510,000 new private-sector members each year just to maintain their share around 12 percent; to increase their share, they would need to attract more than 510,000.[13]

What are the chances that the unions can enroll 510,000 new private-sector members every year? They have been losing the battle for new members, losing badly, and doing an increasingly poor job as time goes on. As one researcher said after reviewing the evidence on attrition, "The steady decline in the union density from 1954 to the present is almost totally explained by the slowing down of the rate of new organizing during this period."[14]

The principal means by which unions add new members is recognition elections supervised by the National Labor Relations Board.[15] When at least 30 percent of a nonunionized firm's workers request an election, the NLRB identifies the employees eligible to be covered by the law (the "bargaining unit") and schedules an election. If a majority of the firm's eligible workers vote to be represented by a union, the union is legally recognized and certified to bargain on behalf of all the workers in the bargaining unit. Hence an election victory, although it does not guarantee that the union will be successful in obtaining a contract, nonetheless constitutes the key step in recruiting new union members.

Unions have fared poorly in NLRB elections. For one thing, fewer workers participate in NLRB elections each year, and because such elections are the principal way that private-sector unions win new members, the declining pool of eligible new members means that even before any ballots are cast, the scope for possible union growth has already greatly narrowed. The percentage of private nonagricultural workers covered by such elections dropped from over 2.4 percent in 1950, to about 1.1 percent in 1965, to 0.5 percent in 1980, to 0.3 percent in 1983. In 1989, only 273,775 private-sector workers, less than 0.3 percent of nonfarm private-sector workers, had an opportunity to vote on unionization in an NLRB election.[16] Because 510,000 new members were needed, but only 273,775 (in 1989) were covered in the elections, the unions had fallen short of their goal by some 236,225 workers before the ballots were even counted.

Within the constricting circle of recruitment opportunity, unions have been faring much worse at winning new members. Fewer of the voters in NLRB elections now vote in favor of unions. The percentage of workers voting for unionization, considering all certification elections together, shrank from 75 percent or more before 1950 to around 60 percent in the 1960s to less than 50 percent in the 1980s; in 1989, just 49 percent of the workers eligible to vote in

NLRB elections cast their ballots for a union. Not surprisingly, the union victory rate in these elections has likewise plunged—from 76 percent in 1950–54, to 55 percent in the 1960s, to 37 percent in 1975–79. In 1988, unions won 1,839 out of 3,670 elections, for a win rate just over 50 percent; but from these elections they gained just 96,771 workers in the bargaining units they won—fewer than one-fifth of the number needed to maintain their 12 percent share of the work force.[17]

The impact of adverse trends on union presence in the private sector has been devastating. New workers won to unionism through NLRB elections as a percentage of all nonagricultural employees declined from 2.0 percent in 1950 to 0.7 percent in 1965; it dropped to 0.2 percent in 1980 and around 0.1 percent in the 1980s. In NLRB elections during the 1980s, unions enrolled fewer than one new member for every thousand workers employed in the private sector.[18] Thus, by the 1990s the unions' efforts to attract new members through the election process yielded only a small fraction of the number needed to maintain even their anemic 12 percent share. Unions gain a few members in other ways (expanded employment in some already-unionized enterprises, for instance, or union recognition achieved without an election), but NLRB elections remain the unions' primary means of access to the 85 percent of the labor force employed in the private sector. In trying to sign up new members, unions have hit a stone wall.

Why Have the Unions Declined?

In popular discussions, the most commonly cited factor in the decline of unions is change in the kinds of industry now prevalent and in the types of workers increasingly present in the labor force. The national economy has transferred its base from goods produced by heavy industries in the Northeast and Midwest to services and light industries located in a variety of areas besides the so-called Frost Belt. So too, the makeup of the labor force has changed to include more women, more white-collar or other nonproduction employees, and more highly educated and younger workers. Because both the industry and labor-force transformations constitute movements away from the traditional sources of union strength, it has sometimes been argued that these structural changes lie behind the eroding union support.[19]

Recent research tends to cast doubt on the central importance of structural and compositional factors in the union decline. The logic of the structural-compositional explanation relies on the assumption that the characteristics of those who were unionized in the past are good predictors of who can be unionized. For example, women historically have had lower rates of unionization than males, so when the labor force shifts to include more women, the structural explanation depicts this change as adverse to union organizing. Yet among unorganized workers, higher percentages of women than men report that they would be willing to vote for a union, and so the underlying assumption may be false.[20] Thus, present or past union characteristics may provide an unsound basis for extrapolation.

Although conflicting findings remain, recent research suggests that structural and compositional factors played an important role during the early years of the unions' decline but a much more limited role beginning in the mid-1970s. Richard Freeman and James Medoff, for example, studied the period 1954–79 and found that structural and compositional factors accounted for more than 72 percent of the union decline. Although, for reasons that they note, this estimate is surely on the high side, it seems likely that these factors did have considerable impact. After the 1970s, however, structural and compositional shifts accounted for far less of the union decline. MIT's Henry Farber, in perhaps the most persuasive study, finds that only about 20 percent of the decline between 1977 and 1984 can be traced to structural and compositional factors.[21]

Among the host of other possible explanations for the unions' declining success at new organizing, four causes in particular have gotten substantial empirical support. First, unions seem to be putting fewer resources into organizing. Paula Voos found that unions' expenditures to organize nonunion workers within their jurisdictions fell dramatically during the period she studied, 1953 to 1977. Richard Freeman and James Medoff suggest that as much as one-third of the decline in new members attracted through organizing may be due to this factor.[22] When unions do invest in organizing campaigns, their return in terms of new members is less than in the past, so some have argued that the unions' shrinking investment in organizing is simply a rational response.[23]

Second, it is clear that the legal environment has become increasingly hostile to union organizing. For example, it has become much more difficult for a union, after it obtains sufficient worker signatures to trigger an NLRB election, to get the Labor Board to hold an election; the opportunities for employers to challenge, delay, and disrupt the election process have substantially expanded. So too, adverse labor-law rulings have greatly strengthened the employers' role in elections and weakened the unions' hand. All efforts to achieve major reforms, such as amending the NLRA to tip the balance in favor of unions, have failed. Indeed, AFL-CIO president Lane Kirkland, reflecting the deep antipathy of unionism to the current legal situation, has termed labor law a "dead letter" and occasionally called for its repeal, saying at one point that workers may be "better off with the law of the jungle. . . . Let us go mano a mano. I think we could organize very rapidly."[24]

Third, many investigators have documented the explosive growth of employer opposition to union organizing. Assisted by burgeoning numbers of "union-avoidance" consultants, employers have developed sophisticated defenses against organizing campaigns, and many observers have suggested that management resistance plays a central role in the unions' lack of organizing success. Richard Freeman and James Medoff assign between a quarter and a half of the decline in union organizing success through NLRB elections to rising management opposition. Henry Farber also finds significant evidence of increased employer resistance to unionization. Indeed, this employer offensive has been so powerful that "decertification" efforts—attempts to dislodge existing unions—have become increasingly successful. In 1989 there were 622 decertification elections, with the antiunion side winning 70.9 percent of them and the unions losing the right to represent 14,809 workers. Although this figure represents a tiny fraction of a private labor force totaling more than 90 million, it looms large when compared to the unions' yield (96,771 in 1989) from organizing: for every 6.5 new members the unions manage to attract, one existing member is lost through decertification.[25]

Finally, and perhaps most disturbingly for the union cause, there is growing evidence to support the conclusion that nonunion workers do not see unions as effective agents on their behalf and that growing numbers of them do not want union representation. Although workers' perceptions of unions are not formed independently of, for example, employers' efforts to oppose unions or the unions' ability to achieve real gains for workers, the unions' task is made immeasurably more difficult if their organizing efforts are not only stymied by law and resisted by employers but also spurned by the unorganized. Yet that conclusion is indicated by the downward trends, already noted, in pro-union votes in NLRB elections. One might expect that workers voting in these elections would be more strongly pro-union than other unorganized workers, because an election typically is triggered only when an organizing team is convinced that it has sufficient support to win. Yet among the limited and presumably more pro-union set of workers who get a chance to vote in these elections, fewer than half (49.0 percent in 1989) cast ballots for unionization. The high rate of antiunion votes in NLRB decertification elections would reinforce this point, although in these elections the voters are workers who already are represented by a union. In the same vein, Henry Farber reports that between 1977 and 1984 the percentage of nonunion workers who said they would vote for a union if given the chance fell from 38.6 percent to 32.4 percent; Farber concludes that the reduction in the demand for unionization played a crucial part in the union decline. Finally, these results parallel the public's increasingly unfavorable image of union leaders: as late as the early 1970s, 20 percent of the public as surveyed by the Harris Poll had "a great deal of confidence" in union leaders, but by the end of the 1980s this figure had slumped to 10 percent.[26]

To summarize, the severe decline in the unionized share of private-sector workers has resulted from the unions' loss of previously organized members and inability to attract new ones. The NLRB elections for union certification engage a declining percentage of the economy's unorganized work force, and voters in these elections are less likely to vote union. Structural or compositional changes in jobs and workers may account for part of the unions' troubles, but more crucial are diminishing union resources devoted to organizing drives, adverse legal changes, a powerful antiunion offensive by employers, and declining interest in unionization among nonunion workers.

The Unions' Response

Union officials, quite understandably, and a number of the unions' friends and supporters, less understandably, have been reluctant to admit the seriousness of the unions' problem. Lane Kirkland, AFL-CIO president, has frequently declared that the bad news is greatly exaggerated. In 1986, in an essay revealingly titled "It's All Been Said Before. . . ," Kirkland wrote: "Labor's obituary has been written at least once in every one of the 105 years of our existence, and nearly that many causes of death have been diagnosed."[27]

On occasion the unions have tried to acknowledge their desperate situation, but even then they have flinched. For example, in the mid-1980s the AFL-CIO Executive Council launched an effort to face up to the hard facts confronting unions. It established a Committee on the Evolution of Work to investigate the decline; the committee's report, called *The Changing Situation of Workers and Their Unions,* was rightly seen as something of a cold shower, candidly addressing many problems, including internal union deficiencies, that the labor movement traditionally has been reluctant to consider. But even the authors of this report felt compelled to cushion the blow; they introduced their work with the statement that none of the adverse developments they surveyed "warrants prophecies of doom and despair regarding the future of the labor movement. Such prophecies were ventured 50 or so years ago, after American unions in the 1920s and 1930s had suffered serious setbacks and the number of unionized workers had declined dramatically; some predicted the demise of the labor movement at that time. In fact the reverse occurred."[28] Nor are union officials the only ones to avoid the unpleasant reality. One otherwise helpful scholarly work, for instance, after an extensive review of the dimensions of the decline that seemingly pointed in the opposite direction, nonetheless concludes, "There has been no sudden, stark, or 'spectacular' decline in either new union organizing or in union growth."[29]

What these observers say is, at one level, quite true: the recent declines do not directly threaten the *organizational* integrity of the House of Labor. The reduced union share still leaves the unions with some 17 million public- and private-sector members, and so as organizations, the unions remain large, well-funded, and powerful; few other organizations can claim such large membership rosters or assured revenues. Whatever the future trend in union density figures may be, the result is unlikely to challenge the principal unions' organizational viability. Neither, however, is it likely to reverse the fact that the unions have come to represent only a small minority of American workers.

The arguments made earlier concerning the causes and effects of the union decline might be granted and yet the conclusion—that collective bargaining cannot serve as the centerpiece of a new system of workers' rights—be denied. It could be argued that the facts point to the need for a rededication to a familiar old strategy: renew the unions, organize the unorganized. The problem is not collective bargaining, this objection would go, but rather the barriers to increased unionization. This argument carries enormous weight, supported as it is by the generations-long tradition of workers' struggles to build unions and by the resources mobilized in behalf of it by today's House of Labor. As Staughton Lynd has argued, "The bulk of nonunionized employees in the private sector *are* covered by the National Labor Relations Act and their obvious first step toward civil liberties in the workplace would be to seek collective bargaining recognition."[30] The negative can never, of course, be proved: that more effort, more resources, and more commitment would not reverse the disastrous trends in private-sector unionization. Indeed, it would be surprising if a major increase in the unions' organizing effort, in quality as well as quantity, would not have some effect. Nonetheless, a slowing or even stopping of the decline in union share would still leave unions with only about 12 percent of the private-sector labor force as members. The chance that a major labor commitment to organizing would significantly increase the union share seems very small. Only about a third of the nonunionized workers in the U.S. economy, when polled, indicate that they want a union at their workplace, and Henry Farber's finding of a declining demand for unionization combined with more recent Harris polls offer no prospect of respite.[31] Finally, on those occasions when the unions have mobilized themselves to make greater organizing efforts, the results have not been impressive. Undoubtedly the unions can fine-tune their organizing campaign and thereby marginally improve their success rates. There seem to be attractive opportunities for better organizing success in smaller workplaces where women and minorities are heavily represented. But even if unions do reorient and improve their organizing, they cannot reverse the adverse structural and compositional changes nor the active employer opposition to unions. When they have tried to obtain significant reforms to redress the hostile legal environment (as in 1977–78), their efforts proved utterly unsuccessful. What is perhaps most serious of all is the apparent lack of support for unions among nonunion workers.

As committed a union activist as Staughton Lynd, writing in 1978, admitted that "if the creation of unions were strictly limited and if most workers were obligated to remain unorganized, there might be cause for focusing on the implementation of specific rights [without unions]."[32] Many years have passed since these words were written, years in which private-sector unions have suffered grievous further losses. Even those who have devoted their lives to the labor movement cannot ignore the adverse trends.

Union leaders and others who worry about the unions' future feel they nonetheless have an ace up their sleeves: the "Big Surge" theory.[33] Implicitly admitting their situation, union advocates point out that "historically, unions have rarely grown at a moderate steady pace. Instead, they have advanced in fits and starts—in sudden spurts."[34] AFL-CIO President Kirkland has pointed to "major breakthroughs" in organizing in declaring that the labor movement's direction is "onward and upward."[35]

Academics have a special reason—fear of contracting Barnett's Affliction—that impels them to qualify and hedge their projections. In 1932 George Barnett, then president of the American Economic Association, made a prediction that became famous in the 1980s: "American trade unionism is slowly being limited in influence by changes which destroy the basis on which it is erected. . . . I see no reason to believe that American trade unionism will. . . become in the next decade a more potent social influence."[36] It has become almost de rigeur to refer to this spectacularly wrong prediction (or a similar one made in the same year by Lyle Cooper in the pages of the *American Economic Review*) when considering unionism's future. Modern academics inoculate themselves against Barnett's Affliction by hedging any predictions of future union decline with references to a Big Surge.[37]

It is true that union growth has occurred by surges rather than along a smooth curve. Explosive growth occurred in the 1910s, 1935–46, and in the public sector from 1965 to 1975. None of these episodes could have easily been predicted, based on existing conditions. Richard Freeman and James Medoff note that these spurts occurred "generally during improving conditions following significant recessions and during the two world wars," but this observation hardly yields a general theory of spurts.[38]

But waiting for the Big Surge is no strategy for union regeneration. Because the events that might trigger such a surge (war, depression) lie outside the control of unions, at best this position would call for maintaining the integrity of existing labor organizations so as to be ready to exploit radically improved conditions when they occur.

Moreover, the Big Surge theory forestalls efforts to understand the likely future consequences of present conditions. Given the intimidating shadow of George Barnett's prediction, it is perhaps not surprising that modern observers are so timid (or hopeful); but Barnett's Affliction does not make a new Big Surge more likely. One who is not intimidated is Leo Troy, a careful scholar of unions who states unequivocally:

> The American union movement is in a permanent state of decline. Decline does not mean extinction. It means that the union movement will continue to represent workers in the industries in which they are entrenched, but that new organization will be minimal and density [share] will continue to slide.
>
> Most likely . . . the American labor movement will continue into its second century a much smaller movement than it is even now. The American labor movement always has been a minority movement in this country, and it will be a smaller one as it enters the twenty-first century.[39]

What of relevance to workplace rights may be concluded from this review of unionism's decline? Most important, unless a Big Surge occurs, which is unlikely, unionism in the private sector will remain restricted to a very small proportion of the work force—12 percent or less. The importance and impact of this decline should be clear: a labor movement that enrolls so few workers can no longer plausibly speak for workers as a whole, nor can it provide a credible threat to nonunion employers in general. Thus, the unions' decline has not just been a numerical slide; it has deeply eroded organized labor's basic position in industry and society, and has nullified collective bargaining's two lines of indirect influence—emulation and statutory generalization.

The Diminished Role for Unionism

Before 1970 unions represented 30 percent or more of the private-sector work force, and those workers were located in the most technically advanced, profitable, and strategic industries. Under these conditions, the unions exerted great leverage. Membership density then probably understated the union's impact: Because union membership was geographically concentrated in the Northeast and Midwest, economically and politically strategic areas, a given national density rate translated into a much higher level of influence. Then too, to gauge the unions' influence properly, one would have to add to the union membership figures those other workers who were greatly affected by union actions—nonmembers in shops governed by a union contract, "exempt" workers employed by a unionized employer, workers in nonunion plants employed by a firm that also has unionized plants, and workers in nonunion firms operating in largely unionized industries. There were clear lines of influence running from collective-bargaining victories to all of these nonunion workers. A given national density rate implied much wider actual reach. The claim of the unions to speak for the "laboring masses" in unorganized shops as well as their own members was plausible.

But the union decline reversed this situation. Unions are now largely located outside the most technically progressive, rapidly growing industries; indeed, almost all of their recent growth has occurred outside the private sector entirely, that is, among public employees. It is no longer plausible to speak of a shrinking union movement, one that organizes only an eighth of the private-sector labor force (and that share contracting), as representing the majority of private-sector workers. The present reality is that even when nonunion workers have a chance to vote on unionization, fewer than half do so. A small percentage of American workers is now covered directly by collective bargaining, and the indirect mechanisms of influence have similarly shriveled. The union-threat effect has withered, and statutory generalization has atrophied. The shrinkage has eroded the unions' political powers as well.[40]

Representing a small minority, unions almost surely will be unable to use collective bargaining as a centerpiece for new rights for workers at large. Undoubtedly unions will continue to use collective bargaining to win new rights for their own members, for example, the historic job-security pacts the United Auto Workers achieved with Ford in 1987 and with General Motors in 1990. But neither emulation, the threat effect, nor statutory generalization seems likely to transmit these collective-bargaining gains to workers at large.

Thus it seems that collective bargaining can no longer be regarded as the core institution for a new regime of workers' rights. Some other basis must be found. This conclusion does not deny that unions and collective bargaining will remain at front rank in the organized sector of the economy, however large or small that sector becomes. Nor does it deny that unions can play a leading role on behalf of workers' interests. Indeed, the proposals explored later in this book may suggest exactly such a role for unions.

Notes to Chapter 4

1. *United States* v. *Bethlehem Steel Corporation,* 315 U.S. 289, 326 (1942). The words are Justice Felix Frankfurter's.
2. See Ronald Berenbeim (1980).
3. Theodore R. Marmor (1973), pp. 5–14.
4. Workers derived several advantages by first trying out rights won through collective bargaining before extending them through statutory generalization. Whereas a direct campaign to extend some benefit to all workers may have been politically infeasible, an effort to generalize an existing benefit was less so. Employers that already provide a benefit may support generalization, if that would mean either socializing any expenses and thereby reducing those employers' costs, or, alternatively, imposing its costs on any competitors that currently escape those costs. Trying out benefits in the union sector before statutory generalization also means that the benefit or right has a history, and it deprives the opposition of many arguments against it based on costs or impracticality. Finally, because the benefit or right already exists for part of the labor force, its generalization involves a smaller impact than would be the case if it were to be started anew.
5. For a historical account of the changing organization of the workplace, including the rise of bureaucratic control, see Richard Edwards

(1979). On theory Y, see Douglas McGregor (1960). The organizational behavior literature of the 1960s is exemplified by Chris Argyris (1965).

6. For a prescient early dissent from the prevailing lack of concern over membership losses, see Solomon Barkin (1961).

7. Unionism's declining fortunes have recently attracted growing scholarly attention. What has caused the collapse of private-sector unionism? The answers can be divided into two groups, depending upon whether the researcher is seeking immediate ("proximate") causes to account for the decline, or a more fundamental explanation. One of the most helpful analyses is that of Michael Goldfield (1987). Similarly, William Dickens and Jonathan Leonard (1985) deal exclusively with proximate causes, whereas Seymour Martin Lipset (1986) aims at fundamental causes.

8. This index is a reasonably accurate measure of the reach and impact of unions within the private sector. Good arguments could be made, however, that this measure alone is insufficient. For example, one might argue that union influence would differ depending upon whether unions represent 12 percent of the workers in every industry, or all workers in 12 percent of the nation's industries; in both cases the union share would be 12 percent. Similarly, political clout or other aspects of union influence undoubtedly depend upon other factors beyond membership share; a highly militant 12 percent might be more powerful than a passive 28 percent. Nonetheless, I would argue that since the 1970s the long-term and continuing erosion of the union share serves well enough as a proxy for the multidimensional decline of the unions, and that in any event there are no counteracting trends in the other dimensions of the unions' organizational lives that would offer relief or mitigation of the story told here. For a more qualitative and institutional analysis of this decline, see Richard Edwards and Michael Podgursky (1986).

9. The calculation of the union share involves choosing between two data sources, neither of which is without problems. The Bureau of Labor Statistics conducts a household survey that questions people at their homes and an establishment survey that draws information from employers. For the numerator of the share calculation there is no dilemma: the better source is the household survey, and its data are used herein; the data derive from inquiries in which each employed person is asked if in his or her "main job" there is a union, or if that job is covered by a union contract. For the denominator, however, each source introduces certain problems. The household survey counts persons, the establishment survey counts jobs. If each person had only one job, the surveys would be identical, except for sampling error. But in cases where one person holds two jobs, a divergence results: for example, for 1990 the household survey puts the total of nonfarm private-sector wage-and-salary workers at 87.9 million; the establishment survey puts the number at 91.6 million; *Monthly Labor Review,* vol. 115 (June 1992), tables 5 and 12. Thus if a person holds two jobs and one is unionized and one is not, using the household survey data in the denominator would cause this situation to be counted as one union member and one labor-force

member, or a share of 100 percent, despite the fact that one job is unionized and one is not; if a person holds two jobs and both are unionized, using the establishment survey data in the denominator would cause this situation to be counted as one union member and two labor-force (jobs) members, or a share of 50 percent, despite the fact that both jobs are unionized. This discrepancy does not, however, alter the trend in union density nor its significance.

10. Richard Freeman (1988), p. 2. See Leo Troy (in Seymour Martin Lipset, 1986) on the implications of the shift in unionism's center of dynamism from the private to public sector.

11. Richard B. Freeman and James L. Medoff (1984), p. 241; see also Michael Goldfield (1987), p. 81.

12. William T. Dickens and Jonathan S. Leonard (1985), table 1; Richard Freeman (1988), p. 16 and exhibit 5. See also Richard B. Freeman and James L. Medoff (1984), chap. 15; and Michael Goldfield (1987), chap. 7.

13. U.S. Department of Labor, *Employment and Earnings* (January, 1990), table 60 and table 63. Nonagricultural private-sector employees in 1988 numbered 88,212,000; see also note 9.

14. Michael Goldfield (1987), p. 81.

15. See William B. Gould IV (1986b), chap. 3. As noted, there are several avenues besides certification elections by which unions can obtain members; however, these alternate avenues only result in small additions to membership. There is also the countervailing trend of decertification elections.

16. Richard Freeman (1988), exhibit 5; and calculated from NLRB *Annual Report*, 1988, and U.S. Department of Labor, *Employment and Earnings* (January, 1990), table 60 and table 63. "RC"-type elections only are included in the calculation. See also William T. Dickens and Jonathan S. Leonard (1985), table 1.

17. Michael Goldfield (1987), fig. 14; William T. Dickens and Jonathan S. Leonard (1985), table 1.

18. Richard B. Freeman (1988), exhibit 5; see also William T. Dickens and Jonathan S. Leonard (1985), table 1; note that their figures reported are based on five-year averages. Calculated from NLRB *Annual Report* and U.S. Department of Labor, *Employment and Earnings* (January), various years.

19. Henry S. Farber (1990, table 2 and p. S77) finds that unionization is heaviest among the following: (1) males, nonwhites, and workers living outside the South; (2) jobs in manufacturing, construction, and the transportation, communication, and public utility industries; and (3) workers in blue-collar jobs. He also found that the union decline between 1977 and 1984 was greatest among the most heavily unionized workers.

20. Thomas A. Kochan (1979); James L. Medoff (1987); Richard B. Freeman and James L. Medoff (1984), pp. 226–28; Michael Goldfield (1987), pp. 134–37.

21. Richard B. Freeman and James L. Medoff (1984), p. 225; Henry S.

Farber (1990), p. S79. See also Henry S. Farber (1985), and William T. Dickens and Jonathan S. Leonard (1985).

22. Paula B. Voos (1983, 1984); Michael Goldfield (1987), pp. 205–07; Richard B. Freeman and James L. Medoff (1984), pp. 228–30.

23. John Abowd and Henry S. Farber (1990) find that union organizing is positively related to the change in the total quantity of quasi rents available to be divided between unions and employers; these rents have decreased with the rise of import competition in the manufacturing industries. However, there remained a substantial downward trend in time spent on union organizing not explained by changes in product market competition.

24. *Wall Street Journal,* "AFL-CIO Chief Calls Labor Laws a 'Dead Letter,' " August 16, 1984, p. 8. On labor law as a fetter on organizing, see Richard Edwards and Michael Podgursky (1986); Michael Goldfield (1987), pp. 187–89; Richard B. Freeman and James L. Medoff (1984), pp. 242–43; and Sorrell Logothetis (1985).

25. Richard B. Freeman and James L. Medoff (1984), p. 239; Richard B. Freeman (1988); Henry S. Farber (1990), pp. S93–S96; and NLRB *Annual Report,* 1988.

26. Henry S. Farber (1990), p. 597i. Harris Poll (Louis Harris and Associates, Inc., Information Services), July 9, 1989; the level of confidence in union leaders was: 1971–75, 16.2 percent; 1976–80, 12.6 percent; 1981–85, 11.0 percent; 1986–89, 10.2 percent. See also James L. Medoff (1987).

27. Lane Kirkland (in Seymour Martin Lipset, 1986), p. 393.

28. American Federation of Labor–Congress of Industrial Organizations (1985), p. 6.

29. Michael Goldfield (1987), p. 231.

30. Staughton Lynd (1978), p. 893.

31. Richard B. Freeman (1988), p. 23. See also James L. Medoff (1987) for an extensive and useful review of attitudes toward unions.

32. Staughton Lynd (1978), pp. 892–93.

33. Lane Kirkland (in Seymour Martin Lipset, 1986); Richard B. Freeman and James L. Medoff (1984); Michael Goldfield (1987); John Thomas Dunlop (1982); Mike Davis (1980a, 1980b).

34. Richard B. Freeman and James L. Medoff (1984), p. 244.

35. *Wall Street Journal,* August 16, 1984, p. 8.

36. George E. Barnett (1933); see also Lyle W. Cooper (1932).

37. Richard B. Freeman and James L. Medoff (1984), p. 244; Michael Goldfield (1987), p. 245; AFL-CIO (1985), p. 6; Lane Kirkland (in Seymour Martin Lipset, 1986), pp. 393–94.

38. Richard B. Freeman and James L. Medoff (1984), p. 244.

39. Leo Troy (in Seymour Martin Lipset 1986), pp. 107, 109.

40. Lane Kirkland (in Seymour Martin Lipset, 1986, p. 401) is probably correct when he notes that "almost without regard to the percentage of the workforce represented (though there are obviously limits), unions will continue to carry out their primary role of representing workers' interests on the job. In this role, even at a 1 percent level of organization, the union

would remain the most significant force in the work life of its members." True, but at the 1 percent level of organization, some 90 million to 100 million private-sector workers will have no union. Even at the current 12 percent level, unions cannot be a significant force in the work lives of the other 88 percent of workers—more than 80 million private-sector employees.

5

The Limited Reach of Statutory Rights

After collective bargaining, statutory provision of rights provided the second fundamental institution of the postwar workers'-rights regime. As the segment of the labor force covered by collective bargaining shrank, advocates of workers' interests almost by default turned increasingly to the political arena. Workers'-rights advocates persuaded Congress and various state legislatures to pass laws directly extending substantive new rights to workers, and the center of gravity in workers' protection shifted to the state. Yet, as is shown in this chapter, statutory provision, like collective bargaining, offers limited prospects of providing a satisfactory general foundation for workers' rights in the years ahead; its limits, however, have rarely been recognized amid the calls for more regulation.

My primary argument is that statutory provision—regulating workplace relations through the state's ability to legislate and enforce rights—is naturally limited in what it can effectively do, and that outside those limits it is clumsy, expensive, and, most telling, highly ineffective. If, in judging how satisfactory statutory provision is, one looks not at the noble intentions of its promoters or the elevated language of its statutes but rather its real impact in the workplace, the limits of its effectiveness become readily visible.

The idea that a duly enacted law may achieve only indifferent enforcement and insubstantial compliance is offensive to everyday American sensibilities. Americans like to think of themselves as a lawful society composed of normally law-abiding citizens. When laws are not enforced vigorously enough to ensure compliance, as in the case of financial manipulations or dealings in illicit drugs, the common and predictable reaction is to charge those responsible for enforcement with incompetence, perhaps even intentional dereliction of their duties, and then to demand more police, prosecutors, and prisons. When changing leaders and beefing up enforcement fails to work, the stage is set for the next round of charges and demands for even tougher action.

The popular belief that laws are to be obeyed accounts for the public's often-reported distaste for plea bargaining, which is seen as somehow compromising with criminals. Yet experts on criminal justice consistently argue that plea bargaining is indispensable to the functioning of the criminal justice system. Indeed, police, judges, lawyers—and the scholars who study them—know that, in practice, accommodations are made all along the line: laws are selectively enforced, immunities are bartered, some violations are routinely ignored, indictments and pleas are traded, and appeals and challenges are used to forestall the timely administration of justice.

This more "realistic" perspective has been taken a step further by scholars in the "Law and Economics" tradition, who apply conservative neoclassical economics to a study of the legal system. The larger project of conservative neoclassicism goes far beyond the law; it has attempted to show that virtually all human behavior—marriage, church attendance, racial discrimination—can be understood as the working out of an underlying market or efficiency logic, and because by axiom markets produce optimal social outcomes, such results contain moral claims.[1] When applied to crime and legal theory, this outlook has led to the proposition that the law's penalties—fines for polluting a river, for example, or even prison terms for assault—can best be understood as a set of "prices" (or disincentives) that society charges for permitting certain types of behavior.[2] Despite its putative predictive power, the Law and Economics approach is unappealing to popular thought because it denies the law's moral authority, the sense that the community has not just set a penalty for violations but has also declared that no one should commit the act. Indeed, a recent study has reconfirmed the importance of normative and moral considerations, as distinct from instrumental or rationally self-interested concerns, in explaining why people obey the law.[3]

But the Law and Economics tradition offers an important truth: laws are more successful in regulating some types of behavior than others. Moreover, laws will have secondary consequences and side effects, because people will not simply respond to a new law by obeying it and leaving their other behavior unchanged; rather, they may alter all their actions in response. For example, an employer may respond to a new workers' right not only by observing that right but by reducing wages and by seeking to exploit legal loopholes.

Public policy must operate somewhere between the two extreme views—at one end the moralistic belief that duly passed laws ought to be obeyed and compliance enforced regardless of the costs, and at the other end the perhaps cynical belief that laws will be broken whenever the efficiency calculus indicates that the benefits of doing so exceed the costs. The law does and should have moral authority, but it is limited. Enforcement buttresses the law's authority, but it too is limited. If the law attempts to regulate behavior where moral authority is weak or enforcement difficult or costly, it will likely be ineffective.

It is understandable that, despairing of collective bargaining and seeing no other alternative, workers'-rights advocates should insist that the federal government certify and enforce workplace rights. Thus there have been repeated calls for new legislation to ban unjust dismissals, require pay based on comparable worth, regulate the introduction of certain technologies, establish family-leave policies, regulate plant closings, mandate health benefits, and create other workplace rights. These pleas have gone hand in hand with demands for tougher enforcement of existing statutes. For example, the authors of a study financed by the Ford Foundation wrote:

> The federal government should reassume its responsibility for regulating the workplace. . . . As workplace regulations erode, and as the free market exacerbates the problems of many workers, the necessity of government intervention will once again be clear. With government having modified and trimmed back the excesses of earlier regulations, the nation

> may be ready for the vigorous and fair enforcement of existing statutes and executive orders. An educated and affluent work force will insist that their elected representatives protect its rights, attend to its interests, and cater to its needs. Sooner or later, then, the pendulum will probably swing back in favor of effective federal regulation of the workplace.[4]

In recommending this course, one has some obligation to determine if statutory provision of rights is likely to help workers. And those seeking to regulate relationships where the law is not an effective instrument perhaps should search for new means of achieving the goal rather than simply continue to demand more effective enforcement of the unenforceable. Indeed, when a statute is inefficient in the sense that losers lose more than winners gain from it, there will likely be relentless pressure on officials to overlook violations as well as informal efforts at evasion, such as side bargains and implicit understandings among those whom the law is intended to regulate. Indeed, both sides may benefit from underenforcement. These points are crucial when considering statutory rights for workers.

The Rise of Statutory Rights

In this chapter I focus primarily on substantive rights created directly by legislation—that is, on rights by which a statute imposes an obligation upon government to achieve a certain outcome, such as a safe workplace or a nondiscriminatory pattern of hiring. The statutory rights considered here are thus claims or protections that workers may exercise directly and that constitute benefits themselves. Statutes are sometimes also used to establish or ensure a worker's access to a legislatively favored process; in this case, the worker achieves a benefit, if at all, indirectly via the outcome of that process. The most important instance of a favored process is workers' right to unionize under the National Labor Relations Act. My focus, however, is on directly mandated rights.[5]

The provision of statutory rights in the United States dates at least to the earliest years of this century, but the modern period can be said to have begun in 1938, when Congress passed the Fair Labor Standards Act.[6] The FLSA, like the NLRA, had its antecedents and partial expression in earlier legislation; restrictions on the length of the workweek, for example, had been included in the National Recovery Act codes of 1933 and 1934. But the FLSA established these rights on a permanent basis. It covers most hourly workers and requires their employers to pay a 50 percent premium ("time and a half") to employees working more than forty hours a week. It also mandates a minimum wage and restricts the use of child labor. In certain industries, it sets restrictions on how employers may organize production; for example, in the manufacture of some women's garments, it proscribes production in the home.

Despite these early efforts at the statutory granting of rights, the collective-bargaining approach dominated the provision of workers' rights during the 1940s and 1950s. Between passage of the FLSA and the 1960s, there was little further advance in statutory rights, either at the federal or the state level. The major pieces of federal legislation passed during this period focused on labor law (and reflected the conservative tide): the 1947 Taft-Hartley and 1959 Landrum-Griffin acts revised the NLRA framework, making it less favorable to unions.

Legislative granting of substantive rights gained new momentum in the 1960s. This change in focus undoubtedly reflected several factors: the fruition of the unions' efforts to generalize collective-bargaining gains through legislation, the growth and success of the civil rights movement, the revival under Presidents Kennedy and Johnson of the New Deal vision of government as solver of social problems, and the increased social opportunities made possible by the long prosperity of the 1960s.

Yet the change in focus also reflected growing disenchantment with the collective-bargaining approach and with unions themselves. Collective bargaining reached a declining share of the labor force, and, significantly, few women and blacks. Union officials tended to be white males, and traditional collective bargaining tended to focus on the interests of male blue-collar workers and, in some areas (for example, the crafts), on white males' interests. Disenchantment was evident in the struggles over integration of some of the union-controlled paths to jobs, especially apprenticeships in the construction crafts. So too, union-won seniority systems seemed to block the progress of minority workers who had only recently gained access to the bottom rungs of job ladders. Activists on behalf of minority rights were soon joined by others operating outside the mainstream labor movement in advocating the statutory granting of rights. Women in particular felt poorly represented by the union hierarchy and believed that their objectives, such as equal access to jobs and training, better conditions for part-time work, day care, and family-care leave, often placed them at odds with male workers, whose interests were likely to receive much higher priority under traditional collective bargaining. So too, some workplace health and safety campaigns originated outside of unions.[7]

The House of Labor was itself often divided by the inclusion efforts. Take, for example, the demands for racial justice. On the one hand, unions, especially the industrial unions, were one of the strongest forces for racial justice in American society. From their 1930s slogan, "Black and White, Unite and Fight!" to their lobbying in the 1960s on behalf of civil rights legislation, unions provided strong support for African-Americans. On the other hand, many craft unions operated what has been variously characterized as a racial caste system or a white cartel, blocking access for blacks to the better jobs. So too, many unions have resolutely defended seniority systems (one of organized labor's greatest prizes in bargaining with employers) against minority efforts to inject affirmative-action criteria into promotion, hiring, and layoff systems.[8]

Similarly, unions found themselves divided on women's issues. Some women's activists, like those who in 1974 formed the Coalition of Labor Union Women, operated mainly inside the union movement or in coalition with unions. Others found themselves fighting unions (and employers) alongside African-Americans in attempting to gain access to jobs and training, end discriminatory wage and promotion practices, and open up the seniority system.[9]

Thus the great campaigns of the 1960s and 1970s for statutory rights emerged from a growing frustration with the collective-bargaining model, with activists believing that statutory rights would substitute for gains not achievable through involvement with unions and collective bargaining. Note that this frustration appeared among advocates of workers' rights, that is, from the Left, as it were. (In the late 1970s and 1980s it would be employers who would walk away from the bargaining table.) To its credit, the leadership of the mainstream labor movement largely supported, and in some cases provided the critical resources to pass, the new legislation.

Within a short span, the statutory-rights campaigns succeeded. At the federal level, the Equal Pay Act (1963) was followed by the Civil Rights Act (1964), the Age Discrimination in Employment Act (1968), the Mine Safety Act (1969), the Occupational Safety and Health Act (1970), the Rehabilitation Act (1973), and the Employee Retirement Income Security Act (1974). Other statutes were later added to this set of protections, most notably the 1986 amendments to the Age Discrimination in Employment Act, the Worker Adjustment and Retraining Notification Act (1988), the Americans with Disabilities Act (1990), and the Family Leave Act (1993). All these laws, and many additional pieces of state legislation, directly granted rights to be exercised by workers as employees.

Are Statutory Rights Effective?

Because two decades of experience has been gained with much of the statutory-rights legislation (and much more history with a few such laws), it is appropriate to ask: Have statutory rights, the second leg of the postwar workers'-rights regime, effectively supported employees' legitimate rights? Given the decline of the union share, is the statutory-rights approach a viable alternative as the primary institutional vehicle for workers' rights?

In evaluating the success of statutory rights, I consider only the most basic issue: their effectiveness in achieving their principal stated purposes. Thus, does the minimum wage law really protect workers from subminimum wages? Does the Employee Retirement Income Security Act (ERISA) in fact safeguard workers' private pensions? Does the Occupational Safety and Health (OSH) Act guarantee or substantially contribute to the provision of "safe and healthful working conditions" for each worker? I leave aside the issue of whether or not the statutory right promoted the public good in some larger sense. I also do not consider the cost-effectiveness of the various statutory measures. These concerns would be essential in a fuller public policy evaluation, but my question is simpler and prior: do the laws work?

In answering this question, it is worth noting that no single assessment fits all protective legislation. Yet my argument is that a twofold pattern emerges: the most successful regulation is that which regulates the simplest aspects of the workplace, and even the most successful regulations have associated with them considerable difficulties in ensuring adequate compliance.

The oldest and most accepted statutory rights are the minimum-wage and overtime provisions of the Fair Labor Standards Act. The FLSA has established norms that appear to provide effective constraints in practice. Formal complaints of violations have been relatively few, affecting less than 2.5 percent of covered establishments each year.[10] The Labor Department estimated that in all industries, the percentage of subject employees who were paid in violation of the minimum wage during a survey week was only 0.8 percent in 1965 and 1.2 percent in 1979.[11]

There has been little public commentary or complaint about the complexity or enforceability of the minimum-wage law, which is consistent with the idea that the FLSA is widely accepted and well observed. When conservatives criticize the minimum wage—arguing, for example, that it deprives teenagers of jobs and increases unemployment—even their attacks are implicit testament to the FLSA's effectiveness, because there would be little complaint if employers could easily evade the law. Of course, as the real or inflation-adjusted minimum wage has declined, the incentive for violating the law has likewise decreased, enhancing the prospects for voluntary compliance. The one clear enforcement problem that does exist concerns workers who are illegal aliens. However, this exception is not related to the minimum wage itself but rather to the workers' reluctance to report abuses out of fear of deportation. Still, regardless of whatever other effects for good or ill the minimum wage law creates, there has been remarkably little criticism of the effectiveness of the FLSA as law. Its provisions are clear, reporting requirements are not burdensome, and it is enforceable.

The requirement that workers who put in more than forty hours a week be compensated at a higher rate also appears to function successfully. Because the FLSA permits but makes very costly the forty-first and subsequent hours, one expected result would be that employers would use less overtime. (Recently, however, costs for medical insurance, social-security contributions, and other benefits

Figure 5-1. Average Weekly Hours Worked in Manufacturing, 1890–1991

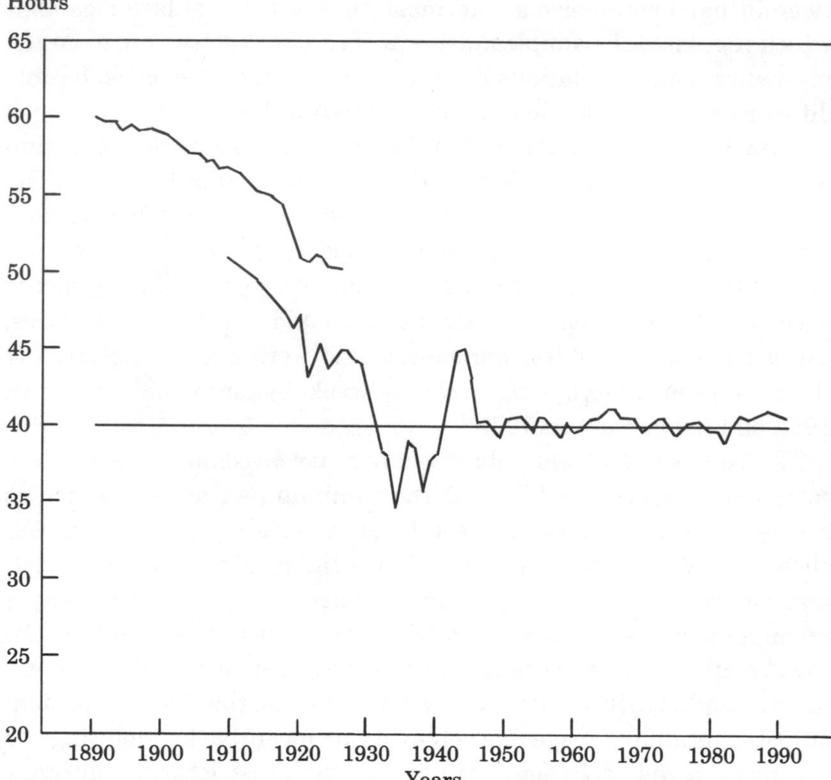

Sources: Bureau of the Census, *Historical Statistics of the United States: Colonial Times to 1970*, pt. 1 (U.S. Department of Labor, 1975), pp. 168–70; Bureau of Labor Statistics, *Handbook of Labor Statistics* (August 1989), p. 304; and *Monthly Labor Review* (May 1992), p. 76.

have become a much bigger percentage of the typical employer's wage bill; to the extent that these costs are fixed per employee and thus do not change as the workweek extends beyond forty hours, the cost of overtime relative to regular work time, even with the time-and-a-half requirement, declines.) As Figure 5-1 shows, after 1940, when the FLSA became fully effective, average weekly hours in manufacturing converged quite strikingly around the forty-hour limit. In this case, one must have less confidence than in the case of the minimum wage that the law necessarily caused the outcome (the standardization of the forty-hour week), because as figure 5-1 shows, average hours worked declined before passage of the law. Perhaps more direct is evidence derived from complaints of violations of the workers' right to receive time and a half. Complaints remain relatively few; based on the official 1965 and 1979 noncompliance surveys (the latest available), the percentage of covered establishments using overtime that violated the time-and-a-half rule declined nearly one-third. Here, as in the case of the minimum wage, the rights created under the law are unambiguous, reporting is minimal, and enforcement is straightforward. The right seems an accepted part of contemporary business relations.[12]

The success of the FLSA is also suggested by the lack of controversy over its enforcement mechanism. The Labor Department's Wages and Hours Division, whose compliance officers are charged with enforcing the law, remains largely anonymous, especially in contrast to the Environmental Protection Agency, for example. When the FLSA is scrutinized (as it was by the Minimum Wage Study Commission, discussed later), compliance issues typically provoke little controversy (despite bitter differences over the wisdom and consequences of a minimum wage itself). This lack of controversy is perhaps the best evidence of the degree of legitimacy the FLSA provisions enjoy.

Here, then, is a statute granting simple, straightforward rights to workers, and considerable evidence suggests that it works; yet even with this statute, it would be unwise to ignore some problems. At the end of the 1970s, the Carter administration appointed the Minimum Wage Study Commission, a bipartisan presidential panel that included conservatives and liberals, management and labor. The commission examined the FLSA's effectiveness and published its findings in a seven-volume report issued in 1982. In the same year, the General Accounting Office studied FLSA compliance; the GAO is the tough-minded, independent, and highly respected investigative agency that reports directly to Congress.[13]

The commission dealt mainly with such issues as the impact of the minimum wage on employment and unemployment, the macroeconomy, and income distribution; but as a subsidiary part of the study it also examined compliance with the FLSA. The commission found that during a surveyed workweek in the final quarter of 1979, about 128,000 of the 2.6 million U.S. business establishments subject to the FLSA—or about 5 percent—were in violation of the minimum-wage provision. Some 236,000, or 21 percent of the establishments using overtime, were in violation of the overtime requirements of the act. Altogether, a total of 343,000—13 percent—of all covered establishments violated either one or both of these provisions during the survey week.[14] That is, noncompliance was more than five times greater than would be suggested by the number of formal complaints or the official surveys.

The most frequent violations of the minimum-wage rule were in retail trade, where 11.7 percent of the establishments broke the law; the lowest percentages were reported in mining (0.4 percent) and manufacturing (0.8 percent). The most frequent violators of the overtime provisions were services (29 percent of establishments violated the law), wholesale trade (25 percent), and retail trade (24 percent).[15]

The *Minimum Wage and Maximum Hours Standards under the Fair Labor Standards Act* report noted that each year about 3 percent of the establishments subject to the FLSA are investigated by the Wages and Hours Division compliance officers. Steven Welch estimates that this enforcement results in detection of only 20 percent of the violations. Moreover, when discovered, employers agree to restore only 54 percent of the total back wages owed, and litigation results in little additional reimbursement.[16] The commission, in a unanimous conclusion, noted the consequences: "The Commission views the overall level of non-compliance with the Fair Labor Standards Act as unacceptable. It is our view that Congress should address this issue by attempting to increase the cost of not complying with the Act."[17] Welch details the many problems in enforcing the law, from limited enforcement resources, to the great evidentiary burden required for successful litigation, to the inherent incentives for employers to break the law. The principal problem, however, is simply that of trying to keep up with employers who willfully violate the law.[18]

The GAO also examined the level of compliance with the FLSA. In a 1981 report, *Changes Needed to Deter Violations of Fair Labor Standards Act*, GAO investigators noted that "there are insufficient deterrents to discourage employers from violating the Act. . . . Habitual or flagrant violators receive no harsher treatment than do employers who inadvertently violate the Act."[19] Four years later, the GAO was instructed to determine what progress had been made toward improved compliance. Not surprisingly, four years into the Reagan administration, which generally had shown little support for statutory protection of workers' rights, the GAO said: "In our 1981 report, we reported that noncompliance with FLSA's minimum wage, overtime, and record-keeping provisions was a serious and continuing problem and that employers who violated these provisions were often not penalized. . . . During our current review, we found that most of the problems we identified in our 1981 report still exist."[20]

The FLSA is a simple law to enforce. For the two regulations considered here, the wage floor and the forty-hour workweek ceiling, the same standards apply to all subject employees, without much variation or tailoring.[21] The items to be checked, wages and hours, are open to ready scrutiny by workers themselves and to compliance officers, and are virtually devoid of ambiguous or contradictory definitions. Employer record-keeping is required by other laws (for example, those concerning taxes and social security), and such records are themselves not complex, unless by design. Retroactive monitoring can be done by recourse to paper or electronic records. All these features tend to simplify enforcement. Even so, the level of noncompliance remains "unacceptable."

A more difficult law to administer is the Employee Retirement Income Security Act (ERISA), designed to safeguard the pensions of workers enrolled in private-employer pension plans. The law does not require employers to have pension plans, but if they do have them, it requires them to administer the plans in accordance with certain standards. For example, employers must register their plans with the Labor Department and file annual reports, they must prepare plan descriptions, develop and distribute summary plan descriptions, follow standard accounting procedures, keep records, and meet fiduciary responsibilities. The law also directly establishes certain rights for covered workers. For example, ERISA in most cases requires that the employer's contributions to pension benefits be vested after five years of employment, and it gives each worker the right to obtain or inspect the actual pension policy.

Unlike the FLSA, ERISA is a long and complicated statute. It specifies in considerable detail the eligibility, reporting, accounting, fiduciary, and other obligations of employers and attempts to provide appropriate regulation for the immense variety of private pension plans and their associated highly differentiated employers. The original statute runs to more than 200 pages in the federal code, and its several major amendments (1980, 1981, 1984, and 1986) have added hundreds more.[22]

Some complexity is inevitably involved in the regulation of pension plans because each private plan can be somewhat different. But there are also some features that mitigate the complexity of pension regulation. First, although individual plans differ, for regulatory purposes their differences do not require information on other matters about each firm, such as its products, markets, technology, profit situation, and competitors; that is, the relevant variations all occur along dimensions well understood in the insurance world. Second, the plans are paper instruments for which records exist and these records constitute the direct target of regulation. This makes the regulator's job much easier compared, for instance, to adjudication of a shop-floor dispute over some act or practice for which written records, if they exist, are already one step removed from the phenomenon to be regulated. Regulating a paper instrument also means that such regulation can be retroactive and can occur at second or third hand. Third, pension plans tend to be fairly static, with changes introduced relatively infrequently. These characteristics tend to simplify the regulatory task.

ERISA can at best be described as only moderately successful at meeting its stated goals. It has been much more successful in requiring employer disclosure than in actually regulating pension plans. At the most basic level, ERISA evidently has successfully compelled employers with private pension plans to register such plans, since ERISA now governs more than 800,000 of them. The law has also caused employers to make their plans available, in principle at least, for employee scrutiny. The act has probably considerably improved accounting and record-keeping procedures in firms, although these procedures have been little studied. Certainly ERISA has heightened employers' perceptions of the need to inform their employees of their pension rights, as made evident by the frequent inclusion in employee handbooks of ERISA requirements. These and other changes stimulated by ERISA undoubtedly have granted workers substantial and effective access to information not enjoyed prior to ERISA's passage.

However, severe problems exist in the regulation of private pension plans, in insuring pensions when private plans fail, and in achieving the other aims of ERISA. In 1985 the Department of Labor held hearings on the impact of ERISA. The Committee on Education and Labor of the House of Representatives also heard testimony on employee benefit plans, in which ERISA performance figured prominently. Finally, a number of private groups have studied ERISA.[23] The picture that emerges from these reviews is one of great gaps in the protection of workers' pensions, a regulatory process overwhelmed by the enormity of the pension plans it is to regulate, and substantial enrichment opportunities for the financial community.

The first problem is simply the complexity of the regulations and their attendant high reporting costs. As noted, the statute itself is long and complicated. The necessary administrative regulations and accounting procedures inevitably add further layers of complexity. The result is a system that only highly specialized experts can understand. As one qualified observer, a friend of workers' rights, put it: "While I am an advocate of more substantive protections for workers, like 3-year vesting, the complexity that we have in the existing laws and regulations is just beyond the comprehension of anyone who hasn't struggled with it. I challenge any Member of Congress to take a pension plan document which has been approved by the Internal Revenue Service for use under prototype plans, which are designed for small employers, to read it and tell me what it means. It complies with all the regulations, but no one could understand it."[24]

The requirement that pension plans conform to ERISA regulations results in high reporting costs, especially for small and medium-size businesses. An unintended side effect is that employers may be deterred from starting plans or induced to abandon them.[25]

ERISA's complexity has also spawned an extensive and lucrative financial-management and consulting industry to administer ERISA-governed pension funds. One government study concluded that "it is not hard to understand why there have been so few detailed inquiries into the [financial] industries fostered by ERISA. . . . The legal and administrative structures of ERISA are intricate to the point of discouraging any but the indomitable. The language is confusing, full of special purpose acronyms (PBGC, SOL, OPWBP), legal shorthand (exclusive benefit rule, prudent man rule), and special numbering (Title I, S406(b), S408)."[26] To avoid liability for any potential violations of their fiduciary responsibilities, employers typically pass on the risk by hiring consultants, much as bookies lay off big bets. The consequences include the payment from pension revenues of an army of costly, redundant advisors; one expert has noted, "ERISA is a make-work program for pension fund consultants." This delegation of control makes it increasingly difficult to assign responsibility for investment performance or any other specific matter, including malfeasance. "No identifiable party is in control. This situation cannot work to the benefit of plan participants."[27]

Nor does the horde of consultants appear to provide any positive investment benefits. ERISA rules create a world in which there are "no special rewards for superior performance and perceived strict accountability for deficiencies." Tying pension fund managers' compensation to performance is "practically non-existent"; one fund manager acknowledged that "you might find a lot of people dropping out of the money management business if they had to perform [that is, produce superior investment returns] to get paid." There is no publicly available source of information to determine the real rate of return achieved by pension funds.[28]

It should not be concluded that all of ERISA's problems are traceable to financial opportunities. Serious problems exist throughout ERISA's operations. There are many gaps in protection; for instance, many part-time workers, people who switch jobs, and others are not covered by ERISA guarantees, even though their employers may have pension plans. Another problem is that failing pension plans are guaranteed by the government (albeit through a reinsurance scheme), whereas plans that amass wealth beyond actuarial commitments can serve as tax-free slush funds for employers. The burden of the plans' failure therefore falls on the government while the fruits of success accrue to employers, creating a subsidy for excessive risk taking and an opportunity for financial buccaneering by the unscrupulous. Administrative responsibilities are scattered among several federal agencies.[29] The principal agency, the Office of Pension and Welfare Benefit Programs (OPWBP), is unable to digest the more than eight hundred thousand reports submitted to it each year. ERISA permits employers to use social security benefits to offset or substitute for a substantial portion of the employer-paid pension, thereby often vitiating a workers' private-pension benefit.[30]

Enforcing compliance is a particular problem. OPWBP lacks adequate litigation resources, and investigations of ERISA violations may take years to complete, a situation that frequently results in the provision of evidence containing some legal defect.[31] The National Pension Forum, a bipartisan panel made up of members of Congress, heads of government agencies, and various other highly placed experts and representatives, concluded in 1985 that "a strong enforcement program is critical to the administration of ERISA. The current program is unacceptable and must be improved."[32] As with the FLSA, the levels of enforcement and compliance are found, by those who study them, to be "unacceptable."

ERISA, then, has proven to be a faulty mechanism for ensuring pension rights. There was much abuse and fraud in the private pension system before ERISA, and it would be an exaggeration to conclude that, on balance, ERISA has made matters worse. But it is also difficult to sustain the belief that it has helped matters much.

The provision of substantive rights by other federal statutes has produced highly mixed results. The Worker Adjustment and Retraining Notification (WARN) Act, which requires employers to give their workers at least sixty days' notice before any layoff or shutdown affecting fifty or more workers, was passed as recently as 1988; soon afterward complaints began to be heard that it was not tough enough ("Employers aren't scared," declared one state-level enforcement official).[33] Certainly the equal-employment provisions (title VII) of the 1964 Civil Rights Act have been successful in ending most overt discrimination by race, sex, and other protected categories.[34] However, they have been much less successful at overturning more subtle, institutional forms of discrimination, and in the process have spawned a substantial monitoring and enforcement bureaucracy that is widely perceived to be onerous and burdensome. Reporting requirements are extensive, as are the associated direct and indirect costs.

A similar conclusion is applicable to the Equal Pay Act of 1963. This law grants workers doing "equal work on jobs the performance of which requires equal skill, effort, and responsibility, and are performed under similar working conditions" the right to be free of pay discrimination based solely on gender.[35] The law has effectively ended overt gender-based pay discrimination of the kind practiced in the infamous Westinghouse case, for example. The Equal Pay Act has also been the basis of substantial court awards to female employees of some major employers. But the law has been much less successful in reducing other disparities, for example, those of the kind fought over in the Sears case. Here the disparity was rooted in informal, implicit practices such as assigning male sales clerks to big-ticket items such as appliances (for which commissions are higher) and female clerks to positions offering less opportunity. After a massive investigation and trial, the courts held that Sears had not violated the antidiscrimination laws.[36]

Perhaps the most complicated and least satisfactory statute concerned with workers' rights is the Occupational Safety and Health Act, which "declares it to be [Congress's] purpose and policy . . . to assure so far as is possible every working man and woman in the Nation safe and healthful working conditions."[37] Rather than specify what is meant by this right to a "safe and healthful" workplace, the OSH act delegates authority to administer the act to the secretary of labor, who in turn delegates it to the Occupational Safety and Health Administration (OSHA), an agency within the Department of Labor. The secretary is directed to promulgate safety and health standards for workplaces "to serve the objectives of this Act." Each employer is then legally obligated to "comply with occupational safety and health standards promulgated under this Act." Finally, the secretary of labor is charged with inspecting and investigating workplaces, issuing citations for violations, and initiating prosecution when necessary.

Has the OSH act produced, "so far as is possible . . . safe and healthful working conditions"? Given the weasel words "so far as is possible," the answer to this question is a matter of opinion. Although the OSH act has stimulated much research into and dissemination of information on occupational hazards, its actual effects on workplace health and safety are less certain. According to a 1989 General Accounting Office study, "OSHA's impact on injury and illness rates is largely unknown."[38]

The exact goal of the OSH act is itself ambiguous or at least arguable. There has been intense debate over whether the clause, "so far as is possible," means that regulation should be aimed at the *technologically* possible, regardless of the costs involved, the *economically* possible, or only the economically *practical*; each interpretation would give a different weight to the cost factor.[39] OSHA itself initially accepted the first formulation, attempting to set standards and hold employers to a technical level of feasibility.

So far as enforcement of the law is concerned, the Supreme Court's opinion is the one that ultimately matters, but the Court itself has not taken a fixed position. On the one hand, the Court in its 1981 cotton-dust decision (the *American Textile* case) explicitly disavowed benefit-cost tests. The Court upheld the OSHA cotton-dust standard and interpreted "so far as is possible" to mean strictly "capable of being done." It indicated that technological and economic feasibility rather than benefit-cost trade-offs should guide OSHA decisions.[40] On the other hand, the Court has at other times indicated that an OSHA standard can be overturned if OSHA fails to demonstrate that the risk reduction achieved would be "significant." This was how the Court reasoned in the 1980 benzene case *(Industrial Union Department, AFL-CIO* v. *American Petroleum Institute)*, in which the Court's reasoning appeared to introduce some leeway for OSHA to use cost considerations in interpreting "as far as is possible."[41] The Reagan administration routinely prepared and used benefit-cost calculations in its interpretation of the law. Thus observers are left to wonder what standard the law requires, with different and evolving interpretations evident and therefore differing opinions on OSHA's effectiveness likely.

Concerning the law's impact, the initial studies of OSHA effectiveness, conducted during the mid-to-late 1970s when the OSH act was five to eight years old, almost invariably concluded that OSHA had no discernible effect on industrial safety. (Virtually all studies eschewed evaluation of health aspects, because the health consequences of OSHA regulations are likely to be evident only after many years, and even then will be confounded by many other influences.) Robert Stewart Smith concluded that "while the incentives to comply with OSHA (in advance of inspection) are weak, perfect enforcement of excellent standards could conceivably reduce injuries by as much as one-third, while perfect enforcement of the current standards could reduce injuries by somewhere between 2 percent and 22 percent in inspected firms. . . . The actual effects of OSHA may be virtually nil."[42] A study of the OSH act's impact in California concluded that in 1974 OSHA reduced the injury rate in manufacturing by at least 2 to 3 percent and cut all occupational fatalities by 5 percent. The most careful work was perhaps that of W. Kip Viscusi, whose 1979 study largely confirmed that OSHA had little impact.[43]

A more recent study, again by Viscusi, analyzed OSHA's impact on workplace safety during 1973–83. Viscusi focused on work injuries in a sample of two-digit manufacturing industries. His evidence concerning the agency's effectiveness was "more favorable than the prevailing view in the literature, but . . . still very mixed."[44] More specifically, he concluded that "the overall injury rate series provides no support of a positive net effect [of OSHA]. The lost-workday . . . data suggest a [statistically] significant effect for 1973–83. . . . On the basis of these results, OSHA's effect appears to be in the range of 1.5 to 3.6 percent of the current lost-workday incidence rate. Viewed somewhat differently, OSHA prevents from 1 to 2 injuries involving at least one lost day of work per 1000 workers annually."[45] Thus a "statistically significant" but otherwise tiny beneficial effect could be traced to OSHA. The most direct measure—the overall injury rate—showed no OSHA effect, but the risk of losing workdays because of workplace injury was reduced 1.5 to 3.6 percent.[46] Other evidence is similarly mixed: for example, although workplace fatalities declined during 1972–84, nonfatal injuries increased.[47]

The econometric studies thus appear to be virtually unanimous in concluding that OSHA's impact on injury rates is on the order of a 1 to 3 percent reduction at best.[48] The early studies in the 1970s found virtually no OSHA impact, and this finding has been only slightly amended by the more recent work. Of course, all these studies could be wrong if they were all vulnerable to the same errors—for example, it could be that the quality of data is simply too poor, or that the data are too aggregated, to uncover the real OSHA impact. As John Mendeloff has pointed out, the crucial data series are not very reliable and may be heavily influenced by such extraneous factors as changes in employers' understanding of reporting requirements and improvements in worker compensation benefits (higher benefits increase workers' incentive to report injuries). Mendeloff has concluded, "The difficulties in developing accurate statistics on workplace injuries and in assessing OSHA's impact are disconcerting. Simplistic claims about the effects—good or bad—of OSHA policy changes should be viewed with skepticism. . . . Not only does the validity of the data as indicators of workplace risk remain uncertain, but there are no studies that control for the important variables."[49] Pending a reversal of findings, however, the evidence provides little comfort to those who would see OSHA as a model of effective worker protection.

OSHA's impact on reducing the incidence of occupational diseases is even more problematic. Because occupational diseases appear only after a long lag, it is probably too early to gauge OSHA's impact, and no really credible studies have attempted to do so. Nonetheless, a priori reasoning suggests a much more likely positive impact for OSHA. The reduced presence of asbestos in workplaces, for instance, given what is known about its deadly effects, seems almost certain to have a major effect on workers' health (so long as the substitute materials do not turn out to be equally deadly). Similar reductions in health risks seem likely to derive from control of other toxic substances, such as cotton dust, lead, and formaldehyde. Unfortunately, OSHA has dealt with only a very few of the suspected dangerous chemicals used in industry; after fifteen years of activity it had issued workplace exposure limits for only ten health hazards.[50] The GAO has concluded:

> OSHA standards fail to (1) cover many health and safety hazards adequately and (2) keep pace with knowledge about new or existing hazards. In the health area, estimates of the number of new chemical products introduced into the workplace range from 1,000 to 3,000 a year. By comparison, as of 1989, OSHA standards regulated only about 630 substances, most of which are accounted for by a single air contaminants standard. This standard specifies permissible exposure levels, but does not include other features, such as exposure monitoring, medical surveillance, and removal. Fewer than 30 substances hazardous to health are regulated by more comprehensive standards. Many of the safety standards initially set are outdated or fail to address important workplace hazards. For example, a presidential task force in 1976 estimated that the standards governing machine guards that OSHA had adopted in 1971 covered only 15 percent of the machine types then in use. As of 1989, these standards had not been updated.[51]

OSHA's ineffectiveness at preventing injuries appears to derive from several sources. First, establishing appropriate OSHA standards is inherently difficult. This is true because what is being regulated—the interaction of workers with machines and materials—is inevitably different in each workplace. Work routines, the particular configuration of the machines, the handling of materials, the layout of the workspace, the quality of supervision, and the attitudes and habits of the workers and employers all vary from workplace to workplace. This makes the job of effective and sensible regulation nearly impossible. But that issue aside, OSHA's general commitment to using standards has problems. John Mendeloff makes the point that OSHA has often used excessively strict standards; the result of such overregulation is frequently a compensatory underregulation in practice. He notes that "conflict between labor and industry goals provides the underlying basis for the slow pace of standard setting. In collective bargaining the two parties have an incentive to compromise their differences, in the interests of reaching an agreement. Delays in reaching agreement are costly to both. But delay in setting standards is often a boon to industry."[52] And why can't OSHA simply run roughshod over the dispute? "Even if the costs and effects of exposure reductions were certain, people would disagree about whether they were worthwhile. But, in fact, they are often quintessentially uncertain. Faced by uncertainty and unclear guidelines from Congress or the courts about the degree of evidence that is sufficient, agencies often lack confidence that they can meet the burden of proof that will be demanded."[53] Across-the-board standards usually will be hopelessly clumsy and inappropriate, and generate political backlash; yet adequately decentralized tailoring of safety planning would require expertise and resources far beyond what nearly anybody expects OSHA could command. Furthermore, all must be done in a context of highly inadequate and unreliable information.

A second problem is detecting violations of OSHA standards. Inspecting workplaces for compliance, given the 5 million or more workplaces and the vast differences among them, is a gargantuan task. OSHA inspects workplaces either as a result of its own enforcement strategies ("targeted" inspections) or upon worker complaints. Each year OSHA inspects 70,000 workplaces. At that rate, a workplace could expect to be inspected about once every seventy-one years. Although the relevant pool of dangerous workplaces with poor safety records is much smaller, the possibility of regularly inspecting all of these seems minimal. The National Safe Workplace Institute, a strong advocate of workers' protections (and a harsh critic of government laxness) admitted in its report, *Beyond Neglect*, "The government—however well funded and staffed—will never be able to comprehensively 'police' U.S. workplaces, even if that objective were desirable."[54] When workers are represented by a union, the union can take the lead in monitoring safety concerns, filing complaints, forcing inspections, and providing necessary follow-through; but of course unions now represent only one out of eight private-sector workers.[55]

Finally, OSHA penalties for detected violations have little deterrent power. The total of fines assessed each year by OSHA in the whole economy has ranged from $6 million to $30 million; in a $5 trillion or $6 trillion economy, such a level seems unlikely to provide major incentives. The average penalty in 1986 was about $57 per violation. Moreover, OSHA itself has little direct clout; according to one study, "Because of the ambiguity regarding OSHA's power and mandate, almost all the difficult decisions are resolved in the courts."[56] The result is typically great delay in resolving any dispute.

OSHA's poor record does not prove that federal statutory provision of rights is always ineffective. The experience of the Mine Safety Act demonstrates that federal regulations on specific and easily identified hazards, when coupled with strong local union organization, can dramatically reduce workplace injuries.[57] OSHA's own performance in dealing with a few hazards, such as asbestos, solvents, and lead, has clearly had a major beneficial effect. Neither does its record demonstrate that there are no effective measures that the agency as currently constituted could undertake to increase its effectiveness. For example, work on scaffolding is one of the most dangerous occupational hazards in this country, yet elsewhere, in Japan for instance, it is much less risky, primarily because other countries have much stricter safeguards on erecting scaffolding and require extensive netting. OSHA's failure to impose these simple and workable rules to make scaffolding jobs safer is a tragic illustration of its inability to protect workers.[58]

Despite some successes, the conclusion seems well founded that OSHA has not compiled an admirable record in reducing overall injury rates. One thoughtful study concluded:

> Much of the public criticism of OSHA has centered on the slowness of the standard-setting process, the infrequency of the inspections, and the size of the fines. The agency has been called stupid, poorly managed, and insensitive to the concerns of both labor and management. Much of this criticism is misdirected. OSHA has been relatively ineffective to date because the existing regulatory structure is simply not capable of addressing the millions of separate problems that constitute the occupational safety and health problem in the United States.[59]

What Has Been Learned?

When a variety of statutes is considered, it appears that the statutory granting of substantive employment rights has had highly mixed or uneven results, including inadequate protection for workers, substantial problems of noncompliance, and unintended side effects. Sometimes the method has simply failed. Statutory rights have typically proven less positive in reality than they appeared to be in prospect.

Statutory provision of substantive rights seems to be a limited and risky mechanism to rely upon as the primary or sole vehicle for protecting workers in an age when collective bargaining touches only a small minority of workers.[60] During the heyday of the postwar rights regime, when statutory rights regulating rather simple aspects of the workplace existed in combination with a vigorous and substantial national union movement, these rights provided workers with important new protections. In particular, when applied to industries such as underground mining or to easily identified regulatory concerns such as a minimum wage or a workweek maximum, statutory protections have proven effective. But as the primary mechanism in a general system to protect workers, statutory provision of substantive rights is flawed, limited, and ineffective.

In concluding, I do not wish to overemphasize my negative conclusion. The question at issue has to do with whether statutory provision of substantive rights should be the rallying point of a new rights regime. A negative answer does not mean that statutory rights provide *no* benefits to workers. It does not mean that *existing* statutory protections should be rolled back, nor does it imply that additional statutory rights should be banned where they will work. Statutory provision will continue to be a crucial device for protecting workers. In some areas, such as minimum wage and antidiscrimination protections, legislation may continue to serve as the primary line of defense simply because no other means have been found to achieve the desired ends. In these ways statutory provision of substantive rights will and should remain part of the arsenal used to defend workers. Moreover, the negative findings reported in this chapter do not extend to all aspects of the statutes; indeed, in the cases of ERISA and OSHA, the laws' requirements of employer disclosure and stimulus to provide workers with vital information appear to be their most effective parts. The essence of the argument here is that statutory provision of substantive rights is only indifferently successful, and a seeming lack of alternative mechanisms for workers' rights should not blind one to this fact.

The Political Dimension of Statutory Rights

Is my conclusion on the limits of regulation merely one final and ironic result of Reagan (and Bush) conservative government? After all, one might argue, Ronald Reagan rode to electoral victory on a wave of antiregulation fervor, and sought to roll back federal regulatory activity; George Bush pledged to continue this effort. If one finding after twelve years of antiregulatory policy is that regulation is ineffective, has anything been discovered about regulation per se? Instead, perhaps observers have simply measured the success of efforts by Ronald Reagan and his followers to make regulation ineffective.

This is a difficult objection to meet because the period covered in this study includes two decades of Republican rule, much of it hostile to regulation, and only four years of proregulation Democratic government. It is thus difficult to set aside the claim that more commitment to regulation, tougher enforcement, more resources, and a more proregulatory climate would not have worked wonders in making regulation effective.[61] (If this trumpet call sounds familiar, it is—it echoes the summons issued by many unionists and union supporters and discussed in the last chapter, to wit, that more commitment and resources devoted to organizing would reverse the adverse trends in union share.)

How much improvement a stronger regulatory commitment might produce is unclear. Certainly the evidence from the Carter years is not encouraging. For example, the Minimum Wage Study Commission report on FLSA effectiveness cited earlier primarily reflected experience under the Carter administration; its findings of inadequate enforcement were based largely on surveys conducted during the final quarter of 1979, toward the end of the third year of Jimmy Carter's presidency—late enough for that administration to have found its bearings and set its course and long enough in advance of the 1980 election for it to have been sheltered from antiregulatory political pressures. The GAO's finding that noncompliance with the FLSA was a "serious and continuing problem" also was based on enforcement efforts during the Carter administration.

Similarly, many of the studies of OSHA effectiveness, for example, the insightful studies by Lawrence Bacow and W. Kip Viscusi, reflect results obtained in part or mostly during the Carter years (for example, Viscusi's study covers 1973–83).[62] The meager benefits from regulation that these studies document describe the activist, proregulatory regime of OSHA administrator Eula Bingham as well as those of less favorably disposed regulators. As one work-safety organizer and activist said, "Despite a genuine commitment to worker safety and health on the part of OSHA head Dr. Eula Bingham during the Carter Administration, the agency was unable to fulfill its promise. . . . Even at its best, OSHA did not have the capacity to eliminate most workplace hazards."[63] Similar evidence exists for other regulatory efforts during the Carter administration. Undoubtedly a more genuine and firmer commitment to regulation would make it more effective, and the Reagan years do not provide good evidence on how effective regulation could be. Still, evidence from the Carter years is not much more encouraging.

Moreover, it is an intrinsic feature of the whole regulatory strategy that regulatory effectiveness is hostage to the predilections and priorities of the regulators. Regulation is unlikely to be more effective than the regulators intend it to be (though it may inadvertently be a good deal less effective). It is surely relevant in assessing the whole regulation strategy to note that in the two decades following the passage of much of the regulatory legislation, several administrations hostile to regulation were elected, and in at least three elections (1980, 1984, 1988), antiregulation rhetoric was a central part of their successful electoral strategy. (President Clinton's campaign eschewed regulation and focused on other issues, which probably contributed to its success.) In this sense the data from the Reagan and Bush years, or any part of these two decades, cannot be dismissed so easily.

The Limits of Statutory Rights

Some patterns are discernible in the mixed results from regulation, and these patterns suggest the bases for successful regulation. First, the most successful regulation is that which regulates the simplest aspects of the workplace. The right to a minimum wage involves a straightforward, easily understandable aspect of the employment relationship; all workplaces pay wages, and the minimum level can be set in the law. The right to a safe workplace is more complex: What is an acceptable level of risk of accident or disease? How should the law treat the employee's responsibility for accidents or disease? But most fundamentally, the definition of a "safe and healthful" workplace defies clear statutory or regulatory definition because each workplace is unique in its geography, architecture, technology, machinery, history, personnel, and shop practices, and all of these factors influence plant safety. Thus, effectively implementing the right to a safe workplace intrinsically involves interpretation based on "close knowledge" rather than on mere ex post monitoring. The difference in regulatory success between the FLSA and OSHA appears mainly to reflect differences in the complexity of the attempted targets of regulation.

Second, even the most successful regulations have associated with them considerable difficulties in ensuring adequate compliance, and so a second characteristic of successful statutory regulation is that enforcement must be relatively straightforward. Compliance will be more problematic to the extent that violations are difficult to detect and that enforcement requires the intervention of technical expertise and professional personnel and depends upon interpretation based on local, particularistic, and specific features of a workplace. When violations are not easily detectable and demonstrable to an external authority, enforcement depends much more on the intervention of inspections, detailed examinations, professional expertise, and interpretation. In Equal Pay Act cases, for example, discrimination based on corporate pay systems that explicitly called for different pay for men and women were easy to eliminate, but more subtle discrimination has been hard to dislodge.[64] FLSA violations are relatively easy to detect and document, whereas OSHA and ERISA violations are much more difficult.

So too, a successful regulatory scheme must have access to an effective enforcement mechanism—not simply an enforcement agency, which can easily be created by Congress or state legislatures, but rather an effective mode of intervention and instruments of enforcement. For example, under ERISA all covered employers are required to have registered and on file with the federal government copies of their pension plans; because this law requires a positive action on the part of the employer, enforcement is in principle straightforward. Virtually all employers already show up in government records (through income tax returns and social security contributions), and so access to an appropriate enforcement mechanism for ERISA rules is simple. Alternatively, enforcement of antidiscrimination statutes is complex because employers are not under ordinary circumstances required to maintain the sort of records that would make enforcement easy; here enforcement agents are mostly required to construct their own cases. When employers are forced to do so (to have or keep federal contracts, for example), the reporting requirements are complex, burdensome, costly, and frequently unhelpful.

Thus statutory provision of substantive rights is likely to be more effective if certain circumstances prevail—the right is targeted to a simple or straightforward aspect of the employment relationship, violations can be easily detected, and an effective enforcement mechanism is available. These characteristics also define the effective limits of statutory rights: the further statute-based rights depart from these circumstances, the more uneven and unsatisfactory their impact is likely to be.

My argument does not, of course, prove that statutory rights lacking these characteristics fail to be in the public interest. The workers' right granted, even if only partially, erratically, or rarely achieved, may nonetheless be so important as to justify the existence of the statute. Rather, the point here is that statutory provision of substantive rights is only one of several mechanisms available to society to shape the employment relationship. It makes sense to rely on this mechanism only if no better alternative exists. As the union part of the postwar rights regime withered, advocates of workers' rights shifted the burden of workers' protections by default to its other support, statutory rights. But as has been shown, the existence of a statute does not automatically produce a corresponding real benefit for workers. Statutory provision succeeds better under some conditions than others, or to state the point negatively, it fails to achieve its ends more commonly under some conditions than others. Choosing the statutory mechanism by default only makes sense if there are no other choices.

I noted that the turn toward statutory provision of rights was stimulated by frustration with the collective-bargaining part of the postwar regime. It is an irony of history that workers' advocates should turn to the state to bestow rights on workers at just the historical moment when the declining organization of workers on the shop floor would render such statutory provision least efficacious. It is an irony to be lamented, but not repeated.

Notes to Chapter 5

1. See, for example, the many papers from this perspective in the *American Economic Review* (May 1987, *Papers and Proceedings 1986*).

2. See Guido Calabresi (1968); Ian R. MacNeil (1982); and Richard A. Posner (1977).

3. Tom R. Tyler (1990) concludes that this study "makes clear that normative issues are central to any effort to understand authority and compliance. . . . The instrumental perspective is clearly insufficient to explain people's view about the legitimacy of authority and their behavioral compliance with the law. Citizens act as naive moral philosophers, evaluating authorities and their actions against abstract criteria of fairness" (p. 165). See also Robert Cooter (1984).

4. Sar A. Levitan, Peter E. Carlson, and Isaac Shapiro (1986), pp. 247–49.

5. Rights may be granted to workers either by establishing a worker prerogative ("Any employee shall have the right to . . .") or by creating a corresponding employer obligation ("Every employer must provide each worker with . . ."); both are treated as workers' rights.

6. In America, antecedents can be traced back to colonial times, when wages and other terms of employment for some crafts were set by statute; see Richard B. Morris (1965).

7. Herbert Hill (1989); Reynolds Farley (1984); James R. Green (1978); Patricia Cayo Sexton (1982), pt. 2 ("Women's Issues").

8. See Michael Reich (1981); and U.S. Commission on Civil Rights (1976, 1982).

9. Patricia Cayo Sexton (1982), preface.

10. Calculated from U.S. Employment Standards Administration, *Minimum Wage and Maximum Hours Standards under the Fair Labor Standards Act,* 1982.

11. U.S. Employment Standards Administration, *Minimum Wage* . . . , 1982, table 5.

12. U.S. Employment Standards Administration, *Minimum Wage* . . . , 1982, table 8.

13. U.S. Minimum Wage Study Commission (1981); U.S. General Accounting Office (1981).

14. U.S. Minimum Wage Study Commission (1981), vol. 1, pp. 151–52.

15. U.S. Minimum Wage Study Commission (1981), vol. 1, p. 152; see also Brigitte Sellekaerts and Stephen Welch (1981), p. 24.

16. U.S. Minimum Wage Study Commission (1981), vol. 1, pp. 156, 157; and Stephen Welch (1981), p. 115.

17. U.S. Minimum Wage Study Commission (1981), vol. 1, p. 161.

18. Stephen Welch (1981), pp. 118–20.

19. U.S. General Accounting Office (1981), "Digest," pp. i, v.

20. U.S. General Accounting Office (1985), pp. 1, 3.

21. The FLSA also contains rules on child labor and some specific industry codes; I do not consider them here.

22. P.L. 93-406 (September 2, 1974).

23. See, for example, the studies by the American Federation of State, County, and Municipal Employees, the Employee Benefit Research Institute, the National Pension Forum, the American Society of Pension Actuaries, and others in U.S. Congress, Committee on Education and Labor, Hearings, March 21, 1985.

24. Testimony of Donald Grubbs in U.S. Congress, Committee on Education and Labor, 1986, p. 170. See also Kathleen Utgoff (1990) for a critical discussion of the impact of proliferating federal pension regulations, especially the substantial increase of the 1980s.

25. See statements by Edward Roybal, pp. 36–39; John Heinz, pp. 39–41; Emily Andrews, pp. 312–49; William Welsh, pp. 363–71; and Karen Friedman, pp. 426–27; all in U.S. Congress, Committee on Education and Labor (1986). See also "Small-Business Pensions Strangling on Paperwork,"

Springfield (Massachusetts) *Union-News,* December 4, 1989, p. 44; this Associated Press wire story reports on "hundreds" of small businesses that are abandoning their pension plans because of the cost and complexity of federal regulatory rules, and quotes Alvin Lurie, former IRS commissioner and chairman of the New York Bar Association's Special Committee on Pension Simplification: "It has become much, much too complicated. It's frightful. People can't afford it, don't understand it."

26. U.S. Congress, Committee on Education and Labor (1986), p. 55, which reprints a report from the U.S. Department of Labor, Office of Pension and Welfare Benefits Program of 1985; hereafter referred to as OPWBP. Page numbers cited refer to the OPWBP pagination, not House committee pages, p. 2.

27. Stephen Ross, in testimony before the U.S. Congress, Committee on Education and Labor (1986, pp. 71–72) [OPWBP], pp. 18, 19.

28. U.S. Congress, Committee on Education and Labor, 1986, pp. 61, 73 [OPWBP], pp. 8, 20, 28.

29. See statement by Lynn Williams, president of the United Steelworkers, U.S. Congress, Committee on Education and Labor (1986, p. 257).

30. Pension Rights Center, "The Case of the Disappearing Pension," pp. 428–43, and Donald Grubbs, "Vesting, Portability, and Integration with Social Security under Private Pension Plans," pp. 113–62, in U.S. Congress, Committee on Education and Labor (1986).

31. National Pension Forum, in U.S. Congress, Committee on Education and Labor (1986, p. 207).

32. National Pension Forum, in U.S. Congress, Committee on Education and Labor (1986, p. 202).

33. "Has the Plant Closing Law *Fizzled*?" *Boston Globe*, March 18, 1991, pp. 9, 11. Quotation is from Julie Sekera, director of policy and planning for the Industrial Services Program of the State of Ohio. A comprehensive review (U.S. General Accounting Office, 1993) suggests widespread noncompliance with the law. For a more cautious appraisal, see Ronald G. Ehrenberg and George Jakubson (1990).

34. P.L. 88-352 (July 2, 1964).

35. P.L. 88-38 (June 10, 1963).

36. The Westinghouse case involved a chart establishing labor grades and wages at a Westinghouse plant. Jobs were ranked on their worth to the company by Westinghouse, using its own criteria. When the company translated these job values into wages, however, male jobs were segregated from female jobs and assigned higher wages for jobs of equivalent value. The separate series for male and female jobs apparently was maintained until 1965, when they were merged. When they were merged, however, male grades one through ten were simply renumbered six through fifteen, thereby preserving the gender differential. See Winn Newman (1976); and Don Treiman and Heidi Hartmann (1981). Re the Sears case, see *New York Times*, "Sears Bias Stand Upheld by Court: U.S. Judge Backs Company in Sex Discrimination Case," January 16, 1988. p. 7.

37. P.L. 91-596 (1970, sec. (2)b).

38. U.S. General Accounting Office (1990, p. 15); P.L. 91-596 (1970), sec. (6)(1) and (5)a(2).

39. *Technologically possible* implies no consideration of costs; the standard for *economically possible* has tended to be whether the OSHA rule would ruin an entire industry; *economically practical* suggests benefit-cost analysis.

40. *American Textile Manufacturers Institute* v. *Donovan*, 452 U.S. 490 (1981); W. Kip Viscusi (1986b), p. 247.

41. *Industrial Union Department, AFL-CIO* v. *American Petroleum Institute*, 448 U.S. 607 (1980).

42. Robert Stewart Smith (1976), p. 70; see also James Robert Chelius (1977); John Mendeloff (1979); and the reviews in Lawrence Bacow (1980), and W. Kip Viscusi (1986b).

43. John Mendeloff (1976) reported in Albert Nichols and Richard Zeckhauser (1977), p. 53; W. Kip Viscusi (1979).

44. W. Kip Viscusi (1986a), p. 578.

45. W. Kip Viscusi (1986a), p. 578.

46. W. Kip Viscusi (1986a). When Viscusi lagged the variable measuring OSHA inspections by one year, the results suggested that OSHA reduced the overall injury rate by about 2.6 percent. However, the variable for current OSHA inspections carried a positive coefficient of nearly identical size, and therefore Viscusi concluded that the net effect of OSHA inspections was nearly nil (−.04%). W. Kip Viscusi (1986a), table 3.

47. Sar A. Levitan, Peter E. Carlson, and Isaac Shapiro (1986), pp. 119–23.

48. One dissenting study is that by William N. Cooke and Frederick H. Gautschi III (1981). They studied Maine manufacturing firms from 1970 to 1976 that had received OSHA citations, and found that citations significantly reduced total lost workdays, thereby providing evidence of a positive OSHA effect. Viscusi (1986a, p. 586) criticizes this study for bias caused by a regression-to-the-mean effect among cited firms.

49. John Mendeloff, "The Hazards of Rating Workplace Safety," *Wall Street Journal*, February 11, 1988, p. 20.

50. Mendeloff (1988), p. 2. Many observers doubt the cost-effectiveness of the measures taken, arguing that lives are saved only at unjustifiable expense. For example, each life saved by the arsenic standard was estimated to cost $70 million; the same amount of money spent in other ways might have saved many more lives. See Viscusi (1986b), p. 247. The point in the text concerns whether lives are saved, not the cost-effectiveness of the measures.

51. U.S. General Accounting Office (1990), p. 21.

52. Mendeloff (1988), p. 137.

53. Mendeloff (1988), p. 138.

54. National Safe Workplace Institute (1990), p. 75.

55. U.S. General Accounting Office (1990), pp. 2, 28–29.

56. Viscusi (1986b); Levitan, Carlson, and Shapiro (1986), pp. 123–24. From time to time, OSHA has also used a "megafine" strategy to levy large penalties on recalcitrant firms; large fines, however, usually extend the period of litigation and increase the level of political interference.

57. Connerton, Freeman, and Medoff (1983).

58. National Safe Workplace Institute (1987), pp. 11–13.

59. Bacow (1980), pp. 49–50. Bacow continues: "Most safety hazards are not subject to control by standards. Uniform standards necessarily result in inefficient allocation of hazard-abatement resources. Regulations cannot be written with enough specificity to accommodate all of the unique conditions encountered in the nation's five million workplaces. Even conscientious and well-trained inspectors can only observe a small proportion of hazards. And fines do not create the necessary incentives to ensure that both workers and managers will properly implement procedures designed to guarantee the safety of the workplace. In short, occupational safety and health policy is ineffective because it is poorly designed."

60. The experience of other countries is relevant, but no other Western or capitalist country attempts to regulate so large, diverse, or traditionally antistatist an economy as that of the United States.

61. This is the claim made by Levitan, Carlson, and Shapiro (1986).

62. Bacow (1981) and Viscusi (1986a).

63. Engler (1984), p. 2.

64. See P.L. 91-596 (1970), section (5)a(1); and "Sears Vindicated in U.S. Appeal," *Wall Street Journal,* January 18, 1988, p. 7.

6

Enterprise Rights in the Contemporary Firm

Many American workers enjoy important work rights in addition to those gained through union contracts and statutory provision. While these rights—which I have termed *enterprise rights*—are more unevenly available and less firmly anchored than collectively bargained or statutory rights, they nonetheless constitute a precious legacy for the employees to whom they apply.

Workers at the National Can Corporation's Oklahoma City plant, for example, enjoy a wide range of enterprise rights. Perhaps most important, these enterprise rights are all clearly spelled out in the plant's employee handbook, which is distributed to each worker. For example, the handbook states that "if ability, qualifications and experiences are relatively equal, the senior employee will be given primary consideration in such matters as promotions, layoffs, recalls from layoff, etc."[1] The right to seniority preference, long rejected by industrial management, was historically among the first demands made by unions after they gained legal recognition, and winning it proved to be a great victory. The reason was simple: seniority preference greatly reduces the scope for arbitrary treatment, favoritism, nepotism, and other management abuses. (Unfortunately it also often creates rigidity and imposes a variety of costs, mostly felt by management but to some extent by workers as well.)[2] Workers at the Oklahoma City plant, although they have no union, reap the benefits of past labor struggles.

Workers at National Can in Oklahoma City also have the right to use eleven paid holidays plus paid vacation that accrues according to a set, published schedule. They have access to an "open line" communication and complaint system, as well as a grievance procedure that can involve personal review by the plant manager and even appeal to an outside impartial arbitrator. Every worker's job is assigned a numerical pay grade; the pay rates are known and pay for similarly rated jobs is standardized. Vacancies for permanent jobs are posted, and current employees may bid for them "on the basis of seniority and ability." Many other enterprise rights obtain as well.

By contrast, workers at Ware Manufacturing possess virtually no enterprise rights.[3] A Massachusetts firm, Ware employs about one hundred fifty people in its sole plant, essentially a big machining room. Ware distributes no employee handbook to its workers nor any other documents detailing their job rights. Ware's workers even find it difficult to get the notifications required by law (for example, on the profit-sharing plan or retirement benefits). Concerning in-plant rights, the management is completely mute: all workers are strictly at-will employees, with no real rights.

Nancy Markham, now a former Ware employee, discovered her lack of rights the hard way. Markham had been hired as the only woman among the male machinists and the lowest-paid machine operator, but she was a quick learner and she soon trained on the CNC machines, the firm's biggest and most expensive pieces of equipment. In the first round of raises after she arrived, Markham got a dollar-an-hour increase, the biggest in the shop. But she immediately got into serious trouble with the foreman for revealing to the other workers the size of her raise. The foreman told her he would fire her if she ever did it again, ending with, "If you have any problems with your money or anything to say about your money, you come directly to me. I respect a man [sic] who comes into my office and says he's worth more money. That's what you should do."

Six months later, however, and only four days after she received her second raise, Markham was fired. Two or three months after her first raise, she had joined with a small group of other machinists to meet secretly and explore the possibilities of starting a union at

Ware. A couple of weeks before the second round of raises was announced, word of the unionizing effort began to get around the plant. On a Monday, the foreman walked around the shop, telling each worker the size of his raise. When he walked over to inform Markham of her raise, he was plainly nervous. He knew that she was expecting at least a dollar, and given her low pay and her work on the big equipment, considerably more might have been justified. He told her that they were raising her fifty cents, assuring her that it was among the biggest raises in the shop. He reminded her not to talk to the other workers about her raise: "Remember, Nancy, let's not have a repeat of last time."

Markham was angry, and protested; despite her good work and experience on the CNC machines, her pay would still be the lowest in the shop and far below that of most of the other machine operators. She told the foreman that her wage was hardly more than she could make in a pizza shop, and she was running a million-dollar machine. "Do you want to know what I think of the raise? I think it sucks, to tell the truth," she said. When the foreman got angry because Markham was not more grateful for the fifty cents, she replied: "Aren't you the guy who told me I should come to you if I thought I was worth more money?" The foreman replied that it had already been decided, and there was nothing he could do.

Telling the foreman what she thought, especially when the bosses were trying to figure out who might be union enthusiasts (despite specific federal guarantees granting workers the right to form unions and not be fired for organizing activities), sealed Markham's fate. On Thursday, the pay packets came with the raises in them. At 3:00 p.m. on Friday she was called into the foreman's office, and he told her that she was being let go: "It just seems that you're not that happy here, and my experience is that an employee that starts out unhappy just never gets happy." As Markham noted, "On anything that has to do with what happens in the plant, vacation time, employee rules, anything . . . any regulation about salary or wages, they don't give you anything because they don't want to have a policy. They have the policy, but they don't want to give it to you."[4] At Ware some privileges are gained in practice, but Ware's workers enjoy virtually none of the rights won in the postwar rights regime. Any special privileges are informal, particularistic, and not officially acknowledged by the company. With no written, official policies, workers at Ware have little basis for challenging management's interpretation of how policies apply in a specific case, for pressing grievances, or for resisting if management simply chooses to ignore them.

Employees have few rights at Ware Manufacturing, much more significant ones at National Can. To some, the enterprise rights extended by National Can may seem to be trivial—after all, employees at most companies get paid vacation and most employers implicitly follow the seniority principle at least to some extent. Yet this reaction is shortsighted in both historical and comparative terms. Moreover, National Can's policies are not just implicit or customary practices; they are all put in writing and distributed to the company's employees.

National Can's policies are powerfully shaped by the company's immediate legal and economic environment. Although the Oklahoma City plant is nonunion, most of the company's other plants are unionized: the San Leandro and Modesto, California, factories are organized by the International Association of Machinists and Aerospace Workers, and the Edison, New Jersey, plant by the United Steelworkers. The enterprise rights at the Oklahoma City plant closely follow rights won in union contracts at National Can's other plants, and the management of National Can undoubtedly has been stimulated to extend enterprise rights in Oklahoma City in part because it hopes to avoid unionization at this new, modern plant. Yet fear of unions does not seem to be the whole reason, and National Can may be equally stimulated to extend enterprise rights by its desire to build and motivate a committed and productive work force. The management works hard to impress upon its workers an appreciation of the rights they enjoy at National Can.

Although the National Can plant is exceptional in the extent of the enterprise rights it guarantees, it is representative in the sense that many employers provide at least some enterprise rights. As is shown in this chapter, employers vary greatly in the kind of enterprise rights they offer and in their commitment to them. The sheer diversity of such rights and the proprietary and private way that information about enterprise rights typically is treated by employers make assessing them difficult. However, any assessment of the status of workers' rights must address enterprise rights because they form a large part, perhaps the most significant part, of the current body of rights the average American worker possesses.

Enterprise rights provide protections on the job to workers who otherwise would not have them. This simple fact makes significant the changes now occurring in enterprise rights; under the impact of rulings in a growing number of states where courts have recognized employee handbooks as binding contracts, employers are "scrambling to take away rights they gave to employees," in the words of one employee-relations expert.[5]

Thinking about Enterprise Rights

Enterprise rights are primarily of interest in nonunion workplaces. Unionized workplaces may also have enterprise rights, but typically the most important rights are made part of the collective contract itself. In nonunion workplaces, enterprise rights to some extent substitute for or play the same role that contract-based rights play in unionized workplaces. Thus in speaking of enterprise rights, I mainly consider the nonunion sector.

Enterprise rights, as the term is used here, must be clearly distinguished from the larger and more amorphous category of "generalized practice or custom" that develops in most workplaces. Enterprise rights are workers' rights that are put in writing, typically in an employee handbook, or are otherwise explicitly stated and acknowledged by the employer. They represent that part of customary practice that achieves the status of explicitly affirmed (written) guarantees. They require some positive action on the part of the employer to accept (or initiate) and formalize them. In contrast, workplace customs and practices, although they also may be of great significance to the workers involved, are informal and implicit. As at Ware, such practices generally develop with nothing more than the boss's conscious forbearance, a kind of tacit approval or silent acquiescence. Such customary practices do not constitute *rights*; they are merely privileges that can be maintained by the worker's (or workers') immediate power.

Neither do enterprise rights reflect simple contract benefits. It is true that employers offer enterprise rights, like contract benefits, as part of their competitive strategy in the labor market. Yet to treat enterprise rights as simply the emoluments of individual employment contracts is to miss something vital. For enterprise rights represent a third category—a bundle of terms and conditions that is generally *not* available for individual employees to bargain over (nor is it bargained over collectively, since I am here considering nonunion employers). Enterprise rights express the explicitly affirmed supracontractual aspects of an employment contract, and thus they represent the presuppositions or the framework for an individual worker's contract bargaining; for example, seniority preference and appeal beyond one's immediate supervisor are almost never items of individual contract bargaining (in the unionized sector, of course, they are bargained for collectively). As will be shown, this difference results in a significant legal distinction with important economic and contractual implications. It would blur important distinctions to agglomerate all terms of employment not based on statutes into the single concept, "contractual benefits."[6]

Employers establish enterprise rights for a variety of reasons. Clearly one motivation is competitive: to attract and retain good workers and motivate them to high productivity. In motivating workers, employers must respond to the workers' own understanding of what constitutes fair treatment and which work rights normally obtain in "good" jobs. Workers come to have expectations based on their experiences or what they think they know about other workplaces; historically, these expectations have been based to a significant degree on the standards and rights gained in unionized workplaces, even among workers for whom no realistic prospect of unionization exists. A second reason for an employer to establish enterprise rights is to preempt or forestall unionization. One of an employers' most persuasive antiunion pitches to workers is the claim that workers already enjoy the rights that unions would try to achieve by bargaining. Finally, some employers may establish enterprise rights because they believe workers deserve rights.

Enterprise rights differ from other workers' rights because, having been granted unilaterally by the employer, they may also be changed, redefined, or withdrawn by unilateral management decision. As recently as the late 1970s the law was clear: enterprise rights are not legally enforceable employer obligations. More recently, however, what was once a clear difference between enterprise rights and other rights has become much less clear. An impressive number of state courts have begun interpreting employee handbooks, and the enterprise rights stated in them, as implicit or implied contracts between an employer and its workers; such contracts therefore become legally enforceable. Thus today a rather fuzzy line divides enterprise rights from other rights.

Enterprise rights are most commonly written out in employee handbooks. Virtually all larger employers and many small and medium-size firms use handbooks as a convenient way to inform new workers of company rules and practices, instruct employees about their obligations, provide incumbent employees with a ready reference for disciplinary procedures and company benefits, and in general let all employees know what the employer expects of them.[7] New employees may be required to sign a form indicating that they have received the handbook and will comply with company rules. Handbooks range from small brochures to thick notebooks hundreds of pages in length. For the purpose of this chapter, if employers' guarantees are nowhere put in writing and made available to employees, they are not here treated as enterprise rights.[8]

Most employers regard employee handbooks as strictly proprietary and private, and they generally refuse requests from outsiders (for example, academic researchers) for copies of them. This attitude has become much more common in recent years as courts have granted some legal status to handbooks.[9] For example, one senior manager who released a handbook for use in this study indicated that he could be fired if other company officials discovered he had done so. Labor organizers regularly collect such documents surreptitiously from sympathetic employees, but they use the handbooks discreetly to avert reprisals.

The significance of enterprise rights is more difficult to assess than that of other categories of workers' rights. It would be incorrect to interpret them simply as hollow promises, because courts have shown a growing inclination to give legal effect to handbooks, and in any event enterprise rights help establish employee expectations and provide workers with important leverage in obtaining the actual exercise of such rights. But crucial limits remain: legal or other outside enforcement authority to require a company to live up to its stated enterprise rights remains weak. Little prevents a company from cynically establishing enterprise rights that it has no intention of respecting—but then neither is it required to do so, and establishing such rights when workers will daily see them disregarded is not only unnecessary but almost a sure recipe for worker unrest.

In the remainder of this chapter I review the kinds of enterprise rights existing in contemporary firms. I have surveyed 112 firms, all private, for-profit, nonunion companies; information about enterprise rights is primarily derived from their employee handbooks in use from 1987 to 1990.[10] This type of data implies some important limitations on the kinds of conclusions I can draw. First, I cannot make statements about actual shop-floor practice, because practice can depart significantly from written policies. This is not a debilitating restriction, given my focus on enterprise rights rather than shop-floor custom or practice, but it should be kept in mind that I am discussing written policies, not practice. Second, I cannot claim that any particular provision or particular company's policy continues exactly as described, because these policies may have been modified since my study. Third, I cannot claim that the group of companies in my survey is necessarily representative of all employers, because it was not constructed on a statistical sampling basis. The panel is, however, highly diverse in terms of region, type of industry, and size of firm. The second and third limitations are not seriously harmful to my purposes either, because all I am attempting to suggest is the nature, variety, and texture of enterprise rights in practice. I have not used statistical tests because I cannot assume that they would be valid.

What Enterprise Rights Do Workers Have?

Enterprise rights, because they are neither required by law nor granted in collective bargaining, reflect the great diversity of the nation's 5 million employers. Nonetheless, certain patterns or common elements are evident in the types of enterprise rights granted. Most enterprise rights granted by employers fall into three general categories: those that provide the employee with "voice," those that promise fair dealing with the employee, and those that establish substantive employee privileges or perquisites.[11]

Enterprise Rights That Grant Voice

One common enterprise right is the "open-door policy." Some 41 percent of the firms studied offer it. Indeed, this exact term is used so similarly by so many different employers that one can easily discern the standardizing impact of management consultants at work. The basic idea is to create an atmosphere in which employees as individuals can speak up. For example, at the Keyes-Fibre Company in Memphis, Tennessee, a manufacturer of molded foam products such as sandwich containers and egg cartons, employees receive the following counseling:

> Every supervisor is responsible for upholding both the spirit and intent of our policy of fairness, impartiality, and open communications by having an open door and open ear.
>
> If your supervisor does not give you a prompt answer, if you are not satisfied with his answer, or if for some reason you do not feel you can discuss it with him, then by all means feel free to discuss it with the Employee Relations Manager.
>
> You are also entitled to a fair and impartial hearing by the Plant Manager without fear of reprisal for having taken the matter up with him.[12]

The IBM handbook contains a similar statement:

> [A] basic IBM communications channel is the Open Door. The Open Door Policy, a reflection of IBM's belief in respect for the individual, is deeply ingrained in IBM's history. It is based on the conviction that every employee has a right to appeal the actions of those who are immediately over him or her in authority.[13]

The open door is by no means restricted to employers with slick or sophisticated personnel departments. For example, A. Duda and Sons, one of the largest produce growers in Florida, states:

> Here at A. Duda & Sons, Inc. we have an "open door" policy. This means that you can take your personal or work prob-

> lems or your complaints to any supervisor, or any member of management you choose to select. You have this *basic right* and *freedom* as an employee of A. Duda & Sons, Inc.
>
> Remember, you may use this "open door" policy without fear of penalty or reprisal.[14]

The worker's right to discuss or complain about a work-related problem with a company official other than an immediate supervisor is, historically, a major advance for workers. The "tyranny of the foreman" was one of the most oppressive but pervasive features of industrial life in the period before the postwar rights regime, and indeed it continues to be so in many informally organized shops today.[15] Under such tyranny the employee faces the stark choice of knuckling under or quitting the job. Giving employees access to a formally sanctioned alternate communications channel places a potentially substantial limit on the scope for arbitrary foreman rule (indeed, it was this attribute that first attracted upper management's interest), and it opens to the employee the wider realm of the company for making complaints, seeking information, and attempting to have disputes arbitrated.

Still, despite its grant of accessibility, the open-door policy is one of the weakest enterprise rights. It formally offers no more than an audience, a hearing in the literal rather than the legal sense. It promises no particular response, follow-up, or other positive action. Undoubtedly its vagueness is, to management, one of its appeals.

A stronger grant of voice occurs when an employer establishes a formal employee-grievance system. Surprisingly, nearly 61 percent of the companies I surveyed had done so, and they reported a great variety of specific mechanisms. This percentage closely matches the findings of a Conference Board study published in 1980. That study also found that the credibility of such systems depends most strongly on two factors: protection from reprisals by supervisors and "the strict impartiality of the ultimate decision maker."[16]

Least innovative and formalized are systems like the one at Perdue, Inc., the big Maryland-based poultry producer. The grievance mechanism (or "complaint procedure," as Perdue calls it) is simple and not well developed. An employee with "a complaint, a dissatisfaction over what he feels is unjust treatment, a misunderstanding, or who has questions about his rights or obligations" first raises the complaint with her supervisor.[17] Appeals may be taken to the department foreman and the personnel department. Merrill Lynch and National Can offer their employees systems similar to Perdue's, permitting the employee to appeal up the managerial ladder and horizontally across the company to a personnel or employee-relations department. A more highly developed system, representative perhaps of the group of formalized complaint mechanisms, was in effect at the Connecticut Bank and Trust Company, a medium-size commercial bank recently acquired by the Fleet Bank system.[18]

Although systems like those at Perdue and CBT are common, there is considerable diversity in how employers offer grievance rights. The Hawthorne Community Medical Group, Inc., is one of the largest multispecialty group practices in Los Angeles, with medical offices throughout southern California. HCMG provides a more meaningful grievance procedure than those discussed above by adding several novel features. First, the HCMG handbook identifies a "grievance" as an employee allegation resulting in a dispute or disagreement between the employee and the company (not merely a company supervisor or officer); thus grievances are lifted above the level of personal "complaints" or "personality conflicts" to matters of substantive policy interpretation. Second, several employee safeguards are introduced. For example, supervisors who do not respond within the allotted time are presumed to have denied the grievance, thereby permitting the grievant to appeal immediately to the next level. Appeal is permitted to the chief executive officer of the company, and protections against reprisals are strongly worded.

Still a different line of innovation can be seen at Consulting Services, Inc., a Massachusetts company employing about a hundred people using social science to analyze government and business problems.[19] One innovation is a statement in the company handbook that employees may file a grievance based on what they see as violations of the company's "implicit policy," as well as its "written policy," an arrangement that greatly expands the scope of possible complaints.

With one exception, the steps in the formal complaint procedure at Consulting Services are similar to those of complaint systems elsewhere. Initially the complaining employee is directed to use a system of informal problem solving; this can be followed by an appeal to the personnel department, and then a formal written grievance. What happens next, however, is novel: the formal complaint is heard by a Personnel Complaint Committee composed of two company officers and two employees "chosen by lot from a pool of eligible and willing employees." All employees except senior management and corporate officers are eligible to be chosen. Alternates are selected for all four positions, and the complainant may request that the designated alternate for any particular committee member serve in that member's stead. (The remaining three members decide if the request is to be granted.)

The Personnel Complaint Committee at Consulting Services renders a final decision, based on the complaint submitted and any additional information it wishes to collect. The Company's board of directors has empowered the committee to "resolve virtually all complaints raised by employees," so the committee's decision is automatically binding on the company. The sole exception is a decision that "involves Board [of Directors] prerogative (e.g., the expenditure of funds, the creation or termination of positions, etc.)," for which board review is required before the decision is implemented.[20]

Consulting Services is unusual in empowering its joint employee-management committee to impose solutions, but the involvement of workers in grievance processes is a more widespread phenomenon. At Budget Car and Truck Rental, for instance, the first stage in the formal grievance process is consideration of the complaint by a grievance committee consisting of two staff members and two managers.

Enterprise Rights That Promise Fair Dealing

Enterprise rights of the second type establish presumptions of fair treatment for the employee—something akin to but typically weaker than the legal concept of due process. All enterprise rights, including the open-door and grievance procedures, are in large part directed toward establishing a general sense of fair dealing, for the very idea of "rights" is one that conveys limits on arbitrary treatment. But the enterprise rights considered here have a more direct relationship to fair dealing.

Probably the most immediate point of contact with the issue of fair treatment is in the matter of discipline. Virtually all employers have rules, and most reserve their prerogative to impose punishment, including dismissal, for violation of their rules. Many employers have only vague and informal systems of discipline, reserving to themselves the maximum flexibility to deal with disciplinary problems. Other employers (about 41 percent of those surveyed) have regularized discipline in ways that offer the employee some predictability and sense of order in matters of punishment. The simplest and most common arrangement is a progressive series of stated disciplinary steps. At many Holiday Inns, including the one in Hollywood, California, for instance, discipline follows the progression of verbal counseling, a first written warning, a final written warning (which may include a suspension), and discharge. This system is intended "to ensure a fair method of disciplining employees" and "to give employees advance notice, whenever possible, of problems with their conduct or performance in order to provide them an opportunity to correct any problems."[21] The employee can appeal any penalty to the personnel department and then to the general manager.

The Budget Car and Truck Rental system calls for virtually the same set of steps (verbal warning, written warning, suspension, and discharge). It adds a forgiveness clause, however: if no further warnings are issued during the nine months following a warning, that warning will be removed from the worker's record. At d'Amour's Big Y, a Massachusetts supermarket chain, a rule infraction is not held against the employee if it occurred twelve months ago or longer.[22] National Can in Oklahoma City also uses the twelve-month rescission rule.

Major electronics manufacturer Texas Instruments employs a five-step process: informal review, oral warning, "guidance report," probation notice, and termination. The first two steps and the last step are self-explanatory. Guidance report is a status, known to the employee and decided upon jointly by several levels of management, that usually entails a thirty-day period during which "the employee is closely observed." Managers are instructed that "guidance does not mean that the employee is on the way out. This is another attempt to save a valuable TI asset—its people."[23] TI's probation notice is "the last chance, so to speak"; the worker stays on probation until the company perceives performance improving or, alternatively, until he is fired.

A less common form of progression is the listing of stated penalties for specific infractions. D'Amour's Big Y divides violations into "serious offenses," usually resulting in immediate termination, and "other offenses" that call for minor discipline such as reprimands and suspensions. Serious offenses include theft, falsifying records, disclosing confidential company information, sleeping on the job, and destroying company property. Other offenses include irregular attendance, lateness, unauthorized smoking or eating, improper language, and horseplay and violation of safety rules.

Finfrock Industries, a Florida company that makes prestressed structural-concrete products, lists thirty-one specific rule violations, along with the penalties for the first, second, and third offenses. For example, "willful failure to use safe equipment or comply with safety rules" brings a written warning for the first violation, then a two-day suspension, and then discharge. "Obtaining materials or tools from the storeroom or other assigned places on fraudulent orders or misrepresentation" brings a written warning the first time and then discharge, whereas "unauthorized possession of explosives on company premises" triggers immediate discharge.[24]

Undoubtedly the most serious and tension-fraught matter involving fair dealing is the process governing dismissal. Most employers carefully preserve their prerogatives by stating that employees are hired "at will."[25] Nonetheless, some employees enjoy significant protections from arbitrary dismissal. Some companies (about 12 percent of those in my survey) promise their employees that any dismissals will be handled by special procedures, separate from other disciplinary and supervisory processes. For example, at Texas Instruments a discharge requires the approval of at least four levels of management; for employees who have worked at TI for fifteen years or more, the company president must personally approve any termination notice. Similarly, at Coast Novelty Manufacturing Company, a California firm that claims to be America's largest producer of cake ornaments and importer of cake decorations, a dismissal requires previous written warning and may be implemented only by a discharge notice signed by the company president. At J. C. Penney, an employee is subject to immediate discharge only for certain specified offenses (for example, drinking at work or bringing dangerous weapons to work). Otherwise, if the employee has completed the initial ninety-day probationary period, no "discretionary discharge" can be effected until he has been placed on review status and given an opportunity to work out his problems.[26] Review status is a kind of disciplinary probation lasting thirty, sixty, or ninety days.

Many employers distinguish between new employees still in the probationary period (typically ninety days) and nonprobationary employees. Workers in the former group may be discharged immediately, with or without cause, and without necessarily having been warned first or informed of the reason. Implicitly, and occasionally explicitly, nonprobationary employees have the right to be warned of any problems in writing before being subject to dismissal, to grieve or appeal a dismissal, and if dismissed to be given a reason.

Some employers promise or imply that they will dismiss employees only for "just cause." Although only a few of the employers in my survey flatly stated that just cause was their standard, 32 percent of the companies provided a statement implying just cause and another 6 percent indicated just cause in one part of the handbook but reaffirmed at-will elsewhere. Hawthorne Community Medical Group states straightforwardly that "it is COMPANY policy . . . after verbal and written warnings, to discharge an employee for just cause."[27] The handbook for National Can's Oklahoma City plant includes a statement in the section on dismissal that "disciplinary action will only be taken for good cause." Many more employers imply that dismissal for just cause is their policy, but add an at-will clause for legal purposes. Merrill Lynch, for example, notes that in the case of a dismissal, "the individual is informed by the supervisor or manager . . . [of] the reasons for the release."[28] This statement is followed by a list of specific "inappropriate actions" that may result in discharge. Coast Novelty Manufacturing tells its workers that "an employee may be discharged for misconduct, violation of company safety rules, insubordination, unreliability, or inability to perform the work for which hired."[29] Although the stated causes for discharge are vague enough to support considerable managerial discretion, they nonetheless constitute a list of "just causes."

Occasionally employers place more stringent limits on their at-will prerogatives. One interesting instance occurs at National Can's Oklahoma City plant. If the company decides, after the usual progressive discipline procedures have been exhausted, that "a regular [that is, nonprobationary] employee's conduct may justify discharge the employee will be notified in writing and immediately suspend[ed] initially for a period of six (6) work days pending determination by the company."[30] During the suspension period, the worker may request a hearing with the plant manager. The company will state the violation and discuss its case. At this hearing the employee may call witnesses to testify on his behalf. One day after the hearing (or if there is no hearing, on the sixth day of the suspension), the company "will confirm in writing to the employee that the 6-day suspension is affirmed, modified, extended, revoked or converted to discharge."[31] The hearing before the plant manager does not, however, exhaust the employee's rights. He may appeal the firing to an outside impartial arbitrator. The company pays the costs of the arbitration hearing, except for the first $100 of the arbitrator's fee, which the worker must pay; in the event that the arbitrator rules in the employee's favor, the company reimburses the $100. The company states flatly: "The arbitrator's decision will be final and binding upon all parties."[32] By establishing this process of appeal and arbitration, National Can has extended enterprise rights offering significant protection against unfair dismissal.

A number of other companies (not included in my survey) also guarantee to their workers an option of appeal to outside arbitrators. Two major ones are Polaroid and Northrop. In these cases, appeal to an arbitrator is only permissible after all internal appeals and mediation procedures have failed to resolve the dispute. As in a union contract, arbitration is the last step in handling a grievance and is binding.[33]

Enterprise Rights That Establish Employee Perquisites

The third group of enterprise rights includes those that directly create substantive privileges or claims for workers. In many cases these enterprise rights replicate privileges or rights won by unionized workers through collective bargaining.

Many employers (29 percent of my sample) promise that they will post job vacancies so that current employees may apply for them before any other applicants are considered. For example, at Simon and Schuster, the New York book publisher, it is noted in the employee handbook that the company "identifies and posts information on job openings as they occur, and gives full-time regular and part-time regular employees the opportunity to apply for these positions."[34] The company pledges that only if it determines that no qualified internal candidates are available will it turn to outside applicants.

Massachusetts Mutual Life Insurance, a medium-size company with headquarters in Springfield, Massachusetts, has a more elaborate system, in effect granting some "turf rights" to employees. Job vacancies are first posted for three days in the division in which the vacancy occurs; only workers employed within the division may apply. If no applicant within the division is selected, the vacancy notice is posted on the companywide bulletin boards, and any worker can then apply. Even during this period, however, if division candidates are still being considered, the vacancy announcement must disclose the fact so that "in this way, employees know that the Company-wide board contains only those positions which actually are open with no pre-selected candidates from the originating division."[35] Only if no acceptable internal applicant is found does Massachusetts Mutual indicate that it will turn to the outside labor market.

These basics of job-posting and job-bidding rights are elaborated and diversified in many ways by different employers. J. C. Penney promises that it will not fill any job at the "associates" level (basically its regular staff level) until the vacancy has been posted for at least three days. At Furtex, Inc., a Tennessee textile manufacturer, vacancies are posted only twenty-four hours before they can be filled, but workers are encouraged to apply for positions even before they become vacant by filling out job-bid forms, which the company keeps on file. At Keyes-Fibre Company's Memphis, Tennessee, plant, the company posts vacancies for "two full days before considering candidates from outside the Company."[36] If an employee of the Memphis plant is selected, the worker has a thirty-day trial period in the new job, during which either the worker or the company may decide that she should return to her original job, with no penalties or loss of pay.

Many employers offer job-bidding rights but place some restrictions on how frequently workers can exercise them; one such company is Accuride, a California firm that has plants in North Carolina, Germany, England, and Japan, and boasts that it is "the largest drawer slide manufacturer in the world." Accuride workers must be employed by the company at least twelve months and have completed six months in their current jobs before they become eligible to bid on promotion or transfer.

The right to seniority preference is closely linked to job-bidding rights, but is broader in application. Surprisingly, 24 percent of those employers surveyed explicitly recognize workers' rights to seniority preference—often considered one of the fundamental victories of American unions; even more surprisingly, some employers recognize a "strong form" of seniority rights that considerably restricts management prerogatives.

The larger group of employers recognizing seniority preference offers only what may be termed a "weak form"—that is, seniority is one entry in a list of criteria determining some benefit. At Lawrence-Allison & Associates, a Houston-based oil and gas engineering firm with operations throughout the West, job vacancies are filled by "the most qualified person based on ability, performance and length of service."[37] At HCMG, the West Coast medical group, "Promotions are made on the basis of merit and qualifications. . . . In the case of two employees with equal merit and qualifications, THEN the promotion will be made on the basis of seniority."[38] At d'Amour's Big Y, "length of service" is listed first among nine criteria for determining who will be promoted.

Some employers elevate seniority rights to a more commanding position. The strong form of seniority preference makes seniority the determining factor, other qualifications being more or less equal. At Perdue, "seniority shall be the determining factor . . . where the following qualifications are approximately equal: skill . . . dependability, [and] work record."[39] At Kayser-Roth Hosiery, "when there are no major differences between candidates [for promotion or transfer], Company length of service will be the determining factor, except for a transfer request [from an employee] based on an approved personal need." At National Can in Oklahoma City, the senior employee will be given "primary consideration" if ability, qualifications, and experience are "relatively equal."[40]

Seniority preference may be applied to a broad range of worker situations. Although it is widely used to determine eligibility for increased vacation time, health and retirement benefits, and other perquisites, seniority has been acknowledged in other personnel areas as well. The most common practice is the recognition of seniority rights in transfer and promotion policies. Some employers, including Perdue, d'Amour's Big Y, National Can, and Kayser-Roth, also recognize seniority rights in layoff and recall procedures, thereby granting extra job security to more-senior workers; d'Amour's Big Y tells its employees, "in case of layoff due to business conditions beyond our control, your seniority insures you of work as long as work is available."[41] At National Can, in the event of a layoff, more-senior employees can bump or displace other workers in equal or lower-rated jobs and even, with some restrictions, in higher-rated jobs. At Texas Instruments, as already noted, an employee with fifteen or more years of seniority can be dismissed for cause only by the company president.

Enterprise rights are also used to grant a wide range of other substantive benefits to workers. One of the most important, but also one of the rarest, is the right to training. Many companies maintain training programs, and a smaller but still significant number offer vague assurances to workers of the availability of further training. For workers in these companies, although there may in fact be considerable opportunities for training, access to it does not exist as an employee's *right*; rather, access to training is a matter of company needs and the employer's choice of whom it will train. IBM, despite its justly earned reputation for extensive and sophisticated employee training, merely assures its employees that "the company offers a wide range of developmental, educational, and training opportunities."[42] It leaves uncertain what access any particular employee or potential employee might claim.

Although virtually no employer offers access to internal training programs as a matter of right, a few do offer workers a right to subsidized schooling. Accuride, the drawer-slide manufacturer, is one. Full-time Accuride workers who have completed at least one year of employment can continue their schooling at company expense. The courses must relate "to your current job or other jobs within the Company to which you aspire."[43] Reimbursement depends upon the grade received. (An *A* is good for 100 percent reimbursement, a *B* for 90 percent, and a *C* for 80 percent; lower grades result in no refund, and a passing grade in a pass-fail course nets 70 percent.) Digital Equipment Corporation, the mid-size Massachusetts computer maker, will pay for all expenses and provide company time for courses that are "job-required." More unusual is the provision that for "career-related" courses, the company will pay tuition and some other fees. (It will not, however, provide company time for such training.) Most unusual of all, even for academic work aimed at "knowledge and perspective broadening," the company pays half of the course tuition (up to $300 a year).

Another enterprise right granted only infrequently (by only 11 percent of my sample) is severance pay. Marathon Oil, a subsidiary of USX, is one employer that makes a specific guarantee. If a worker is laid off because of the closing of a Marathon facility or to a reduction in the work force, within certain restrictions she will be paid a "termination allowance" equal to one week's pay for each year of company employment. At Viking Penguin, the New York branch of the British publishing house, severance pay is granted to any employee discharged due to "no fault of the employee"; dismissed workers receive one week's pay for each full year of employment up to ten years, and two weeks' pay for each year of employment over ten years.

Another important group of enterprise rights concerns the division between work time and the employee's nonwork leave time. Fairly standard features include paid vacation, sick leave, and retirement pay. Some employers have gone further: at Connecticut General Insurance Company, for example, some workers get as many as five days' leave for personal business. Paid personal leave is also guaranteed at Vanguard Electronics Co., a California-based small electronics manufacturer of inductive devices for military and industrial uses; there, full-time workers get credited with a half day of personal leave for each month worked, up to six days per year. Unused personal leave time can be sold back to the company at the end of the year.

A significant number of companies grant workers the right to take unpaid leaves of absence for disability, medical, maternity, and military reasons.[44] A few grant employees the right to take unpaid leave for other personal reasons and still retain their job rights. Unichem International, a New Mexico-based chemical company with operations in twelve states and eight foreign countries, grants personal unpaid leave "upon presentation of appropriate justification"; such leave is not treated as a break in service with the company. Perdue grants personal leave for up to two weeks with the approval of lower-level management; the maximum personal leave, thirty days, must be approved by the director of employee relations. Prestige Stations, Inc., a retailing subsidiary of the oil giant ARCO, grants unpaid leave for personal business of up to two weeks, contingent on the immediate supervisor's approval; an additional two weeks, contingent on the division vice-president's approval; and lengthier leave on approval of higher management. One of the most liberal policies is that of A. Duda & Sons, the Florida produce grower. For "personal illness or injury, or circumstances creating family hardship," Duda grants leave of up to ninety days, with extensions possible up to one year. Virtually no employer permits workers to take personal leave unless they experience an injury, family difficulty, or similar problem. In general, workers have no enterprise right to unpaid leave for reasons unrelated to problems (for example, to build a house or help launch a family enterprise).

Other enterprise rights regulating time exist as well. Some companies guarantee a minimum for "call-in" pay; that is, a minimum number of hours' worth of pay for any extra period for which the worker is called to work. At Keyes-Fibre's Memphis plant, for example, any worker who reports for work without having been notified not to report is guaranteed at least four hours' pay; a worker recalled to work after completing a regular shift is guaranteed at least three hours of pay (calculated at the time-and-a-half rate). A few employers also guarantee a minimum amount of work time. J. C. Penney, for example, promises its regular, full-time workers who have five or more years of continuous employment forty hours of work during any week that they work. More junior employees are also given a guarantee, but for fewer hours.

The 112 company handbooks I studied are filled with other enterprise rights granting substantive perquisites. Relatively common are provisions concerning health insurance, pension rights, paid holidays, and benefit buy-back provisions. These more common enterprise rights are often supplemented by idiosyncratic provisions (for example, a Woolworth worker's entitlement to a 10 percent discount on any purchase of store merchandise and a Perdue worker's right to paid funeral leave).

The cases cited above are restricted to enterprise rights granted by private, for-profit, nonunionized employers. They show the great diversity in enterprise rights, but they also suggest that enterprise rights are pervasive and can have a powerful impact on the work lives of employees in these firms. The enterprise rights enjoyed by another substantial segment of private-sector workers—employees of private, *non*profit institutions—are frequently even more extensive and more secure than those that obtain in the for-profit sector.[45]

Limitations of Enterprise Rights

Despite their importance and pervasiveness, enterprise rights have certain intrinsic shortcomings as a mechanism for protecting workers' interests. When enterprise rights are considered as a possible foundation for a new workers'-rights regime, these flaws become particularly striking. One problem is that many employers, perhaps a majority, offer virtually no enterprise rights at all. Numbers and percentages of employers (or of workers affected) are not very meaningful indicators here, given that enterprise rights encompass such vast differences in type, strength, and quality of entitlement. The issue, more precisely, is uneven protection of workers—the reality that an unknown but arguably large number of workers exercise essentially no effective enterprise rights at all.

Unlike uneven coverage, the fact that not all workers enjoy the *same* enterprise rights is not a problem but instead quite possibly an important strength. After all, one strong point of the collective-bargaining system is that contracts can be tailored so that working rights and conditions match the particular features of individual workplaces; obversely, the absence of flexibility is often the fatal flaw in trying to apply and enforce the rights granted by statute. So, having many different employers who offer distinct packages of enterprise rights coexisting in the marketplace is generally a desirable feature. The problem of uneven coverage, by contrast, is that many workers have few or no enterprise rights at all.

A second problem is the secrecy that surrounds enterprise rights; secrecy creates the information asymmetries that may produce market failures, as discussed in chapter 3. Job-seekers generally cannot easily obtain reliable information on enterprise rights to compare such rights among employers. As noted earlier, many firms treat employee handbooks and enterprise rights as proprietary and private information. Typically an employee only receives a handbook after being hired; indeed, employers often require new workers, on receiving a handbook, to promise to return it when she leaves the company. Job-seekers can find out by word of mouth about job rights in a particular plant, and pirated copies of employer handbooks no doubt circulate. But to be informed via these channels, a job-seeker has to have acquaintances who work for the prospective employer.

Moreover, except for workers who are in especially strong demand, job applicants are likely to be highly inhibited about requesting information on job rights from an employer during the hiring interview; such a request (an instance of what is sometimes termed "negative signaling") seems a surefire way not to get the job.[46] The secrecy surrounding handbooks and enterprise rights in general means that someone looking for a position typically cannot compare enterprise rights available in different jobs. Lacking a ready and reliable means of comparison, the job seeker must decide where to work using partial and probably faulty information or by ignoring enterprise rights altogether.

A third problem with enterprise rights is that, as unilateral grants, they can also be changed, even abrogated, at the employer's discretion; this is the problem, as discussed in chapter 3, of lack of contract enforceability. A worker may seek employment with a certain employer specifically because it grants certain desired enterprise rights; but after taking up employment with the firm, perhaps after investing a number of years in the firm, the worker may suddenly find the enterprise rights changed, distorted, reduced, or even withdrawn.

Even if the employer does not alter the set of rights it offers, it may nonetheless refuse to honor them. Enterprise rights represent employer *promises* of rights, but except where courts treat them as implied contracts, these promises lack either the force of statutory law or the legal obligations of contract. Moreover, with no union or other outside authority or source of assistance to appeal to, the individual employee typically stands powerless before an employer that either unknowingly or cynically refuses to live up to its promises. (See the discussion in chapter 3.)

When enterprise rights simply reflect the way the employer prefers to do business, the workers may perhaps rely upon the employer's self-interest to keep it faithful to its enterprise-rights promises. When a firm has a large stake in maintaining its reputation as a good employer, workers may find some protection in that interest. But as noted in chapter 3, such incentives are likely to be weak enforcement mechanisms. When enterprise rights are taken by the workers, and advertised by the employer, as constituting a real restriction on the arbitrary actions of the employer, that is, when enterprise rights are understood to be binding promises that may prevent the employer from pursuing its perceived immediate or long-term self-interest, even in changed circumstances, the lack of enforceability constitutes a serious flaw.

Finally, a perhaps more fundamental flaw is that enterprise rights are invariably *individual* rights, and the collective or shared needs of workers gain no recognition or means of advancement from them. (This attribute is undoubtedly attractive to many employers.)

Until about 1980, courts refused to view enterprise rights as legally enforceable promises. Judges declared that legal enforceability could only be imposed by statute or agreed to in contract. By definition, an enterprise right is not imposed by statute, and therefore the only remaining question was if it constituted a valid contract. The courts answered in the negative, viewing employee handbooks and similar statements of employer policies, both written and oral, as no more than employer benefices, that is, as gratuities bestowed on workers by their employers and therefore not contractually binding.[47]

How the courts reached their conclusion is revealing. The judges argued that promises contained in employee handbooks could not be enforceable as contracts because they can be changed unilaterally by employers; contracts, in the judges' eyes, must be mutual and reciprocal. Moreover, unless the employer and individual worker (or a union, representing workers) made a specific and express contract stating terms and conditions of employment, including of especial importance the length of the contract, courts consistently interpreted the employment relationship between them as being at will. The courts reasoned that because either party, and of relevance here, the employer, can terminate an at-will employment at any time for any or no reason, clearly an employer can legally evade any promises made in a handbook merely by dismissing the worker.

Hence, by this reasoning, the promises or enterprise rights must simply be unilateral employer grants, made for the benefit of the employee, not the quid pro quo terms of an enforceable contract.[48]

Various courts found additional reasons to support their traditional interpretation. For example, some courts concluded that where the handbook was distributed after the worker was hired, it could not constitute part of the employment contract because that contract had already been established. Other courts decided that handbooks and similar statements were simply general declarations of employer policy and lacked the intent to constitute contractual obligations. Still other courts found that the lack of a definite statement concerning the term of the contract, or the failure of an employee to show that he had provided some additional consideration (beyond work) in exchange for receiving the handbook policies as employer obligations, left the employer's promises as simple unilateral grants.[49]

The traditional interpretation thus ran as follows: employees serve "at will" unless they have an explicit contract to the contrary, and unilateral employer promises are gratuities. The labor law of every state was founded upon this doctrine, which was accepted throughout American jurisprudence. In the context of the postwar regime, it made sense: explicit contracts were to be negotiated for workers by their unions, and the National Labor Relations Act provided definite and protected procedures to encourage workers to unionize if they wished. If there was neither a union contract nor a specifically bargained individual contract, the courts could reasonably assume that the parties intended the employment to be at will. Hence, there was a certain compelling logic to saying that, absent an explicit agreement to the contrary, at-will status could be presumed, even if in practice the NLRA did not always permit workers an uncoerced choice of unionizing or not.

In the changed circumstances since the mid-1970s, this logic is unconvincing. When enterprise rights are made supracontractual by employers, thus explicitly preventing individual bargaining over such rights, and when union strength has declined so greatly that courts can no longer presume that workers have a realistic option to unionize, the traditional interpretation of enterprise rights no longer suffices. Sensitive to the changed situation, many courts are no longer persuaded by their own earlier reasoning.

Notes to Chapter 6

1. National Can Corporation, "Employee Handbook," p. 12. All company quotations cited below are from company employer handbooks or equivalent documents unless otherwise noted.

2. For one interesting study, see Robert McKersie and Werner Sengenberger (1983).

3. All information and quotations concerning Ware and Nancy Markham are derived from the author's interview with Nancy Markham, October 14, 1987. The names of the firm and the interviewee have been changed at her request.

4. Interview with Nancy Markham (1987).

5. Joseph Golden, quoted in "Employee Handbooks Important Tool Despite Some Problems, Experts Say," Bureau of National Affairs, *Employee Relations Weekly,* vol. 6 (1988), p. 772.

6. This desire may facilitate the theorist's game, but as I argue later, it masks some important real differences. Robert M. Solow (1980, p. 3) stressed that workers pay a great deal of attention to "principles of appropriate behavior, whose source is not entirely individualistic," such as the reluctance of those out of work to undercut those who hold jobs. Albert Hirschman (1981, p. 304) has noted that the impact of observing these moral-social norms on the working of the labor market "make it less perfect from the point of view of self-clearing, but certainly *more* perfect from almost any other conceivable point of view!"

7. Handbooks also serve a variety of other functions. For example, by stating company policies against discrimination and sexual harassment, they may also be used to defend a company from having to share legal liability in suits brought against one of its employees.

8. When enterprise rights are not outlined in an employee handbook, they may be expressed in personnel-procedures materials available in a manager's office. For example, in *Woolley* v. *Hoffman-La Roche,* discussed later, the court noted that the manual in question was "apparently not distributed to all employees ('in general, distribution will be provided to supervisory personnel')"; *Woolley,* 491 A.2d 1257 (N.J. 1985) at 1265 (internal quotation from Hoffman-La Roche manual). Companies that wish to keep a tighter control over distribution of such materials may require workers to visit a manager's office to inspect them.

Where workers have leverage resulting from, for example, a skills monopoly or a high level of militance, custom and practice may provide privileges that are in fact more firmly anchored than written rights. But outside the union sector (where these privileges may be noted in the contract) and except in unusual circumstances, they are not legally enforceable nor do they constitute *rights.*

9. One casualty of this hardening attitude is historical research; see chapter 7, note 50.

10. I included in the group for study all firms fitting the criteria and for which I could obtain employee handbooks or similar information. The sample consists of handbooks or other appropriate personnel documents. Handbooks were obtained from a variety of sources (the firms themselves, employees, management consultants, former employees), so at least from the method of collection it is not biased in any obvious way (for example, self-selection only by employers with extensive enterprise rights). However, inclusion in the sample requires that firms have employee handbooks or similar documents, so firms without handbooks (or enterprise rights?) are excluded. Some companies such as National Can may have facilities, plants, and subsidiaries that are unionized; in those cases, I consider only the nonunionized portions of the companies. Given the panel's construction, the percentages that are reported in the text should be interpreted as useful for establishing orders of magnitude but are not precise. I also collected but do not report here similar data for unionized companies, nonprofit institutions, and public-sector employers; see note 45.

11. The most certain element in the handbooks is restatement of some of the employee's statutory rights. For example, about 88 percent of the handbooks surveyed included a statement that equal-employment opportunity was company policy. Slightly smaller proportions indicate the nonexempt employee's right to overtime pay for work in excess of forty hours and the employee's right to be free of sexual harassment.

12. "Keyes-Fibre Employee Handbook," pp. 19–20.

13. IBM, p. 31.

14. A Duda & Sons, Inc., p. 14; emphasis in original.

15. See Edwards (1979), chaps. 2 and 3; and Nelson (1975).

16. Berenbeim (1980), p. 9. The study noted (p. 8) that "many executives [who were surveyed in the study] cited formality as the single most important factor in deterring employees from using a complaint system. As one of them put it: 'The more you insist on set rules, the fewer grievances you have. The easiest way to stop complaints is to: (1) require that they be in writing, (2) on the right form, (3) signed, (4) sent to the right person, (5) with no assistance given to the employee in preparation. Then when you get no complaints you can pat yourself on the back and say we have no problems.' " For complaint systems in use (at least before 1980) at Xerox, Levi Strauss, TWA, Northrop, and elsewhere, see Berenbeim (1980), exhibits 1–10.

17. Perdue, Inc., p. 22.

18. Connecticut Bank and Trust, since acquired by Fleet Bank, had a complaint mechanism that established both an informal procedure and a formal "Employee Hearing Program." The latter involved providing a complainant and her supervisor with a forum to present the issues before a hearing committee, which issued a written, final judgment within seven days.

19. "Consulting Services, Inc." is a pseudonym for a company whose

handbook was made available only on assurances of confidentiality. On systems with arbitration, see also Ronald Berenbeim (1980), pp. 17–21.

20. Consulting Services, Inc., pp. 4–7.
21. Holiday Inns, p. 11.
22. D'Amour's Big Y, p. 28.
23. "Texas Instruments Supervisor's Handbook," pp. D-1, D-2.
24. Finfrock Industries, pp. 6, 7.
25. As noted elsewhere, "at will" signifies an employment relationship that is for an indefinite rather than a fixed term, that can be terminated by either party at any time, and in which workers can be fired "for good cause or for no cause, or even for bad cause." *Payne* v. *Western & Atlantic Railroad,* 81 Tenn. 507, 518–19 (1884). This decision was consistent with the famous "Wood Rule" enunciated in Horace Wood (1887), p. 272. For discussion, see Richard Harrison Winters (1985), sec. 2; and Kelly McWilliams (1986), sec. 2.
26. J. C. Penney, p. 29.
27. Hawthorne Community Medical Group, p. 16.
28. National Can, p. 23; Merrill Lynch, p. 19.
29. Coast Novelty Manufacturing Co., p. 6.
30. National Can, p. 23.
31. National Can, p. 24.
32. National Can, p. 24.
33. David W. Ewing (1989), pp. 106–07.
34. Simon and Schuster, Inc., p. B-1.
35. Massachusetts Mutual, p. 28.
36. Keyes-Fibre, p. 16.
37. Lawrence-Allison & Associates, p. 29.
38. Hawthorne Community Medical Group, p. 15; d'Amour's Big Y, p. 15.
39. Perdue, Inc., p. 6.
40. Kayser-Roth Hosiery, p. 17; National Can, p. 12.
41. D'Amour's Big Y, p. 25.
42. IBM, p. 28.
43. Accuride, p. 35.
44. These situations may be governed by various state or federal statutes. For example, military leave is governed by the Military Selective Service Act of 1967, as amended.
45. I collected handbooks (see note 10) for unionized, nonprofit, and public-sector enterprises; the results from surveying these employers support the findings reported in the text, although with some differences. Unionized companies provide significantly more rights than nonunion companies, through the collective-bargaining contract. Nonprofit employers tend to offer significantly more extensive and formalized enterprise rights than employers in my survey of nonunionized companies, although not always (for example, churches tend to offer fewer enterprise rights). Public employers tend to provide many rights that are established in law (for example,

through civil service rules) and rely less on enterprise rights. In all three areas, there are extensive constellations of specific workplace rights.

46. Philippe Aghion and Benjamin Hermalin (1990), and David I. Levine (1991).

47. Richard Harrison Winters (1985), notes 22, 23.

48. Kelly McWilliams (1986), pp. 347–59; Richard Harrison Winters (1985), section 3.

49. Kelly McWilliams (1986), notes 102, 103–105.

7

The Legal Revolution in Enterprise Rights

Dissenting from his court's 1987 decision in *Hoffman-La Roche, Inc.*, v. *Hugh Campbell*, Justice Maddox of the Alabama Supreme Court complained, "I can only conclude that the Court has now adopted a principle of law that an employment terminable at will can be changed by the unilateral action of the employer in issuing an employee handbook or manual."[1] With these words Justice Maddox acknowledged the arrival in Alabama of a dramatic change in legal thinking that has swept through state courts across the nation. Recent decisions have revolutionized the interpretation of laws governing enterprise rights, especially those contained in employee handbooks.[2] In recent years this area of the law has been in great flux, primarily because judges in state courts have had to grapple with the issue of how binding an employer's unilateral promises should be. In state after state, judges have decided that those promises should be kept.

The legal changes derive almost exclusively from jurisprudence rather than legislation, and they are of enormous importance to the future of workers' rights.[3] The specific direction that the judges' decisions have taken is what imparts a momentous significance to these developments. Although the legal evolution has not proceeded linearly and therefore includes many ambiguities and inconsistencies, the movement is almost entirely toward extending legal recognition to enterprise rights. Indeed, it is not unreasonable to envision a time when enterprise rights have the full force of contractual obligation. As one legal expert said, "Employers who have been trying to build a family environment are now being advised that their words may be construed as a contract. . . . [They] have been saying their organization is a great place to work, but now their lawyers are advising them not to put it in writing."[4]

The complex legal developments are contained in a large and rapidly growing case law. They involve hundreds of cases in many different jurisdictions. Almost all of the relevant decisions have been made in state courts, because federal statutes generally do not cover contract disputes (except where unions are involved). The arguments turn on arcane extensions and applications of obscure legal doctrines.

The legal changes are made more confusing by the fact that two related but distinct aspects of employment law, the enforceability of enterprise rights and changes in the at-will doctrine, have typically been conflated. Judges' decisions and legal scholarship have primarily viewed the issue of handbook (or enterprise-rights) enforceability through the prism of its effect on at-will employment. This was perhaps inevitable, because the at-will doctrine was the biggest obstacle to handbook enforceability and because the most bitter disputes, and hence those most likely to be litigated, concern dismissals. But the at-will doctrine has a separate and distinct legal genealogy, an independent rationale with its own case-law precedents and real-life concerns, and it has been powerfully affected by other decisions that have no bearing on enterprise-rights enforceability. This interweaving of handbook enforceability and at-will employment has led to a lopsided development of law in which the changes are more clearly defined for enterprise rights related to dismissal than for other enterprise rights.[5]

Despite confusion and ambiguity, the scope of legal developments in recent years concerning handbook enforceability has been little short of startling, particularly in contrast to the tone and general barrenness of federal policy toward labor during the Reagan and Bush administrations. The judges' new interpretations are currently being reviewed, criticized, and argued in the pages of court decisions and dissents and in the nation's law journals.

Three Precedent-Setting Cases

The legal revolution has had one central theme: it interprets enterprise rights, and especially the handbook promises of employers, as terms of an enforceable *implied contract*. The South Carolina Supreme Court reasoned that "if company policies are not worth the paper on which they are printed, then it would be better not to mislead employees by distributing them. Due to the potential for gross inequality. . . a majority of states has determined that a handbook can alter the employment status. . . South Carolina, as a progressive state which wishes to see that both employer and employee are treated fairly, now joins those states."[6] The courts engineering this innovation see the employment relationship as a contract that incorporates the employer's policies as well as the exchange of pay for work.

The Michigan Supreme Court insisted that "having announced [its personnel] policy, presumably with a view to obtaining the benefit of improved employee attitudes and behavior and improved quality of the work force, the employer may not treat its promise as illusory."[7] The New Jersey Supreme Court was more caustic: "It will not do now for the company to say it did not mean the things it said in its [employee] manual to be binding. Our courts will not allow an employer to offer attractive inducements and benefits to the workforce and then withdraw them when it chooses."[8] In this emerging understanding of the law, at least some employers' handbook promises have become real workers' rights.

To reach the new interpretation, courts have had to undo nearly a century of alternate reasoning. The first erosion of the traditional treatment came, ironically, with respect to enterprise rights other than those governing dismissal. For example, as early as 1958 a New Jersey court considered a case in which an employer had stated in a handbook that it would provide severance pay to a certain class of employees; the court found that the statement constituted a contractual offer that employees could accept by continuing to work for the employer. Other courts have elevated similar statements concerning vacation pay and tenure rights to the status of contractual obligations binding on the employer.[9]

During the 1980s state courts triggered their legal revolution by accepting the argument that employee handbooks and similar employer statements represent implied contracts that could impose binding obligations on employers. Whereas in 1980 that proposition was not firmly established in any jurisidiction, by 1990 courts in at least forty-one states and the District of Columbia had recognized employee handbooks, under at least some circumstances, as implicit contracts; the leading cases are listed in the appendix.[10]

Three cases proved to be particularly influential in imparting the new direction to legal thinking: a 1980 Michigan case, *Toussaint* v. *Blue Cross & Blue Shield*; a 1983 Minnesota case, *Pine River State Bank* v. *Mettille*; and a 1985 New Jersey case, *Woolley* v. *Hoffman-La Roche*.[11] These cases are repeatedly cited in the decisions of other states' courts.

Charles Toussaint was hired by Blue Cross and Blue Shield of Michigan for a middle-management position. He asked about job security, and Blue Cross gave him an employee handbook, which outlined disciplinary procedures and noted that the company discharged employees "for just cause only." Toussaint worked for Blue Cross for five years and then was fired. He sued, alleging that he had been dismissed without just cause and that the employee handbook was part of his employment contract. The trial court found for Toussaint, but the court of appeals reversed this decision, holding to the traditional position that whether or not the handbook was part of the employment contract, the at-will doctrine prevailed.

The Michigan Supreme Court then took up the case. It upheld the trial court on the grounds that the handbook statements should be construed as contractual rights. The court noted that an employer was not obliged to issue a handbook, but if it did so, "we hold that employer statements of policy, such as the Blue Cross [handbook], can give rise to contractual rights [for] employees."[12]

In the second case, Richard Mettille worked as a loan officer for the Pine River State Bank in Pine River, Minnesota. After he completed the standard six-month probation, the bank gave Mettille an employee handbook in which the company's discharge and disciplinary policies were stated. Later, when the bank evaluated Mettille's job performance, it found that he had mismanaged some loan accounts and used excessive sick leave. The bank fired Mettille, and it also sued him to recover two notes owed to the bank that were in default. Mettille responded by claiming that he had been unjustly dismissed because the bank had failed to follow the termination procedures as stated in the handbook. Mettille won his case in trial court.

The bank appealed *Pine River* to the Minnesota Supreme Court, which upheld the trial court's ruling. The court stated flatly that "personnel handbook provisions, if they meet the requirements for formation of a unilateral contract, may become enforceable as part of the original employment contract."[13]

The third case involved Richard Woolley, hired by the huge Hoffman-La Roche pharmaceuticals concern as an engineering-section head at its Nutley, New Jersey, facility. A month after being hired, Woolley was given an employee handbook that outlined the company's policy on termination. The handbook stated that the company would "retain to the extent consistent with company requirements, the services of all employees who perform their duties efficiently and effectively."[14] It also listed Hoffman-La Roche's five specific causes for dismissal.

Nine years later, Hoffman-La Roche fired Woolley because his manager had lost confidence in Woolley's work. Woolley sued, complaining that he had been fired without just cause and without benefit of the dismissal procedures outlined in the handbook. Woolley lost in trial court and in the appellate court, because these courts refused to consider the handbook part of his employment contract. Woolley then appealed to and won in the New Jersey Supreme Court, which held that "absent a clear and prominent disclaimer, an implied promise contained in an employment manual. . . [may be] enforceable against [an] employer."[15]

Toussaint, *Pine River*, and *Woolley* represented clear and direct affirmations of the enforceability of employee enterprise rights.

State Courts Rewrite the Law

Courts in other states have taken the reasoning used in *Toussaint, Pine River,* and *Woolley* and adopted, added to, modified, and extended it to fashion a wholly new doctrine. In the words of Justice Maddox, these courts have "adopted a principle of law that an employment terminable at will can be changed by the unilateral action of the employer in issuing an employee handbook or manual."

Toussaint, Pine River, and *Woolley* would be important under any circumstances, because as state supreme court decisions they determine law for all lower courts in their respective states. But their impact has been much broader because the courts decided the cases widely, on the basis of the full legal issues, rather than narrowly, on some technical feature. The *Pine River* court, for instance, stated the issue broadly: "Can a personnel handbook. . . become part of an employee's contract of employment?"[16] And the *Woolley* court observed, "We believe another question. . . is involved: should the legal effect of the dissemination of a personnel policy manual by a company with a substantial number of employees be determined solely and strictly by traditional contract doctrine? Is that analysis adequate for the realities of such a workplace?"[17] Courts in other states have faced the same dilemma.

To reach their conclusions, the courts in *Toussaint*, *Pine River*, and *Woolley* were driven to overcome several obstacles to handbook enforceability. The biggest problem was simply the iron logic of the at-will doctrine itself. By legal tradition, courts held that if an employee did not have an explicit contract for a definite, fixed term, his employment contract was presumed to be at will and he could therefore be fired at any time "for good cause, no cause, or even bad cause." Here was the rub: suppose that an at-will employee demands some benefit stated in her handbook (for example, termination only for just cause). What is to prevent the employer from simply immediately exercising the overarching at-will prerogative and firing the employee on the spot, thereby vitiating the employee's claim? According to this reasoning, because the employer can easily and legally evade the effect of the handbook's provisions, the handbook cannot be a contract. Or, to turn the problem around, to make handbooks enforceable, the courts would have to declare that the employment relationship in question was not at will, or at least not at will in the sense that that status was customarily understood.

Loosening the tight grip of the traditional at-will doctrine was made easier for judges because for some issues their reasoning proceeded in parallel with legislatively approved immunities, especially those termed "public-policy exceptions." In fact, judicial decisions usually led the process, but Congress and various state legislatures have mandated that an employee is protected from at-will dismissal for discriminatory reasons based on race or sex, for unionizing activities, for refusing to commit a crime, for absence required by military service and jury duty, for reporting workplace violations of the law (whistle blowing), and for various other public-policy reasons.[18] In effect, these legislative acts stipulated that at-will employees could be fired for good cause, no cause, and maybe for some bad causes, but *not* for the *specified* bad causes; they thereby ratified the weakening of the strictest interpretation of at will.

The courts, however, were forced to challenge the at-will doctrine in an entirely new arena, without legislative guidance. In *Pine River* the court attacked the doctrine directly, by arguing that the at-will rule is only a "rule of contract construction, [not] a rule imposing substantive limits to the formation of a contract."[19] Therefore, the at-will rule should not take precedence over other considerations obtaining in ordinary contract theory. This approach was also adopted by, among others, the Nebraska Supreme Court in *Johnston* v. *Panhandle Cooperative Association*. It was accepted by the Illinois Supreme Court in *Duldulao* v. *Saint Mary of Nazareth Hospital*, in which the court noted that the at-will rule creates only "a presumption which can be overcome by demonstrating that the parties contracted otherwise."[20] The Iowa Supreme Court, in *Cannon* v. *National By-Products*, followed this lead by indicating that "whether the written personnel policies became part of the plantiff's contract is to be determined on the basis of plantiff's reasonable expectations. Even if it was not [the] defendant's intention that these policies confer contractual rights, a contract may be found to exist if this was the plantiff's understanding and defendant had reason to suppose that plantiff understood it in that light."[21]

Likewise, in *Toussaint*, Michigan's court held that its at-will rule did not require that an employment contract of indefinite duration *must* be at will, only that absent other information, it would be construed as at will: "To the extent that courts have seen the rule as one of substantive law rather than construction, they have misapplied language and principles found in earlier cases where the courts were merely attempting to discover and implement the intent of the parties. If no definite time is expressed, the court must construe the agreement."[22] In chastising lower courts for "misapplying" the lessons of earlier cases, the *Toussaint* judges were being a bit disingenuous, because clearly they were announcing a new interpretation of the at-will doctrine. Nonetheless, with admirable (if somewhat suspect) deference to *stare decisis* in *Toussaint*, with less concern for precedent in *Pine River*, *Duldulao*, and *Johnston*, and with a forthright overturning of precedent in *Woolley*, state courts declared their intention to cast aside the traditional understanding of the at-will doctrine.[23]

Once freed from the hold of an absolute (or "substantive law") at-will rule, the issue of the enforceability of handbooks was opened up to be decided within the confines of ordinary contract law. Here, handbooks would still be required to pass several more specific tests in order to be construed as valid contracts. In essence, traditional contract theory develops a set of criteria or standards for courts to use in determining if a contract is legally valid and binding. These tests have to do with both the process of making the contract (rules of "construction") and the content of the contract itself (rules of "substantive law"). If a contract fails one or more of the tests, it may be declared invalid.[24]

Within ordinary contract law, judges have confronted four objections in particular to the interpretation of handbooks as contracts. First, a traditional barrier to the enforceability of handbooks is the requirement of "mutuality of obligation," that is, the doctrine that a contract is valid only if it imposes reciprocal obligations on the contracting parties. As a Nevada court stated the doctrine, "Mutuality of obligation requires that unless both parties to a contract are bound, neither is bound."[25] But employee handbooks, as unilateral statements by employers, are perceived in the traditional interpretation to impose no obligations on workers. (This is surely an instance of extreme judicial blindness, since handbooks are full of requirements, duties, proscriptions, obligations, dress codes, and diverse rules that employees must observe.) Because they impose no obligations, traditional reasoning goes, handbooks fail the test of "mutuality" and hence exist as mere "gratuities" rather than as contracts.

Recent court decisions have overcome the mutuality objection by rejecting its application to employment contracts. In *Pine River* the Minnesota Supreme Court declared that requiring mutuality would in effect involve the court in an inquiry into the "adequacy of consideration" (that is, into whether the mutual obligations were adequate or, in nonlegal language, whether the contract was fair or balanced enough to be legal), and that such an examination is forbidden to courts, in Minnesota as in many other states. The court noted that "the demand for mutuality of obligation, although appealing in its symmetry, is simply a species of the forbidden inquiry into the [fairness of the contract terms]."[26] In *Toussaint* the Michigan court had previously argued that while mutuality is a useful "rule of construction," it is not necessary; to be valid, contracts simply require consideration (that the side making a promise get something, some act or forebearance, in return), not mutuality. The Superior Court of Pennsylvania, which as recently as 1983 had required mutuality, determined in 1987 that mutuality of obligation was "a thoroughly discredited notion."[27]

The decline of mutuality has led to a resurrection of an analysis, found in common law but traditionally not applied to employment contracts, called "unilateral contract theory." In the case of unilateral contracts, only one party makes a promise or undertakes an obligation; mutuality obviously has no role in such contracts, yet the contracts are construed as valid.[28] The *Pine River* decision in particular explicated and relied upon this theory, and its reasoning has carried other courts with it. For example, the Alabama Supreme Court, in deciding *Hoffman-La Roche* v. *Campbell*, found that "the unilateral contract analysis set out in *Pine River* [was] both consistent with sound traditional contract principles and in accord with existing Alabama case-law."[29]

Likewise, the Illinois Supreme Court praised and adopted *Pine River*'s analysis of employee handbooks in terms of traditional contract formation in deciding *Duldulao*. The South Carolina Supreme Court, in *Small* v. *Springs Industries*, noted that Small's employment agreement, "like most employment agreements," was a unilateral contract. It upheld the argument that a handbook constituted an enforceable offer or promise.[30]

The mutuality objection is closely related to the second obstacle from traditional contract theory: "additional consideration." As noted, courts traditionally have held that unless there is a definite and specified length for a contract, employment is presumed to be at will; for workers lacking a fixed-term contract, courts required that there must be an additional consideration beyond the usual performance of duties by a worker for the provisions of a handbook to be made contractually binding. In effect, courts required that if they were to render the employer's unilateral grant of promises into an enforceable obligation, they must have evidence that the worker had also provided to the employer something extra in the employment bargain, an additional obligation on the workers' part, or at least evidence of bargaining, to compensate for or justify making the terms of the handbook enforceable.[31] In the case of handbooks, of course, workers have usually provided no such additional consideration.

Those courts taking the lead in forging the new employment law have rejected the doctrine of additional consideration on several grounds. The Iowa court, in *Cannon* v. *National By-Products*, simply rejected the claim outright: "We find it to be particularly inappropriate to require an independent consideration for modification of an agreement which is conceded to have been a mere contract at will by defendant. . . . We find no need to resort to the adjunct rule of interpretation which requires a showing of additional consideration."[32] In *Pine River* the court viewed additional consideration as only a rule of construction: if present (that is, if the worker did assume some new obligation), it was positive evidence that the handbook was intended to be part of the employment contract; if absent, the intent was uncertain and if the parties wished to incorporate the handbook without additional consideration, nothing in law prevented them from doing so.

Other courts followed *Pine River*'s lead. The *Woolley* court reasoned that "the manual is an offer that seeks the formation of a unilateral contract—the employees' bargained-for action needed to make the offer binding being their continued work when they have no obligation to continue."[33] *Woolley* was following other courts that had already begun treating continued employment as itself sufficient additional consideration. More would follow: for example, the West Virginia Supreme Court of Appeals, in *Cook* v. *Heck's, Inc.*, accepted an employer handbook as constituting an offer of a unilateral contract, and "an employee's continuing to work while under no obligation to do so, constitutes an acceptance and sufficient consideration to make the employer's promise binding and enforceable."[34] A California court combined this latter argument with the critique of mutuality cited earlier to deny a claim for additional consideration; the court reasoned that such a claim would improperly involve scrutiny of the adequacy (or "fairness") of the actual terms of a contract: "there is no analytical reason why an employee's promise to render services, or his actual rendition of services over time, may not support an employer's promise both to pay a particular wage (for example) and to refrain from arbitrary dismissal."[35]

A third obstacle in traditional contract theory is the presumption that there cannot be a contract without an express or explicit mutual agreement. Usually, parties are not deemed to have made a contract unless they *intended* to make a contract; the way they signify this intent is by some explicit action, such as signing an agreement. In the case of employee handbooks, however, typically no explicit and specific agreement is made. The court in *Toussaint* rejected the requirement of express agreement for employment contracts. It found that handbooks can create contractual rights for employees even

> without evidence that the parties mutually agreed that the policy statements would create contractual rights in the employees and, hence, although the statement of policy is signed by neither party, can be unilaterally amended by the employer without notice to the employee, and contains no reference to a specific employee, his job description or compensation, and although no reference was made to the policy statement in pre-employment interviews and the employee does not learn of its existence until after his hiring.[36]

The Connecticut Supreme Court, in *Finley* v. *Aetna Life and Casualty Company*, agreed that statements in an employer's personnel manual may form the basis of a contract, and in the absence of "definitive contract language," the court declared, "the determination of what the parties intended to encompass in their contractual commitments is a question of the intention of the parties, and an inference of fact."[37] The *Woolley* court went further, declaring that

> no pre-employment negotiations need take place and the parties' minds need not meet on the subject; nor does it matter that the employee knows nothing of the particulars of the employer's policies and practices or that the employer may change them unilaterally. It is enough that the employer chooses, presumably in his own interest, to create an

> environment in which the employee believes that, whatever the personnel policies and practices, they are established and official at any given time, purport to be fair, and are applied consistently and uniformly to each employee.[38]

The court noted that Hoffman-La Roche, the employer, contended that the manual was just an expression of the company's "philosophy" and therefore was free of contractual consequences, whereas Woolley claimed that the manual consisted of policies intended to be followed by the company in the same manner "as if they were expressed in an agreement signed by both employer and employees." The court agreed with Woolley: "We conclude that a jury, properly instructed, could find, in strict contract terms, that the manual constituted an offer. . . [setting] forth terms and conditions of employment."[39] The Supreme Court of Oklahoma went even further, declaring that mere publication of personnel policies "is the equivalent of constructive knowledge on the part of all employees not specifically excluded."[40]

A fourth obstacle in contract theory, closely related to the question of an express agreement, is the traditional requirement of an appropriate "validation device." A validation device is any exchange or act that makes a promise enforceable, that is, that indicates that the promise has been transformed into a contractual obligation. Normally, promises are validated by a seal (a signature on an explicit agreement) or by consideration (whatever the promisor gets in return for making the promise).[41] Enterprise rights stated in handbooks lack an obvious validation device.

Courts have overcome the validation-device objection in two ways. Some have argued that the worker's continued employment after the issuance of a handbook (whether that occurred before or after the worker was hired) constitutes an adequate validation device. In *Pine River*, for example, the Minnesota court interpreted the employee handbook as a unilateral offer of a contract, communicated via the employee's receipt of the handbook; the worker could signify acceptance of this offer by continuing (or taking up) her employment. This line of reasoning was also followed by the *Toussaint* and *Woolley* courts.[42]

A second way of overcoming the validation-device objection is termed "reliance." This means that if employees could reasonably expect that the handbook promises would be kept, and had relied on this expectation in their subsequent behavior, then the promises would be validated. In *Toussaint*, the court had noted that because the employer had issued a manual containing elaborate disciplinary procedures, workers "could justifiably rely on those expressions and conduct themselves accordingly."[43] The Supreme Court of Arkansas, in *Gladden* v. *Arkansas Children's Hospital*, adopted this reasoning to modify that state's traditional at-will doctrine: "Where an employee relies upon a personnel manual that contains *an express provision* against termination except for cause he may not be arbitrarily discharged in violation of such a provision."[44] Among others, the Colorado Supreme Court adopted this view as well (in *Continental Air Lines* v. *Keenan*). The *Woolley* court, which went farthest in this direction, simply presumed that employees would rely on the handbook provisions, and it declared that this presumption alone constituted a sufficient validation device.[45]

These four objections have dominated most of the legal discussion of how traditional contract theory should be applied to handbooks; various other obstacles to the new doctrine have been raised, but mostly they have been brushed aside. On the other side, contract theory has provided new arguments in favor of interpreting handbooks as contracts, and occasionally the issues raised have proved decisive for the courts in question. For example, in a Texas case (*Aiello* v. *United Air Lines*) decided in the U.S. Court of Appeals, the detailed nature of the employee handbook's provisions swayed the court. The appeals court reviewed prior Texas cases that had supported the traditional view that handbooks are not enforceable, but came to the conclusion that those cases "involve handbooks which do not contain specific detailed discharge and disciplinary procedures. . . . The detailed procedures for discipline and discharge are of great significance in this case."[46] This feature was crucial to the Alabama court in *Hoffman-La Roche* v. *Campbell* as well, and recognized (but to the detriment of the employee) by the Minnesota Supreme Court in *Hunt* v. *IBM*.[47]

In *Toussaint*, *Pine River*, *Woolley*, and their multitudinous progeny, the courts have thus given a firm negative answer to the question posed in *Woolley*: "Is [traditional contract] analysis adequate for the realities of [the modern] workplace?" By setting aside the harshest form of the at-will doctrine and overcoming the various objections from traditional contract theory, state courts have dramatically reshaped and redefined the fundamental law of employment. It is remarkable how quickly and how widely this legal revolution has occurred. The controlling or most important cases are listed in the appendix, state by state. As can be seen, forty-one states have adopted the new reasoning, and all the important cases were decided in the 1980s. The few remaining states, given the overwhelming change in thinking elsewhere, could expect great pressure to fall into line.

The legal evolution has not proceeded evenly, nor have all states accepted all parts of the new doctrines. In the early 1990s, Florida, Indiana, Missouri, and several other states continued to treat handbooks as mere employer gratuities, imposing no enforceable obligations on employers. Among the states accepting handbooks as enforceable contracts, important differences in interpretation remain. For example, in *Pine River*, the court was clear that for an implied contract to exist, the employee must know of the handbook's provisions, whereas the *Toussaint* court declared this was unnecessary and the *Woolley* court created a presumption of reliance, recognizing an implicit contract where the employee clearly was not even aware of the handbook's provisions. Some states have been left with peculiar legal inconsistencies. In Illinois, for example, the relevant decisions seem to indicate that if an employee is given a handbook after being hired, his continued employment satisfies the validation requirement, whereas if the handbook is received before hiring, it does not. Not only does this stand on its head the traditional argument, wherein a handbook distributed after hiring was thereby precluded from being part of the (original) employment contract, it is simply illogical; if employment after receiving a handbook works as a validation device, it should serve regardless of when the handbook is delivered. Similarly, Illinois courts seem to accept written contracts, but reject oral ones whose terms explicitly incorporate an employee handbook in the employment contract; yet any difference between written and oral contracts is irrelevant to the issue here.[48]

The unevenness and inconsistency that characterize this revolution in legal thinking is a common corollary of judge-made law. The unevenness is exacerbated by the fact that virtually all of the changes have originated in state courts, and so divergent lines of reinterpretation are almost guaranteed.

Employer Response to the Changing Legal Climate

While judges have recast the law, employers have been quick to respond. Some of the decisions have resulted in huge settlements; having been widely reported, they have caught management's attention directly. Juries in particular have made big awards. Such litigation sets in motion its own dynamics. As one legal advisor to managers rather delicately put it, "The negative publicity generated by wrongful discharge suits brought by disgruntled employees often compels the employer to settle out of court and, accordingly, the plaintiff's bar has become receptive to handling wrongful discharge cases on a contingency fee basis."[49]

More generally, management consultants, corporate legal staffs, and labor-relations experts have carried to management the message that traditional handbook promises might turn out to be enforceable.

Employers have responded in diverse ways. Virtually all have restricted access to their handbooks; for example, while university research libraries formerly collected handbooks routinely, today employers are no longer willing to release them.[50] Some employers have stopped using handbooks altogether, preferring to rely on oral presentations (for example, at orientation sessions). Many more have rewritten their handbooks, as IBM apparently has done, either to present a hazy general picture of company employment policies that is too indefinite to pass muster as a valid contract or to drop costly enterprise rights from the manual.[51]

These various and conflicting pressures have caused the appearance, in many handbooks, of three new features. One is an explicit disclaimer that the handbook constitutes a contract. Simon and Schuster, for example, informs employees in bold capitals on the first page of its manual:

> **THE POLICIES AND STANDARD PRACTICES DESCRIBED IN THIS HANDBOOK ARE NOT CONDITIONS OF EMPLOYMENT. THE LANGUAGE IS NOT INTENDED TO CREATE A CONTRACT BETWEEN SIMON AND SCHUSTER OR ANY OF ITS COMPANIES AND THEIR EMPLOYEES.**[52]

Keyes-Fibre Company states on page 1 of its handbook: "This Employee Handbook is **not a contract of employment** between the Company and any employee. It is **merely a guide**."[53] Many other handbooks now contain similar language.

Second, many employers include an explicit at-will statement. At Consulting Services, Inc., for example, the handbook includes a statement that "the relationship between CSI and its employees is and remains mutually terminable at will. That is . . . employees are subject to discharge at the complete and unrestricted discretion of the company with or without the customary notice."[54] Other employers, undoubtedly at the urging of company lawyers, have begun inserting similar clauses in their handbooks.

Third, employers have started requiring that employees sign to acknowledge receipt of a handbook. For example, at Lawrence-Allison & Associates, employees are required to sign a statement that reads in part: "I have received a copy of the Lawrence-Allison & Associates West, Inc. Employee Handbook. I understand that I am to become familiar with [its] contents. . . . I further understand and agree that my employment is terminable at will. . . . Finally, I understand and agree that nothing in this Handbook in any way creates an express or implied contract of employment between the Company and me."[55] The signature form, in the case of Lawrence-Allison, may have several purposes: to gain the worker's verification of at-will status, to disclaim legal enforceability of enterprise rights, to extract from the worker a promise to abide by the company's rules and practices, and even to obligate the worker to return the handbook when she quits working there. (At Consulting Services, the handbook is doled out in numbered copies, apparently in an attempt to control unauthorized distribution and reproduction.)

Thus, while judges have made handbook provisions more enforceable, employers have tried to weaken them. Two countervailing pressures, however, limit what employers can do. The first is a matter of law: it is not clear what the legal significance of various devices to limit legal enforceability will be. The second is a matter of economics: employers need handbooks and the provisions they guarantee to attract the quality of workers they desire.

The legal problem is illustrated in the contradictory advice given by management's legal advisors. Whereas some lawyers counsel omitting any language relating to discharge, thereby relying on the traditional at-will doctrine, others insist that termination procedures should be written out precisely and distributed to all employees, so that an employer can defend itself against complaints that it did not follow its own procedures. Some advisors strongly recommend that current and future workers be required to sign explicit statements affirming their at-will status, whereas others caution that courts often brush aside such defenses when confronted with evidence of oral agreements that supersede at-will provisions, or for other reasons.

The courts themselves have not spoken decisively on the legal effect of disclaimers. On one side, one could place the New Jersey *Woolley* court, which (as quoted above) found that "absent a clear and prominent disclaimer," the Hoffman-La Roche handbook was an enforceable contract; although the court did not indicate what its decision would be if "a clear and prominent disclaimer" were present, the implication of its statement seems to be that such a disclaimer would be controlling. Some state courts have directly spoken to the issue to find that a disclaimer was controlling.[56]

On the other side, however, some courts have swept aside such disclaimers. For example, the U.S. Court of Appeals for the Fifth Circuit ruled in exactly such a case. In *Aiello* v. *United Air Lines*, described above, United claimed that its handbook did not alter Aiello's at-will status because the company had included an introductory statement that the handbook's regulations and policies "are not intended to be, and do not constitute, a contractual arrangement or agreement between the company and its employees of any kind. . . [and] that all employment is 'at will.' "[57] This disclaimer was followed, however, by specific procedures and regulations providing that no employee could be discharged without good cause, and United had agreed in pretrial that its personnel policies prohibited it from firing an employee without good cause.

The *Aiello* court was not impressed by the disclaimer. "Because of the detailed nature of the company regulations and the understanding that employees and supervisory personnel have with respect to them being part of a binding employment contract, we find that the employment at-will principle does not apply. Under these circumstances, we cannot find that the purported disavowal of the detailed regulations as constituting a contract, contained in the introduction to the regulations, is controlling. *It is a truism in the law that such disavowals are not controlling*" (emphasis added).[58] Other courts as well have swept aside disclaimers as noncontrolling.[59]

It remains unclear if employer efforts to affirm at-will status, or more generally to deny that enterprise rights contained in a handbook are intended to form a contract, will hold up in court. The U.S. Court of Appeals, at least, held that it was a "truism" that such efforts would not hold up. In a more limited ruling, the Kansas Supreme Court in *Morriss* v. *Coleman Co.* also refused to be swayed by a disclaimer.[60] In effect, judges will be forced to decide the legal meaning of internally inconsistent or self-contradictory documents, for example handbooks that both assert an at-will relationship and promise substantive enterprise rights seemingly inconsistent with at-will status. Only a small number of cases on this point of law have been decided, and so the matter has not yet been definitively settled.[61]

The economic problem in an employer's effort to evade legal liability is that this effort runs exactly counter to the purposes for which the employer establishes enterprise rights in the first place. Employers grant enterprise rights to attract good workers, motivate them, and avoid unionization. Informing workers, indeed, forcing them to sign statements that their employment is at will and that any employer promises are not really enforceable, is hardly the way to achieve these ends. As one group of management advisors ruefully admitted, "It may be difficult to recruit well-educated professionals or middle-level managerial employees by informing them that their employment may be terminated at any time and for any reason."[62] Another respected employer advisor, the Commerce Clearing House, noted that "disclaimers, while they may make the difference between winning and losing a lawsuit, have their drawbacks. In order to be effective, they must clearly state the employer's intention that employment is at will and can be terminated at will. However, that is a harsh reality that may sound unfair and unjust to a lot of present and prospective employees. The result may be that employees are distrustful of the employer, and that could have a detrimental effect on employee morale and, in turn, on productivity."[63] Commerce Clearing House points out other drawbacks as well: for example, if the disclaimer states that the handbook is not a contract, the employer may not be able to enforce its provisions against the employee, either.

Should employers believe the *Employee Relations Weekly* ("Employee Handbooks Important Tool Despite Some Problems, Experts Say") or the Scripps Howard News Service ("Handbooks Can Be a Minefield for Employers")?[64] Employers are caught between their need to make believable promises to workers and their desire not to have these promises taken seriously by courts.

The Current Situation

Both the economic impact and the legal effectiveness of the various employer countermeasures remain uncertain. It is not clear that employers can devise enterprise-rights systems that will simultaneously attract and motivate good workers yet legally remain mere "gratuities." It is also uncertain that judges will accept general disclaimers inserted at the beginning of a handbook whose provisions are intended by employers to produce the benefits of a contract-like relationship and whose promises are understood and relied upon by workers to be contract-like employer obligations.

The manifold inconsistencies, gaps, and unevenness that characterize enterprise rights and employment law are but part of the wider phenomenon of the breakdown of the postwar workers'-rights regime. When workers had a reasonable opportunity to form unions and bargain collectively, judges apparently were content to uphold the at-will rule, perhaps because in their minds unions represented the appropriate mechanism for redressing the inherent bargaining inequality between an individual worker and his employer. Or at least this reasoning provided an acceptable rationalization for the way judges did in fact decide such cases. But the collapse of the union share has shaken the judges' assurance and confronted them with the harshness of the at-will rule when the individual worker stands alone before an employer. In reaction, judges have rewritten the law.[65]

New legal doctrines are emerging quickly, and they are marked by divergent and often contradictory results. New employment relations are also developing, shaped by the countervailing pressures of increasingly intense global competition, the shrinking share of the domestic labor force represented by unions, the growing enforceability of handbook-articulated enterprise rights, and the employers' own self-contradictory desire to benefit from enterprise rights but not be bound by them. For these reasons lawyers' groups, workers'-rights advocates, legal scholars, judges, and others have called for legislation to replace court decisions as the appropriate path for future development.[66]

Notes to Chapter 7

1. *Hoffman-La Roche* v. *Hugh Campbell*, 512 So.2d 725 (Ala. 1987) at 740.

2. This section on legal developments leans heavily on two papers, one by Kelly McWilliams (1986), to which the reader is referred for more extensive discussion and references, and the other by Richard Harrison Winters (1985). On the broader causes behind the changing legal interpretations, see William B. Gould IV (1986a, 1986b).

3. An important exception to the pattern of judge-made law is Montana Code Ann. @ 39-2-504(3) (1987), as of 1993 the only comprehensive state-level wrongful-discharge statute in the United States.

4. Joseph Golden, quoted in Bureau of National Affairs (1988b), p. 771.

5. An example of other decisions that affect at-will, but not enterprise rights generally, is the "public policy exception"; see Kelly McWilliams (1986). An example of the kind of problems caused by conflated development is the following: a significant and growing number of jurisdictions recognize an employer's statement in a handbook that workers will be dismissed only for "just cause" to be a legally binding implied contract, but the precedents cited are largely taken from the legal pedigree of the at-will doctrine and the arguments made are mostly directed toward justifying decisions in light of at-will doctrine. Thus the status of other enterprise rights, aside from those relating to abrogation of the at-will doctrine, remain largely unexplored. Decisions involving other benefits have a much earlier case law; see, for example, *Dolak* v. *Sullivan*, 144 A.2d 312 (Conn. 1958), on retirement benefits; *Tilbert* v. *Eagle Lock Co.*, 165 A. 205 (Conn. 1933), on employee benefits; *Cain* v. *Allen Electric & Equipment Co.,* 78 N.W.2d 296 (Mich. 1956), on severance pay; and the cases cited in *Toussaint* v. *Blue Cross,* note 32.

6. *Small* v. *Springs Industries, Inc.,* 357 S.E.2d 452 (S.C. 1987) at 455.

7. *Toussaint,* at 895.

8. *Woolley,* at 1266. The *Woolley* court (at 1264, references omitted) also chastised other courts: "We conclude that when an employer of a substantial number of employees circulates a manual. . . the judiciary, instead of 'grudgingly' conceding the enforceability of [its] provisions, should construe them in accordance with the reasonable expectations of the employees."

9. This is perhaps not surprising, in retrospect, given that the at-will doctrine constituted such a central tenet of employment law that judges rejected any assault upon it until they were under great pressure; by contrast, they were likely to be more open to arguments concerning more marginal aspects such as vacation pay or severance allowances. On the cases discussed, see Kelly McWilliams (1986), notes 90, 91, and 92. The *Toussaint* court, in rejecting the argument advanced by a dissenting justice, explicitly denied any relevant distinction between other benefits (for example, termination pay, death benefits) and employment security; *Toussaint,* at 884, 908.

10. William B. Gould IV (1986a, 1986b); Michael A. Chagares (1986, 1989).

11. William B. Gould IV (1986a), note 6. The cases discussed are *Toussaint* v. *Blue Cross & Blue Shield of Michigan,* Mich. 292 N.W.2d 880 (1980); *Pine River State Bank* v. *Mettille,* 333 N.W.2d 622 (Minn. 1983); *Woolley* v. *Hoffman-La Roche, Inc.,* 99 N.J. 284, 491 A.2d 1257 (N.J. 1985), *modified,* 101 N.J. 10, 499 A.2d 515 (N.J. Super A.D. 1985). Other important cases are: *Weiner* v. *McGraw-Hill, Inc.,* 57 N.Y.2d 458, 443 N.E.2d 441, 457 N.Y.S.2d 193 (1982); *Carter* v. *Kaskaskia Community Action Agency,* 24 Ill. App. 3d 1056, 322 N.E.2d 574 (1974); and *Pugh* v. *See's Candies, Inc.,* 116 Cal. App. 3d 311, App., 171 Cal. Rptr. 917 at 925 (Cal. 1981). An important countercase is *Banas* v. *Matthews International Corp.,* 502 A.2d 637 (Pa. Super 1985).

12. *Toussaint,* at 892, 15.

13. *Pine River,* at 627.

14. Quoted in Kelly McWilliams (1986), note 141.

15. *Woolley,* at 1258.

16. *Pine River,* at 625.

17. *Woolley,* at 1260.

18. Judge-led changes include refusal to commit a crime, where the seminal case, *Petermann* v. *International Brotherhood of Teamsters,* 344 P.2d 25 (Cal. Ct. App. 1959), found it to be a wrongful discharge in violation of public policy for an employer to fire someone for refusing to commit perjury when the company was being investigated; jury duty, where the lead case, *Nees* v. *Hock,* Or., 536 P.2d 512 (Or. 1975), declared it to be a tort to fire an employee for serving on a jury; and whistle blowing, where in, for example, *Palmateer* v. *International Harvester Co.,* Ill., 421 N.E.2d 876 (Ill. 1981), the court protected a whistle-blower despite the absence of a relevant statute. On public-policy exceptions, see Michael Chagares (1989) and Kelly McWilliams (1986).

19. *Pine River,* at 628.

20. *Johnston* v. *Panhandle Cooperative Association,* 408 N.W.2d 261 (Neb. 1987) at 266. *Duldulao* v. *Saint Mary of Nazareth Hospital Center,* 505 N.E.2d 314 (Ill. 1987) at 318.

21. *Cannon* v. *National By-Products Inc.,* 422 N.W.2d 638 (Iowa, 1988) at 640.

22. *Toussaint,* at 885.

23. Some clarification concerning *Woolley*'s overturning of the at-will doctrine is necessary. The court recognized the doctrine's continuing claim in individual employment contracts where such contracts arguably might provide job protection; it distinguished such cases from those like Woolley's on the grounds that the latter involved an employment manual applicable to the entire work force.

24. Contract theory imposes many standards beyond those discussed in the text, and any particular handbook may fail to be enforceable because it fails these other tests. For example, there are tests of definiteness and certainty, requiring that any valid contract not be so vague or indefinite as to render reasonable interpretation of its conditions impossible. One objection from traditional contract theory to the enforceability of handbooks, which relates specifically and only to at-will status and so is not discussed in the text, is that because an employee handbook does not list *all* the conditions and terms of employment, employment should still be terminable at will. According to this reasoning, terms and conditions that are not included—especially any statement of the fixed length of the contract—leave at-will status intact, even if the handbook is accepted as part of the contract. See Richard Harrison Winters (1985), p. 203 and note 38.

25. *Sala & Ruthe Realty, Inc.,* v. *Campbell,* 89 Nev 483, 487, 515 P.2d 394, 396 (1973).

26. *Pine River,* at 622, 629; Kelly McWilliams (1986), p. 357 and note 99. This line of thinking was also followed in *Weiner*. The adequacy-of-consideration test is related to "unconscionability," a doctrine developed to protect the disadvantaged party in a grossly one-sided contract; see *Woolley,* at 1267, note 9.

27. Kelly McWilliams (1986), p. 357, note 99. The 1983 Pennsylvania case is *Richardson* v. *Cole Memorial Hospital,* 466 A.2d 1084 (Penn. 1983) at 1085; quote from *Greene* v. *Oliver Realty Co.,* 526 A.2d 1192 (Penn. 1987) at 1200.

28. A textbook example illustrating the distinction between unilateral and bilateral (mutuality of obligation) contracts is: "If A says to B, 'If you walk across Brooklyn Bridge, I promise to pay you ten dollars,' A has made a promise but he has not asked B for a return promise. He has requested B to perform an act, not a commitment to do the act. A has thus made an offer to a unilateral contract which arises when and if B performs the act called for. If A had said to B, 'If you promise to walk across Brooklyn Bridge, I promise to pay you ten dollars,' his offer requests B to make a commitment to walk the bridge. A bilateral contract arises when the requisite return promise is made by B." J. Calamari and J. Perillo (1977), pp. 1–10.

29. *Hoffman-La Roche* v. *Campbell,* at 731.

30. *Duldulao,* at 318; *Small* v. *Springs Industries,* 357 S.E. 2d 452 (S.Car. 1987) at 454.

31. Richard Harrison Winters (1985), p. 202, note 28.

32. *Cannon* v. *National By-Products,* at 641–42.

33. *Woolley,* at 1267. See also *Pine River,* at 622, 629; Kelly McWilliams (1986), p. 357. The court in *Yartzoff* v. *Democrat-Herald Publishing Co.,*

Inc., 281 Or. 651, 576 P.2d 356 (1978), indicated that continued employment was sufficient consideration.

34. *Cook* v. *Heck's, Inc.*, 342 S.E.2d 453 (W.Va. 1986) at 459. This reasoning has been followed by other courts as well; see, for example, *Hoffman-La Roche* v. *Campbell*, at 733.

35. *Pugh* v. *See's Candies, Inc.*, at 925. Richard Harrison Winters (1985), notes 84 and 85, gives citations of cases in many jurisdictions.

36. *Toussaint,* at 881.

37. *Finley* v. *Aetna Life and Casualty Company*, 520 A.2d 208 (Conn. 1987) at 213, quoting *Bead Chain Mfg. Co.* v. *Saxton Products, Inc.*, 439 A.2d 314 (Conn. 1981).

38. *Woolley,* at 1268.

39. *Woolley,* at 1265.

40. Oklahoma court quoted in Richard Harrison Winters (1985), p. 210, from *Dangott* v. *ASG Industries*, 558 P.2d 379, 383 (Okla. 1976).

41. Kelly McWilliams (1986, note 72) notes that there are four principal validation devices in contract law: consideration, promissory estoppel or detrimental reliance, the seal, and moral obligation.

42. *Pine River,* at 626–27; see Kelly McWilliams (1986), pp. 360–61 and notes 122 and 150. *Toussaint,* at 883; *Woolley,* 491 A.2d at 1267; also see *Carter* at 1059 and 576; see Kelly McWilliams (1986), note 99, and Richard Harrison Winters (1985), pp. 206–09.

43. *Toussaint,* at 893.

44. *Gladden* v. *Arkansas Children's Hospital,* 728 S.W.2d 501 (Ark. 1987).

45. *Continental Air Lines, Inc.* v. *Keenan*, 731 P.2d 708 (Colo. 1987). *Woolley,* 491 A.2d at 1267; Kelly McWilliams (1986), p. 364. This type of argument is called "promissory estoppel"; one textbook defines it as "a promise which the promisor should reasonably expect to induce action or forebearance on the part of the promisee or a third person and which does induce such action or forebearance is binding if injustice can be avoided only by enforcement of the promise" (Restatement [Second] of Contracts [1981], #90). Promissory estoppel is sometimes included by courts within the broader concept of "consideration." See also *Carter*, at 576; and Richard Harrison Winters (1985), p. 206.

46. *Aiello* v. *United Air Lines*, 818 F.2d 1196 (5th Cir. 1987), at 1201.

47. *Hoffman-La Roche* v. *Campbell*, at 734. *Hunt* v. *IBM Mid America Employees Federal*, 384 N.W.2d 853 (Minn. 1986). A second example of the positive use of contract theory is the whole line of "good faith and fair dealing" cases. These decisions rely on an assumption that all contracts, including employment contracts, impose a duty of good faith and fair dealing on both parties to the contract. In some jurisdictions, courts have decided that if, for example, an employer's decision to dismiss an employee was not made in good faith, the employee is entitled to relief. See for example *Hall* v. *Farmers Ins. Exchange,* 713 P.2d 1027 (Okla. 1986); *Fortune* v. *National Cash Register Co.,* 364 N.E. 2d 1251 (Mass. 1977); Michael A. Chagares

(1989), third column of appendix table; in *Morriss* v. *Coleman Co.*, see the lists on pp. 850–51.

48. Kelly McWilliams (1986), notes 9 and 101; and William B. Gould IV (1986), note 64; Kelly McWilliams (1986), pp. 371–72; and Richard Harrison Winters (1985), p. 208.

49. Martin Wald and David W. Wolf (1985), p. 545.

50. The library at Cornell University's School of Industrial Relations, America's premier collection of industrial-relations documents, has for many years collected employee handbooks as well as union contracts, corporate records, and other materials; the collection contains a historical record covering thousands of companies and documenting the evolving industrial relations of the past several decades. However, the librarians report that since the early 1980s companies have refused to supply handbooks, creating a gap in the historical record; as the library's collection ages, the gap grows.

51. Compare for instance the 1943, 1963, and 1988 IBM handbooks. The 1943 handbook was brief and direct, but it mainly contained instructions and rules for employees, with very few enterprise rights. The 1963 handbook is more discursive and overt in its attempt to appeal to workers; its rules are mixed in with many more enterprise rights. The 1988 handbook has eliminated almost every precise statement of an enterprise right, creating instead a fuzzy but appealing atmosphere of cooperation and opportunity. Of explicit language defining enterprise rights, there is almost nothing.

52. Simon and Schuster, p. i.

53. Keyes-Fibre, p. 1.

54. Consulting Services, Inc., pp. 2–17, 18.

55. Lawrence-Allison, p. 49.

56. See, for example, *Fournier* v. *United States Fidelity and Guaranty Company*, 82 Md. App. 31, 569 A. 2d 1299 (1990), and *Castiglione* v. *Johns Hopkins Hospital*, 69 Md. App. 325, 517 A.2d 786 (1986), where Maryland courts accepted disclaimers. In Colorado, *Cronk* v. *Intermountain Rural Electric Association*, 765 AP.2d 619 (Colo. App. 1988), and *Allabashi* v. *Lincoln National Sales Corp.* [Case no. 89-CA-1346 (January 31, 1991)] held that a disclaimer was not controlling, but *Ferrera* v. *Nielsen*, 799 P.2d 458 (Colo. App. 1990), held that disclaimers were valid and controlling. Courts in Hawaii (*Courtney* v. *Canyon Television and Appliance Rental*, 899 F.2d 845 [9th Cir. 1990]), Maine (*Libby* v. *Calais Regional Hospital*, 554 A.2d 1181 [Me. 1989], and Virginia (*Sullivan* v. *Snap-On Tools Corp.*, 4 IER Cases 439 [E.D. Va. March 8, 1989]), among others, have upheld the legitimacy of disclaimers.

57. *Aiello* v. *United Air Lines* at 1198.

58. *Aiello* v. *United Air Lines* at 1200.

59. Other decisions in which courts refused to accept disclaimers: in Illinois, *Perman* v. *Arcventures Inc.*, 196 Ill. App. #d. 758, 554 N.E.2d 982 (1980); in New Mexico, *Zaccardi* v. *Zale Corp.* 856 F.2d 1473 (10th Cir.

1988); and in Wyoming, *McDonald* v. *Mobil Coal Producing, Inc.* 789 P.2d 866 (Wy. 1990).

60. *Morriss* v. *Coleman Co.* at 844, 849.

61. In one case, *Chambers* v. *Valley National Bank,* 3 I.E.R. Cas. (BNA) 1476 (D.Ariz., 1988), the judge held the disclaimer to be valid, arguing that publication of it amounted to a unilateral offer of a modified employment agreement, which offer could be construed as having been accepted by the additional consideration of the employee continuing to work for the employer. See also Michael A. Chagares (1986).

62. Walter B. Connolly, Jr., Gary E. Murg, and Clifford Scharman (1983), p. 57.

63. Commerce Clearing House (1985), p. 563.

64. Bureau of National Affairs (1988b), pp. 771–72. "Handbooks Can be a Minefield for Employers," *Chicago Tribune,* March 3, 1991, p. 18.

65. William B. Gould IV (1986), pp. 895–99. See also the sources cited in Kelly McWilliams (1986), note 18.

66. See, for example, William B. Gould IV and others (1984); Kurt H. Decker (1983); American Federation of Labor–Congress of Industrial Organizations (1987); Richard Harrison Winters (1985); Paul Weiler (1984); Martin Wald and David W. Wolf (1985), sec. 4.

8

Contemplating Common Ground

The postwar workers'-rights regime once constituted common ground between employers and workers: at least in the economy's core sector of large-scale enterprises, generalized oligopoly, and significant unionization, it formed part of a social compromise that organized the labor relations of the American economy's long postwar boom. The compromise did not eliminate conflict on the larger contested terrain that is industrial relations, but it did provide institutions that effectively enforced workers' rights while permitting employers to be competitive. But now the core-sector structure and the rights regime associated with it have largely disappeared. Both employers and workers have departed the common ground.

Employers now face an increasingly competitive transnational economy. In part, they have responded by trying to reduce the costs of managing their labor forces, including the costs of workers' rights, and to increase the flexibility with which they can deploy their workers. Rosabeth Kantor, then-editor of the *Harvard Business Review*, in reviewing the new learning on how to compete, noted that "in a volatile, intensely competitive world, success comes from the capacity to respond and act."[1] In this environment it is perhaps not surprising that employers should look favorably on a situation in which workers would have few or minimal rights. Yet in part employers have responded to countervailing pressures as well: because the new competitive economy is driven by information and technology, high-quality skills and a highly committed labor force have become essential weapons in the competitive struggle. So, to become or remain competitive, employers have had to develop new ways to attract, retain, and motivate their workers, including the extension of new rights to them.

On their side, workers have no less need of workplace protections than before. Individual workers may find themselves with few rights and subject to the mercy of arbitrary bosses. Seven out of eight private-sector workers have no union to protect them, and the decline of unionism has inexorably diminished the ripple effects from collective bargaining on nonunion workers. Neither can workers look for much help from federal or state statutory protections, because the complexity and intrinsic limitations of centralized regulation combined with the hostility of the regulators has weakened regulation's bite to a hardly noticeable nibble. In reaction, workers have increasingly appealed to the courts for redress and relief, and while the judges have been responsive and juries have frequently been generous, even overly generous, judicial arbitration remains inconsistent, inaccessible to most workers, expensive, and often capricious. No one but lawyers seriously suggests that courts are the best venue for the administration of industrial relations.

Employers and workers need to find new common ground. They must develop a new strategy for workers' rights, organized on the basis of new principles and cognizant of the new economic realities. The workers' stake in a new rights strategy may be apparent; without it, workers will continue to face uncertain and ineffective protection. But why should employers support the emergence of a new workers'-rights regime?

Employer Stakes in a New Rights Regime

Consider the problem: workers' rights are claims that employees may exercise to protect themselves from the established workplace governance. If the employer is the source of established workplace governance, how then could workers' rights ever be in the employer's interest?

Employers have several substantial and compelling reasons to support a new rights regime. The most important and overarching reason is simply their interest in having an effective, accepted, and responsible system of industrial governance. After all, each employer and its workers have a sufficiently shared stake in the health of their enterprise so that both can benefit from a system that achieves high productivity, encourages positive relations, and resolves disputes efficiently and reasonably amicably.

Responsible industrial governance is the employers' general stake; it envelops some more specific reasons for them to support workers' rights. I consider four reasons here, proceeding from the negative (avoiding bad outcomes) to the positive (realizing real benefits).[2]

First, employers have a stake in avoiding outcomes more unfavorable to their interests than a properly constructed new rights regime would be. In this century American workers have not long remained without rights or some organized means of articulating their interests. Industrial workers' powerlessness in the 1920s was followed by the explosive growth of CIO unions in the 1930s; civilian employees' lack of voice in the growing postwar public sector led to the rapid unionization of teachers, police, transit and hospital workers, and others; and the exclusion of blacks, women, and nonunion workers from power in postwar industrial governance resulted in a torrent of statutory protections in the 1960s and 1970s. Although these specific responses are unlikely to be repeated, some response is virtually inevitable.

The point is that a world of minimal workers' rights is not the only alternative to a new rights regime; extensive new regulation is also possible. Employers may be correct in largely dismissing the threat of a serious revival of unionism, but they can hardly be so sanguine about further statutory provision. For the political irony is that while statutory provision (for reasons described earlier) only provides effective workplace protections under highly specific circumstances, many people have an implicit faith in its wider efficacy and legislators seem willing to support it. Deprived of other avenues of redress, workers'-rights advocates are certain to press for further centralized statutory protections. After all, even in the hostile atmosphere of the Reagan and Bush era, these advocates achieved significant new federal regulation in the areas of age discrimination, plant-closing notification, and rights for people with disabilities; and many state legislatures also created new rights for workers. Family leave legislation was passed early in the Clinton administration. Unions, advocates for minorities and women, and those concerned about older workers, health and safety issues, and other labor issues have made additional legislation their highest priority. Waiting in the wings are bills on "cafeteria-plan" benefits, child care, the introduction of certain new technologies, privacy rights, health hazards from video display terminals, comparable-worth pay, and other issues. Additional proposals would reform labor law, toughen enforcement of the Occupational Safety and Health Act and antidiscrimination laws, restrict dismissals except for just cause, and reinvigorate regulation in various other ways.

The decline of unionism, in a context where there are no alternate rights strategies, will surely increase the demands for government regulation of the world of work; it would be remarkable if these demands were not over time acceded to, and, having been acceded to, did not impose further regulatory costs and restrictions on employers (despite producing rapidly diminishing benefits for workers). The threat of extensive additional legislation is made more real by the fact that state judges have begun to rewrite labor law, in particular the at-will doctrine that lies at the foundation of so much American labor practice. Thus regulation may enter by the back door of the courts rather than (or in addition to) the front gate of the legislature.

Second, employers have a vital stake in avoiding excessive and unpredictable litigation costs and, more generally, in finding low-cost and effective methods of resolving industrial disputes. According to a 1988 estimate, lawsuits under statutes protecting employment rights account for the largest single group of civil filings in federal courts.[3] The extensive and growing case law reported in the previous chapter, although it reviews only enterprise-rights cases and omits litigation having to do with other alleged wrongful acts by employers (for example, race, sex, and age discrimination; sexual harassment; defamation; and civil rights violations), begins to suggest the scope of the problem for employers. As the new legal standards become consolidated, litigation by workers is likely to become more common and more routine. In effect, the courts are beginning to stand in for the dispute-resolution mechanism lost when the purview of collective bargaining shrank.

Some estimates exist of the direct economic costs of the new litigation. First, there seems little doubt that such cases are rapidly increasing in number. One study found that cases doubled between 1982 and 1987; another estimated that in 1987 there were 25,000 wrongful-discharge cases pending in federal and state courts.[4] In these cases the plaintiffs (that is, the workers) frequently prevail. A study of 260 cases in a nationwide data base collected by Jury Verdict Research found that plaintiffs recovered damages in 63.9 percent of the cases (78.9 percent in defamation cases; 70.0 percent in sex-discrimination and harassment cases; 58.4 percent in wrongful-discharge cases). In this study the damage awards ranged from $500 to $17.48 million. The average jury award in the 166 verdicts for the plaintiff was $602,302 (this figure is high because of a few large awards, but even the median was $158,800). In a study of California awards between 1982 and 1986, workers in at-will trials won 73 percent of their cases, with an average award of $652,100—fourteen times higher than the employers' average settlement offer and nearly double the plaintiffs' own average original settlement demand. A study by James Dertouzos and colleagues at the Rand Corporation of 120 wrongful-discharge jury trials in California between 1980 and 1986 concluded that plaintiffs won 67.5 percent of those cases. The average award was $646,855, and the median $177,000. Another study in California found that in 1987 plaintiffs won 61 percent of the time and the average award was $596,340.[5]

These sketchy findings suggest that wrongful-discharge litigation can be expensive and unpredictable. To calculate the final costs paid by employers, one must consider several additional factors. Dertouzos and his colleagues found that employers paid an average of $83,000 in legal fees to defend themselves. On the other side, however, they also found that posttrial actions by defendants usually reduced the size of jury awards, shrinking the average final settlement to about 48 percent of the initial award. Considering all these factors, these results imply that the employer's probability of losing one of these cases is about two-thirds and that the average cost of such a loss is $390,628; even if the employer wins, the legal fees—which, as noted above, average $83,000—must be paid.[6]

Thus employers have a direct cost incentive to find more effective means of structuring and regulating labor relations. How significant these litigation expenses loom in employers' overall costs of managing their labor forces is unclear; Dertouzos and his colleagues argued in 1988 that they were not yet significant, principally because cases going to jury trial were still relatively rare. Also to be considered, however, are the many more disputes that are settled before trial. (These outnumber disputes that go to litigation by twenty to one, according to Dertouzos and colleagues.) Finally, employers must also be concerned about the unpredictable size of settlements and the possibility of large and damaging awards.

Undoubtedly the biggest cost to employers is the indirect impact of the litigation explosion. These costs take many forms: changes in employment practices to limit exposure to liability, the diversion of managerial time and attention, the negative impact on reputation and business relations, and the lingering employee bitterness and emotionality, with consequences for morale. Consider just one element: like doctors practicing defensive medicine, employers must think defensively; they must begin to formalize, document, and justify personnel decisions in ways that will appear rational and nonarbitrary to judges and juries who might view the decisions ex post facto with little knowledge of the particular business involved. James Dertouzos and colleagues note, "In response to wrongful termination suits, administrative costs may rise substantially."[7]

Indeed, a second study by Dertouzos, undertaken with Lynn Karoly, documents just how significant the indirect costs of increased litigation are. The authors focus just on the costs of wrongful-termination suits (not all suits related to enterprise rights) using a sophisticated statistical model, and their results are startling: the indirect costs on employers "are 100 times more costly than the direct legal costs of jury awards, settlements, and attorney fees."[8] Considering just the reduced employment that results, they conclude that "the threat of wrongful termination suits changes firms' human-resource practices in a manner that increases the costs of doing business. . . . In effect, firms have responded to increased wrongful-termination liability by treating labor as more expensive."[9] How much more expensive? The decrease in employment is reckoned to be about the same as would be produced by a 10 percent wage increase.

Directly, and with literally a hundred times more force indirectly, the costs of this litigation have already placed substantial burdens on employers. (And, as Dertouzos and Karoly point out, while the litigation affects workers who have been fired, the costs of the litigation have a negative impact on the enterprise's incumbent employees, as well as on the employer.) Because the change in legal standards has been quite recent, one can suppose that these costs will likely increase as familiarity with them becomes more widespread within the labor force.

Third, employers have a stake in a new rights regime because rights are essential for building employee morale and maintaining high productivity.

As is made abundantly evident by the long U.S. history of adversarial and rancorous labor relations, when workers feel that they have no rights or that their rights are violated, they are less likely to be cooperative partners in production; the consequence is usually a management strategy that focuses on designing simple jobs that permit "close" supervision and the application of heavy discipline for infractions. In such a work climate, employers are denied the benefits of a work force that is highly motivated. This cost is often deplored as a lack of loyalty, the decline of standards, or the demise of the work ethic; it seems, instead, an entirely understandable response to a work life without rights.

On the positive side, the most responsible (and happily, some of the most successful) employers have discovered that a system of employee rights is good business—indeed, this is why they have gone to the considerable trouble and expense of promulgating enterprise rights in the first place. There seems little question that their efforts pay off. Although there is not much hard data here, the point is supported by the variety, bulk, and virtual unanimity of the evidence that does exist.[10] Successful firms are those that can instill in their workers a sense of identification with the company, pride, commitment, and loyalty. As the authors of the MIT study *Made in America* noted about the manufacturing companies they examined, "Best-practice firms have recognized that improvements in quality and flexibility require levels of commitment, responsibility, and knowledge on the part of the work force that cannot be obtained by compulsion or cosmetic improvements in human-resource policies."[11] Employees regularly report that what most motivates them in their work is the work they do, more than salary or other job attributes.[12] Being treated fairly, having a right to one's say, and having other workplace rights are fundamental to this motivation.

Fourth, and most important for the future, employers have a stake in supporting a new rights regime because it may well be essential to implementing new management strategies. The decline of American competitiveness has been traced to many factors, but certainly important among them are the traditional practices of American management. But introducing new forms of management may require and certainly would be aided by a new rights regime.

This is not the place to review management problems and philosophies, but a brief explanation of the connection to a rights regime will be given. Private-sector employers in the postwar American economy tended to divide into three groups: those small and medium-size businesses (and a few large firms) where at-will status resulted in truly contingent and precarious employment for their workers, employers of all sizes where unions provided protections against arbitrary treatment, and medium-size and large employers that developed sophisticated personnel systems offering what both employer and worker expected would be long-term, perhaps lifetime employment.[13] As has been shown, the second group has shrunk to a tiny fraction of the labor force.

For employers in the third group, the increasing global competition faced by all employers has triggered a particularly momentous change. It speeded up the product cycle and introduced much larger sales fluctuations and thereby vastly heightened the importance of their ability to adjust quickly to changed conditions. Developing their flexibility, however, often meant for their work forces the breaking of those long-term implied promises; this was seen most dramatically in the laying off of employees to whom the company had given an implied promise of lifetime employment.[14] But virtually all employers exposed to competition have also recognized their greater need for employee commitment to product quality, cost-effectiveness, and the other elements of successful competition; can they expect greater employee commitment from their remaining workers in the face of reduced employer commitment?

Responding to these pressures, employers have been driven in one of two directions. Some, especially small and medium-size businesses, have chosen to pursue a low-wage, few-rights, and highly contingent labor strategy. They have responded to the intensifying competition by moving closer to the deprived labor conditions that workers experience in less developed countries. This has produced, for example, increased attempts to decertify unions, to cut back on job-related benefits, to evade or violate statutory protections, and to employ a growing number of part-time and other contingent workers. Some evidence suggests that, while important, this strategy affects fewer jobs than the one followed by other firms.[15]

Other employers, perhaps responding to different circumstances, have followed another path: even while eliminating labor rigidities, they have sought to introduce new managerial styles that rely on engaging the workers' best efforts. Intensified global competition has stimulated the appearance of many new management philosophies and techniques, including flexible specialization, *kaizen* (continual upgrading), zero defects, quality-control circles, worker participation, labor-management cooperation, and total quality management.[16] Although there are important differences among these approaches, they all rely on or attempt to foster greater identification on the part of employees with the goals of the firm. It is now widely understood that a crucial ingredient in an employer's competitive edge is *involved* workers; this is especially true in areas of business that demand high levels of skill, technology, service, and innovation. Although the specific techniques differ, the universally understood means of involving workers is convincing them that they will receive fair treatment in the workplace.

Efforts to bring Japanese-style management to the American workplace provide a particularly relevant instance of the need for sensitivity to workers' rights. Many observers have pointed out that in transferring a management model from one society to another, the cultural preconditions for the model are likely to be left behind, making adaptation (rather than simple transfer) essential. In the U.S. context, the limited success of efforts to transplant Japanese management techniques may be traceable to American workers' greater insistence on individual rights, even in the workplace. Thus, a system of workers' rights based on American tradition may well be a prerequisite to effective introduction of Japanese-style management.

The fundamental point is that individual employers can do little more than make promises (as some do in handbooks), but a rights regime, properly constructed with employer participation, could provide credible guarantees. Without unions to represent them, statutes to protect them, or credible employer commitments of lifetime employment, workers have little reason to accept employer promises on faith. Indeed, the evidence of the previous chapter is that a growing number of workers lack such faith, and are instead going to court to enforce compliance. Employers could look to a new rights regime as an important aid to their efforts to reformulate their management practices.

Thus employers have a number of substantial reasons to support and even promote a new rights regime. Some involve avoiding bad outcomes, and others are based on the prospect of realizing important benefits. As in previous social compromises, this arrangement would have to provide tangible benefits to both employers and workers to be effective.

Toward a New Common Ground

The analysis of the previous chapters offers some suggestions of where a new common ground might lie. Both workers and employers must recognize that they have traveled beyond the postwar regime's defining landmarks of collective bargaining and statutory provision. Collective bargaining and statutory provision are too feeble and too confining to serve as the central features of a new regime, as I argued in chapters 4 and 5. But while they cannot be central, neither will they nor should they disappear; both are likely to, and ought to, play somewhat different roles from those they had in the postwar regime.

Collective bargaining will likely play a role similar to that of civil service rules in guaranteeing workers' rights. Access to collective bargaining represents one path, eligibility for civil service protections another, by which a small but significant minority of employees—at 17 million, the number of government employees is roughly equal to the number of union members (18 million)—can gain rights.[17] Both collective bargaining and civil-service protections likely will continue to serve as examples of special employment conditions that demonstrate new rights, new benefits, and new employment rules. Both will therefore continue to model for other employees some of the more humane possibilities that the employment relationship may take, and they may also model some of the costs and rigidities of adversarial or overly bureaucratic labor relations. Most important, however, both must be seen realistically as special circumstances. Just as it would be impractical to extend the public sector's inflexible job-tenure rights to the economy as a whole, so it would be unrealistic to expect that collective bargaining would become generalized.

Statutory provision of substantive rights ought to play a different role, one that is at once more general and more restricted. Its great strength is that it can be and usually is applied to all or nearly all workers; for example, the minimum-wage and overtime provisions of the Fair Labor Standards Act apply in principle to virtually every worker who needs such protection. But this attribute is also its great limitation: except for the simplest regulations, it has proven nearly impossible to devise appropriate regulatory strategies and to staff the regulatory agencies with sufficiently competent and disinterested personnel so as to administer workplace regulation effectively. This combination of strength and limitation suggests that statutory provision ought to be reserved for guaranteeing only the most important and unambiguous of workers' rights, where enforcement can be straightforward and should be vigorous. This restriction would rule out reliance on statutory provision as the primary means of administering a detailed set of work rights in the industrial relations system.

Statutes need not be the principal source of the rights that workers possess, at least in the sense of direct mandating of rights. It is understandable that the wrong assumption is often made: workers'-rights advocates, seeking to compensate for the decline of collective bargaining, have seen statutory provision as the only alternative means of guaranteeing rights; they have therefore sought maximum rights through law. But statutory provision need not be the only path to workers' rights.

Finally, rights should be constructed and construed as strong but not absolute claims. The workplace is a continuing social system, much like a village; after a dispute is resolved, the parties to the dispute must continue to work together, and so the system functions best where accommodation, compromise, respect, and remediation rule. Rights must have a place, but they must be matched with responsibility. Mary Ann Glendon has criticized the contemporary American rights discourse for "its legalistic character, its exaggerated absoluteness, its hyperindividualism, its insularity, and its silence with respect to personal, civic, and collective responsibilities."[18] But as she successfully demonstrates, this is not the only possible rights discourse, and in both the workplace and civic society, other conceptions are likely to prove more beneficial to all the participants.

In what direction, then, may new common ground be found? I begin by listing the desiderata for a new rights regime implied by the analysis of previous chapters. Experiences with collective bargaining, statutory provision, and enterprise rights suggest six considerations.

Rights Diversity

The vision of workers' rights—how they are defined and understood—must be broad enough to permit rights to be different in different workplaces. In chapter 2 I noted that rights derive from membership in a group; statutory rights assume that the proper group to which to attach rights is all workers, but for many rights the appropriate rights-defining group is the enterprise work force. A rights regime should offer the possibility of tailoring the menu of rights operative in any particular workplace to the peculiarities of that workplace. Unlike constitutional rights, which in principle are identical for all citizens and are not mitigated by circumstance, workplace rights in a new rights regime must be permitted to be different in each workplace, while not lacking in any.

Workplaces (and the employment relations therein) differ greatly from each other, because of the requirements imposed by the different technologies or production processes in use and because of the different entrepreneurial and organizational choices made. The flexibility to adapt to these differences has always been a great strength of the collective-bargaining model; the lack of this flexibility is a great weakness of statutory provision. Collectively bargained contracts could and did reflect the vast diversity of workplaces, protecting worker interests by means of diverse sets of rights. The bargaining presumably led to those accommodations least antagonistic to the employer's needs; that is, given whatever bargaining strengths workers brought to the negotiations, the employer could in effect choose (or at least shape) those ways of accommodating the workers' interests that least disrupted its business. Statutory provision, in contrast, generally gives the employer little choice as to how to meet fixed standards.

For almost all industrial-relations issues, choice and diversity are preferable to uniformity. Perhaps excluding the basic protections such as a minimum wage, overtime provisions, basic health and safety protections, and a secure pension system, no optimal set of rights emerges as appropriate for the entire work force. Great flexibility in the provision of rights is needed to accommodate workers with differing preferences, patterns of mobility and commitment that vary among occupations, industries that have widely different needs for flexibility, and other sources of diversity within the economy.

A Legal Framework

Workers' rights should be set in a legal framework that is stimulative and permissive, that is, one that stimulates some action by the affected parties while permitting a range of choices as to the particular action to be selected. First, workers' rights need a clear legal basis. The central guarantees of the postwar regime, the collectively bargained contract and the statute, functioned effectively because each had an unambiguous legal foundation. Although disputes over specific interpretation and applicability persisted, the issue of their legal enforceability was not in question. (One indicator of the breakdown of this regime is the rising tide of litigation challenging its operation.[19]) However, the central weakness of enterprise rights, and the aspect that has increasingly drawn the courts into redefinition of employment law, is exactly their ambiguous and shifting legal status. A successful workers'-rights regime requires legal recognition of the announced work rights.

Although a clear legal status is essential, the direct statutory grant of work rights is only one of the ways the law can recognize rights. A method likely to be superior is one that underlies the collective-bargaining model. In particular, the National Labor Relations Act (NLRA) guarantees workers (under specified conditions) the right to organize and bargain collectively through a union, and requires that their employers bargain in good faith, avoiding unfair labor practices. The specific content of the bargaining, and the terms and provisions of the contract that may emerge, are left open to the parties themselves. The legal framework is stimulative but permissive, and this method is, in most industrial-relations applications, likely to be superior to direct statutory mandate, because it permits the tailoring of specific employment conditions to the circumstances of particular industries or employments. It introduces room for local initiative and expertise into the legal recognition of rights, creating an opening for decentralized efforts that are essential in the diverse and complex American economy.

Such scope for voluntary action must be paired with an effective stimulus to action. Absent a sufficiently powerful prod, permissiveness can simply encourage evasion. This is what has happened during the 1980s to federal labor law. The NLRA can hardly be called stimulative any more because the employer's opportunity to avoid unionism has become so great and the penalties for violating federal rules on the right to organize, good-faith bargaining, and unfair labor practices have become so slight. But there is no rational bar to incorporating an adequate stimulus, and the price of failing to do so is likely to be additional direct statutory provision.

Public Disclosure

Workplace rights in effect in any workplace should be publicly disclosed and be provided to job applicants before they are hired. Like rights presently granted by statute or obtained in collective contract, but unlike enterprise rights, all workers' rights should be clearly and publicly stated.

No good public purpose is served by the present practice of making workers' rights secret, mysterious, and proprietary. Access to information about such rights is clearly crucial for job holders and job seekers to be able to evaluate alternative employments, yet much evidence suggests that workers typically know little about the basic rights attached to the jobs for which they have been hired. In the landmark cases of *Toussaint* and *Woolley*, for example, the prospective employees were not aware of what their job rights would be. Withholding such information hurts workers and distorts and impairs the functioning of the job market. Requiring disclosure, as is now mandated by the Employee Retirement Income Security Act for pension policies, would serve a clear public purpose.

Employers cite three main reasons for their unwillingness to disclose enterprise rights or personnel policies generally. One is that such information is "competitive" and disclosure could help competing firms. An analogy is sometimes made to the firm's productive technology, which for competitive reasons an employer may work hard to prevent other producers from stealing. Yet with a little effort, any competitor (like any diligent union organizer) can obtain the appropriate handbook or company policies from current or past employees or others. Because such policies must be distributed to employees or at least must be made known to them, little competitive advantage can be gained from keeping them secret. If obtaining such information were worthwhile, competing firms would surely have sufficient incentive and resources to do so. The main interested party from whom information is effectively secreted is the job applicant, who might wish to compare job offers. Yet surely there is a strong public purpose in having clear information available to workers about the conditions of their current or anticipated employment.

The second employer concern about disclosure is that making such information available might subject firms to unfavorable comparisons by union activists, academic researchers, and others. Certainly their unwillingness to disclose hinders such comparisons. Yet it only hinders general comparisons, not the specific ones that employers worry about. Obtaining the relevant information for any particular company and a few of its competitors is easy work for even a novice investigative journalist, not to mention a veteran union organizer or reasonably energetic researcher. This second concern thus seems a weak objection against the obvious public benefits.

The third reason cited, and perhaps the most powerful in employers' minds, is that public disclosure will somehow lead to increased litigation and legal liability. As the management consultant quoted in chapter 7 said, "the plaintiff's bar has become receptive to handling [such cases] on a contingency fee basis," and public disclosure might just provide further encouragement. Yet this process is already occurring, and surely lawyers (like competing firms and union organizers) can obtain such documents if they choose to. This concern does, however, strengthen the argument for an effective dispute-resolution system (see below).

In short, employers' objections to requiring public disclosure seem weak compared to the public benefits that may be derived. Moreover, whatever force these objections have for the question of any individual firm disclosing its policies in isolation, the objections completely lose their force if all firms are required to disclose, because all firms would be in the same boat. Moreover, public disclosure need not limit other prerogatives of the employer. For example, because I am here considering workers' rights (that is, written entitlements that apply to groups of or all of a firm's employees), express contracts for individual employees who are especially sought-after would continue to supersede such general or implied rights and would remain secret.

Effective Dispute Resolution

Workplace rights should be joined with an enforcement system that fosters quick, simple, inexpensive, and "legitimate" dispute resolution. Again, the experience with collective contracts, statutory provision, and enterprise rights provides an instructive guide.

Collective bargaining tends to produce grievance and arbitration mechanisms that have several desirable characteristics. These mechanisms for resolving disputes can be administered by the partners themselves. When further adjudication is required, a professional arbitrator, chosen according to a prearranged scheme, hears the case. The arbitrator's decision is binding, preempting a lengthy appeals process. Arbitrators base their decisions on the case precedents as they evolve out of contract administration.[20] The arbitration process tends to promote negotiated settlements and is quick and comparatively inexpensive. Arbitration cases are heard under less restrictive and formalistic rules than those required in courts and they are more accessible to ordinary people. Their outcomes are more likely to be accepted as legitimate by the contracting parties. The costs of dispute resolution fall on the parties themselves, not the taxpayer, with useful incentives deriving therefrom. Recourse to courts is minimal, or at least it was before the collective-bargaining system began to break down.

Dispute resolution with statutory provision and enterprise rights is less satisfactory, though for opposite reasons. Resolving conflicts under statutory provision is legitimate but highly cumbersome and costly. It almost always involves administrative regulation backed up by the threat of litigation. The enforcement task, as was shown in chapter 5, is made difficult by the fact that those responsible for enforcement (the regulators) are external to the enterprise itself. The lack of a continuing working relationship, when combined with the opportunities for employer evasion and the evidentiary burden on the regulators if they attempt to pursue litigation, promotes secrecy and strategies of avoidance. Although the eventual decision may be viewed as legitimate, the process is likely to be long and expensive, and to require the involvement of lawyers and other outside professionals. For these very reasons, coverage is likely to be spotty.

By contrast, conflict resolution for enterprise rights is typically straightforward and prompt but generally lacks legitimacy. For example, the internal grievance mechanisms surveyed in chapter 6 typically required hearings and higher-level responses within days. Few relied on outside experts, and none required lawyers. But the arbitrators are also likely to be higher-level managers who are involved, or will be perceived as being involved, in the substance or implications of the grievance itself. Hence, as arbitrators, the managers are placed in a position of conflict of interest that undercuts the legitimacy of their decisions. It is presumably to bolster workers' perception of the legitimacy of such decisions that companies such as Consulting Services and Budget Car and Truck Rental use management-worker committees to hear grievances and that National Can in Oklahoma City offers outside arbitration of dismissal cases. Such efforts definitely mitigate, although they cannot eliminate, concerns about legitimacy.

Routine adjudication of workers' rights within an effective industrial-relations system requires a dispute-resolution mechanism that can operate on a similarly routine basis—one that fosters mediated solutions and that is simple, prompt, inexpensive, and legitimate.

Determining Rights at the Appropriate Level

A new rights regime should establish mechanisms for determining rights—whether market bargaining or political contestation—at the appropriate level of aggregation. In general, this consideration requires determination that is neither at the individual-worker level nor at the level of state or national statutes.

As noted in chapter 3, individual bargaining is an inappropriate mechanism for elements of the employment relationship characterized by local public goods or economies of scale. For one thing, it is too disaggregated to be appropriate for enterprise rights. Individual workers may be able to bargain effectively concerning their wages and other quid pro quo job conditions; for example, even where the employer maintains a fixed wage schedule, job applicants can usually bargain about where on the schedule the applicant will enter or how much credit will be allowed for previous experience or training. By contrast, individual bargaining over such general employer policies as dismissal for just cause or at will, the company's grievance procedures, and access to promotion opportunities, where not impossible, is likely to be inefficient; such bargaining is also likely to put workers at a disadvantage and and thus reduce the provision of rights. Employers typically refuse to bargain with individual workers on these issues.

By contrast, market bargaining or political contention over workers' rights that occurs at the state or national level may occur at too high a level of aggregation. For some matters, state or national determination may be appropriate, but for most enterprise rights, more local determination is likely to be better. In general, if the public-goods or economies-of-scale characteristics of workers' rights are fully exploited at the level of the firm, then the efficient level of bargaining is also the firm. The level of bargaining needs to be established at the point most likely to produce optimal results.

Building on Existing Rights

Rights within a future regime should be built upon or rooted in rights currently exercised in workplaces. Although the temptation to recommend a list of preferred or desirable rights is great, it is, like most temptations, better resisted. This is so for several reasons. One is that such recommended lists imply a set of rights to be uniformly applied to all workers; but as noted above, workers' rights need to be defined flexibly in response to real differences in workplaces. A second is that such lists are typically idiosyncratic and thus lack political credibility. But perhaps most persuasively of all, the abrupt introduction of rights de novo into current, functioning productive systems would be likely to cause great disruption, including most probably the unintended effect of hurting those workers most in need of protection.

Rather, efforts to bring forth a new rights regime should focus on building upon those rights already extant in the workplace. The likely building blocks for such efforts are existing employee handbooks.

The six desiderata I have outlined do not invariably lead to any one system or "solution." Neither do they constitute absolute requirements, the sine qua non of future rights development. Rather, they are reference points for reorienting thinking about any proposed workers' rights. They serve as signposts directing attention toward promising common ground.

Notes to Chapter 8

1. Rosabeth Kantor (1990), p. 7.

2. Another reason is that workers' rights provide a good mechanism for upper management to ensure that middle management is carrying out company policy; the presence of these rights also puts pressure on middle management to deal constructively with personnel problems. See Richard Edwards (1979); David W. Ewing (1989).

3. "Labor Letter: Worker Complaints," *Wall Street Journal*, May 31, 1988, p. 1.

4. Ira Michael Shepard, Paul Heylman, and Robert L. Duston (1989), p. 21. "It's Getting Harder to Pass Out Pink Slips," *Business Week*, March 28, 1988, p. 68, quoting Columbia University professor Alan F. Westin. See also James N. Dertouzos and Lynn A. Karoly (1992).

5. Ira Michael Shepard, Paul Heylman, and Robert L. Duston (1989), pp. 20–23. William B. Gould IV (1986a), p. 905, notes, "Clearly, plaintiffs are winning, the verdicts are large, and both employees and employers systematically underestimate the amount of damages that a jury will award." James N. Dertouzos, Elaine Holland, and Patricia Ebener (1988), p. 26; Bureau of National Affairs, "California Statistics for 1987 Suggest Stabilization in Plaintiff Awards," *Daily Labor Report*, no. 25, Feb. 8, 1988, p. A-3; see also James N. Dertouzos and Lynn A. Karoly (1992); Walter B. Connolly, Gary E. Murg, and Clifford Scharman (1983), p. 59.

6. James N. Dertouzos, Elaine Holland, and Patricia Ebener (1988), calculated from tables 16 and 18.

7. James N. Dertouzos, Elaine Holland, and Patricia Ebener (1988), p. x.

8. James N. Dertouzos and Lynn A. Karoly (1992), p. xiii.

9. James N. Dertouzos and Lynn A. Karoly (1992), p. 63.

10. Thousands of studies over the past few decades have focused on the impact of employee morale and commitment on productivity. The evi-

dence runs the gamut from the opinions of managers, to experimental studies, to case studies, to analyses of in situ data from workplaces. Research design and variable measurement flaws are common, the results differ, and there are many viewpoints about which variables are causal and which merely correlated, but certainly the level of employee morale and commitment is highly associated with the level of productivity. For an extensive review, see Thomas Kochan, Henry Katz, and Robert McKersie (1986). The authors of the MIT study *Made in America* declare that an imperative for restoring American competitiveness is that "employees will be expected to give so much more of themselves to their work" (Michael L. Dertouzos, Richard K. Lester, and Robert M. Solow, 1989, p. 135). For a consideration of the new managerial interest, see "New Regard for the Ideas of Workers," *New York Times*, July 5, 1988, p. D10. For anecdotal evidence, see Sharon Cohen, "Firms Reap Profits When Workers Become Empowered," Springfield (Massachusetts) *Sunday-Republican*, December 2, 1990, pp. D1–D2.

11. Michael L. Dertouzos, Richard K. Lester, and Robert M. Solow (1989), p. 124.

12. See, for example, the Hewitt Associates 1990 poll of 120,000 employees (*Boston Globe*, January 6, 1991, p. 78).

13. Richard Edwards (1979).

14. Such layoffs were reported with increasing regularity in the press during the late 1980s and early 1990s: for example, "Digital Breaks Its No-Layoff Tradition," *Boston Globe*, January 10, 1991, p. 51; "Texas Instruments Lays Off 725," *Boston Globe*, January 18, 1991, p. 67. Similar stories have appeared about Polaroid, Xerox, banks and financial companies, and many other corporations. And firms (for example, the auto companies) that have often had layoffs of blue-collar workers have now increasingly placed their service, technical, sales, and professional personnel in an equally vulnerable position.

15. This is the conclusion, for example, of Gary Burtless (1990), p. 7. Burtless argues that the growing earnings inequality within the male labor force, and particularly the declining wages of low-skill workers, is evidence of the fall in demand for less skilled workers. This explanation is less persuasive for female workers.

16. See Peter F. Drucker (1990); Genichi Taguchi and Don Clausing (1990); and Rosabeth Kantor (1990). Several papers in Samuel Bowles, Herbert Gintis, and Bo Gustafsson (1993) discuss the need for and problems associated with workers' greater involvement.

17. They are, of course, overlapping groups because nearly 40 percent of public employees are also union members; see figure 4-1.

18. Mary Ann Glendon (1991), p. x.

19. Robert J. Flanagan (1987); Richard B. Freeman (1988).

20. This should be recognized, of course, as a simplified description of a complicated process. What arbitrators base their decisions on is a fascinating and understudied question; for two excellent analyses, see James A. Gross and Patricia A. Greenfield (1986), and James B. Atleson (1983).

9

Reconstituting Workers' Rights

When workers' advocates or employers search for proper public policies toward workers' rights, the set of choices they consider is too limited to offer either a common meeting ground or guidance to the way forward. Workers' advocates tend to look backward, hoping for the revival of the postwar paradigm of collective bargaining and statutory rights. Employers, believing they see the future, gaze longingly at a vista even further removed: the "free labor market" of the pre-CIO, pre–New Deal days. These choices do not appear to offer much common ground, because they fail to answer one part or other of the basic question: in an internationally competitive economy, how can the employer's need for flexibility in its operations be reconciled with workers' legitimate aspirations for basic protections and fair dealing at work?

The desiderata for a new rights regime, described in the last chapter, suggest that employers and workers must reorient themselves to expand their range of choices. As has been shown, American workers have enjoyed extensive enterprise rights promising fair treatment yet offering uncertain legal effect. These enterprise rights are the legacy bequeathed to today's workers by prior generations of workers who sacrificed and struggled to make such promises seem a common and expected part of today's workplace. They are not appropriate subjects to leave for individual workers to bargain for in the market, yet neither traditional collective bargaining nor direct statutory provision is likely to serve well either. The new choices that are needed must provide some means to guarantee these enterprise rights while permitting employers sufficient flexibility to allow their enterprises to compete effectively.

The purpose of this chapter is to sketch some possible general lines of advance toward a reconstitution of workers' rights. They are unlikely to be the first choices of either employers or workers'-rights advocates, but in time they may come to be seen as offering genuine common ground.

My proposals entail using statutory law to stimulate some action, while permitting private-sector actors to determine the course of the action. Rather than attempt to impose uniform national standards on a highly diverse economy, they would instead stimulate action but encourage diversity. These proposals are also intended to apply only to larger employers; employers with fewer than twenty workers should be encouraged to participate but not required to do so.

Make Employee Handbooks Mandatory and Public

Employers should be required to provide an employee handbook that would set forth the employer's statement of the workplace rights enjoyed by its workers and would be available for public scrutiny.

American society has a direct interest in the wider dissemination of information about workplace rights. This interest is no different in principle but surely vastly greater in import than its concern in other areas where the law intervenes to ensure openness—for example, requiring that lenders accurately disclose the interest charged on loans, or that vendors of new merchandise spell out their warranties, or that producers of food products list their ingredients. Legal intervention in these cases is used to require honest disclosure of important aspects of the proposed transaction, aspects that may be crucial to an individual's decision but for which an individual typically cannot obtain the information for herself. So too for work rights.

Providing more information to job holders, job seekers, and the public is both directly beneficial in itself and a prerequisite to the other reforms discussed below. In chapter 3 I outlined the market inefficiencies created by informational asymmetries, and in chapter 7 I reviewed the extent to which employers, in the absence of legal constraints impinging on all firms, found it to be in their individual competitive self-interests to withhold information concerning enterprise rights. Viewed from a social perspective, or even from the collective perspective of employers or of workers, maintaining secrecy about enterprise rights makes little sense. Even if workers' rights are to be left entirely for individual workers to contract in the marketplace, efficient bargaining requires adequate information.

This proposal would transform employee handbooks from secret, proprietary materials into public documents recognized in law and open to scrutiny. Each employer would be required to specify clearly, in a legally meaningful way, what the terms and conditions of employment are, and current employees and job seekers would be able to learn these conditions and, if they so desired, compare alternative employments.[1]

Consider more closely how such a requirement might work. First, each employer whose work force surpasses the numerical threshold would be required to have a handbook. In this context, a *handbook* would simply be a fuller and more explicit employment contract, one that spells out the full range of conditions, including enterprise rights, governing the employment. Most medium-size and larger employers already have handbooks, so this part of the proposal would impose nothing new on them. For others, a simple statement of company policy would be all that would be needed to fulfill the requirement. To meet the requirement, the employer would need only to file the handbook (or handbooks, if different ones applied to different groups of employees) with the designated appropriate agency, such as a state labor commission or the National Labor Relations Board. A crucial part of this proposal is making handbooks publicly available; this could be done by opening to public scrutiny the handbooks filed for certification. Employers would also be required to distribute the handbooks to current employees and job applicants.

This proposal would not infringe in any way on the employer's right to determine the content of the handbook. However, to prevent employers from completely undercutting the intent of the requirement by, for example, stating only that employment is at will, there should be a few key areas in which the employer would be obligated to state what the company policy is; those areas might include layoffs, promotion policy, reasons for dismissal and dismissal procedures, the complaint or grievance system, disciplinary procedures, and benefits (health insurance, vacation, sick leave, and pension). Most handbooks include all these elements already, but this requirement would inhibit employers from issuing trivial documents that say nothing but technically satisfy the legal requirement. Even so, determination of the handbook's contents would remain the prerogative of the employer.

A special public-private employee rights commission could be charged with drawing up a standard handbook. It would contain model or prototype provisions in the areas specified. The standard handbook would serve two purposes. First, it would be offered at no cost to employers that currently do not use a handbook, thereby providing them with a legally acceptable document free of any costs of development or distribution. Second, it would provide a default option that would take legal effect in any workplace where the employer, after a reasonable grace period, had failed or refused to promulgate a handbook.

This proposal would make it much easier for job applicants to compare employers' policies, and so it would result in the operation of a labor market based on fuller, more adequate information. It would end the dilemma for job-seekers of having to choose between accepting employment in ignorance of or with only hearsay information about the rights attached to the prospective job, or taking the risk of sending a negative signal during the hiring process by requesting such information. Comparison would also strengthen the voice of current workers within an enterprise to obtain rights comparable to those granted by other employers.

Most employers, and certainly responsible employers, would also benefit from such regulation. At a minimum, to the extent that employers intend to honor their enterprise-rights promises, they would not be harmed, because they would retain complete autonomy over the menu of enterprise rights they would grant. But if matched with an effective arbitration system (see below), enforceable handbooks could provide real benefits to employers: stable industrial relations and regular and reliable industrial governance, and a diminution of the expensive and disruptive litigation they now face—

exactly what the current system of uncertain enforceability and erratic damage awards cannot provide.

Set against the advantages of mandating a handbook and requiring disclosure are various concerns on the part of both employers and workers. Employers have expressed concerns that public disclosure would erode firms' competitive advantages, subject their policies to unfavorable public scrutiny, and increase litigation; all three concerns were dealt with in the previous chapter. In general, however, a firm with superior policies ought to benefit from disclosure. Employers offering low-quality employment may suffer by comparison with competitors, but there seems little compelling reason to shield such employers from effective market competition by keeping potential workers (and all too frequently, current employees) ignorant of their policies.

Labor's biggest concern would be a fear that this proposal would result in mere paper advances: recalcitrant or exploitative employers might not change their office or shop-floor practices at all. Yet the advantages to workers even in that situation should not be overlooked: employers could not write promises into handbooks without either meaning them or risking some form of legal intervention, promises not included in the handbook would stand exposed as unenforceable, and legal recognition would be extended to enterprise rights currently lacking it.

Workers should not underestimate the power of competition to work in their favor. Employers must compete to attract and retain committed, diligent workers, and virtually all employers, to varying degrees, now advertise enterprise rights and employment conditions in their efforts to recruit workers. But with no unions and ambiguously enforceable handbooks, these promises are easily made and easily broken. Regulation could change that (as the courts are now increasingly doing anyway), with obvious advantages to workers.

Make Employee Handbooks Enforceable

State laws (or better, a federal statute) should require that employer handbooks be written in understandable language and that they be recognized as binding and enforceable contracts. In chapter 3 I reviewed how a lack of contract enforceability impedes efficient market functioning. This is not simply a theoretical issue, because, as shown in chapter 6, workers currently enjoy extensive and significant entitlements or enterprise rights extended to them by employers—enterprise rights that now constitute an implicit contract between employer and worker, widely understood in practice as an agreement and relied upon by workers as valid. Yet except in Montana, statutory law nowhere recognizes the handbook as a binding contract.[2]

The current discrepancy between reliance in practice and lack of recognition in statutory law is bad public policy. Economists as much as anyone have contributed to this unfortunate situation. By defining an employment relationship as primarily an individual contract in which wages are exchanged for labor, they have failed to incorporate the third important element intrinsic to any employment relationship: the conditions under which the labor is performed. Judges have at least partially rescued workers from the narrowness of the economic vision, and enterprise rights, expecially those relating to dismissal, have achieved substantial recognition from state courts. However, this acceptance is partial, uneven, often contradictory and capricious, and does not yet usually extend to the full range of enterprise rights. Although it offers much-warranted redress, judge-made law remains intrinsically limited and inferior to an appropriate statute.

Society has an interest here, and the law an obligation, to ensure that the contract entered into by workers and employers is clearly understandable, is indeed understood by both parties, and is enforceable as understood. The requirement of understandable language would not be novel. Many states now successfully require simplicity and clarity in the language of insurance policies and product warranties. Handbooks should likewise be written in simple, direct language.

Contract enforceability ought in principle to be supported by all parties concerned about efficient operation of the labor market and the prevention of misrepresentation. Those who would place greater weight on "self-enforcing" contracts or "reputational" effects may well argue that such a law is superfluous, and that pressures within the marketplace itself provide adequate enforcement mechanisms. But this argument is hardly a reason to avoid making enforcement legally unambiguous, for three reasons. First, if market pressures do the job alone, no appeal to the law will need to be made, and having such a law will do no damage. Second, market pressures may work to enforce contracts *in general*, but they do not guarantee enforcement for *every* individual worker; hence, a law is needed for individual justice even if (by hypothesis) not for general compliance. Third, the current extensive litigation suggests that, empirically, self-enforcing pressures are not sufficient. Only transparently self-serving arguments favor continuing the present situation, in which employers can make promises they are not required to keep.

This proposal would require only that employee handbooks be recognized as valid contracts having legal effect. Even when placed together with my first proposal, it would not alter the freedom of employers to choose the enterprise rights they would grant their employees, that is, the contents of their handbooks. It would not, directly at least, create any new rights except that of a worker, when receiving a handbook, to be assured of its enforceability. As proposed here, the law would not, for example, prevent an employer from issuing a handbook that retained at-will status, offered no grievance system, and in other ways granted few or no rights. It would simply ensure that whatever employers promised to their workers would be enforceable.

Despite its limited impact, there are several compelling reasons arguing in favor of this proposal and few contrary ones. Most important, it would render legally unambiguous the employer's contractual obligations when enterprise rights are promised to workers. It would end the travesty of "implicit contracts"—hollow promises of enterprise rights that employers can abandon when compliance is not longer profitable. By transforming often secret and legally uncertain enterprise rights into true rights, this proposal would allow labor-market pressures to result in usable, that is, enforceable, implicit contracts. As employers compete with each other in the labor market to recruit high-quality labor, enterprise rights should represent real obligations on which employees can legitimately rely. Especially if combined with the dispute-resolution system outlined below, it would effectively safeguard enterprise rights.

Requiring adoption of handbooks and making them public and enforceable would go a long way toward preserving the precarious legacy of enterprise rights that today's workers enjoy. But it would do so while preserving maximum flexibility for the employer to structure its operations so as to remain competitive.

Establish an Independent System for Resolving Workers'-Rights Disputes

To secure workers' rights in practice, employers and workers need to have access to an alternative, independent system of dispute resolution. Such a system should foster quick, simple, inexpensive, and legitimate resolution of rights disputes. A public system for mediating and arbitrating industrial grievances, carefully limited in jurisdiction, should be established.

To see the public interest here, one should first look at what is wrong with currently available systems. These systems—arbitration within collectively bargained agreements and litigation for statute-based rights—derive from the twin pillars of the postwar rights regime, and unfortunately they reflect their flaws as well.

Arbitration under collective bargaining has proven quite effective in settling disputes, but its sphere is shrinking. It is remarkably inexpensive, its procedures are relatively informal, and the "arbitral culture" surrounding it accommodates interests so as to permit the parties to continue to work together. Because the decisions of professional arbitrators reflect expertise and are based on the common arbitral law of past decisions, the results are highly predictable. Given the predictability of decisions, arbitration tends to promote settlement at the early stages of a grievance procedure because the disputing parties can judge for themselves if a proposed settlement is substantially different from what an arbitrator is likely to award. The problem with arbitration is that the area it covers is highly limited and rapidly shrinking. The decline of the union sector has correspondingly shrunk the scope of union-based grievance arbitration for settling industrial disputes. For the most part, nonunionized employers do not use arbitration; National Can in Oklahoma City is an exception in this regard. Lacking a union, most workers are denied access to arbitration.

The second settlement mechanism, litigation, has its own problems. Although ostensibly available to all, in practice it is slow, costly, overly formal, and highly capricious. The significant costs of pursuing a legal remedy often put litigation beyond consideration except in cases where damage awards can be expected to be very large. Even then, workers are often required to pay significant amounts of money up front; and as the Rand study found, employers' average legal fees—win or lose—in wrongful-termination cases are $83,000.[3] Many of these costs are traceable to the highly formal character of the court proceedings, desirable in serious criminal cases but unnecessary, and even detrimental, in industrial disputes. The intricacy of the procedural safeguards built into court proceedings typically produces long delays between the time a suit is filed and its final disposition.

A further problem is the unpredictability of the outcome. Widely diverging decisions may be traced to the lack of expertise with industrial cases, on the part of judges, who must deal with all types of law, and even more so on the part of jurors, who rarely serve on more than one case. Throwing industrial disputes into the general court docket means that there can be little routinization of decision-making, the result being highly unpredictable outcomes. Not only does this produce a lack of horizontal equity (that is, similar cases may produce widely varied damage awards), but also that the very unpredictability of the outcome means participants cannot predict what they will obtain in court. Thus, they may be less likely to settle beforehand.

Perhaps the most unfortunate consequence of litigation in industrial disputes is that it produces winners and losers rather than mediates disputes. In fact, the courts are costly but otherwise work tolerably well in assessing damages after an employment relationship has broken down, and they serve the task of mediating and repairing a continuing relationship very poorly. The adversarial culture of litigation promotes disruption and bitterness, more commonly resulting in separation than reconciliation.

Where unions are not present, many employers have, as was shown in chapter 6, instituted complaint and grievance systems themselves. In some cases these systems establish joint management-employee committees to hear grievances, as at Consulting Services, Inc.; others call upon outside arbitrators, as at Northrop, Polaroid, and National Can in Oklahoma City. But for the great majority of nonunion employers, the complaint and grievance systems are little more than promises of review by higher management officials. Such systems justifiably bring upon themselves the suspicion of conflict of interest, inasmuch as company officials are likely to think beyond the actual merits of the grievance immediately before them and worry about such matters as the besmirching of the firm's reputation, showing support for the supervisory staff, and the implications of a decision for other employees. If workers are to have rights in practice, they need assurance of a more independent forum in which to have disputes resolved; indeed, it is exactly recognition of this need that has prompted state courts to enter industrial disputes with such vigor.

What is needed is an alternative system for resolving disputes that is aimed at mediating settlements; that is speedy, informal, inexpensive, and binding; and that is reasonably independent and disinterested. A dispute-resolution system superior to those currently available would combine the procedures, expertise, and arbitral culture of the arbitration system derived from collective bargaining with the independence and legitimacy of the courts.

The idea of alternative systems for resolving labor disputes is not new. A special panel of the California State Bar proposed an arbitration system in its report, "To Strike a New Balance." University of Texas professor John Allison, among others, has urged greater use of what have been termed alternative dispute-resolution techniques, which include arbitration, mediation, rent-a-judge (private employment of a judge by the parties to a dispute), summary jury trial, and minitrials. David Ewing, former editor of the *Harvard Business Review*, has called for "corporate due process" for resolving grievances in the nonunion workplace. Also, a limited system dealing with discrimination cases was proposed by the Bush administration.[4]

The most promising approach to dispute resolution would be to establish a public system of labor arbitration to resolve industrial disputes concerning rights granted through statute or employee handbooks. The jurisdiction would be rigorously limited to these rights and would not extend, for example, to wage disputes or normal contract bargaining. Arbitral decisions could therefore be firmly based on application of specific documents (statutes and handbooks), just as arbitration under collective bargaining is based on the negotiated contract.

A worker's complaint would be handled as follows. First, the employer's in-house complaint procedure would be invoked. Only if that procedure failed to produce a mutually satisfactory resolution could the worker file a claim or grievance with the arbitration board. At filing, each side would be required to provide a deposit toward payment of the costs of arbitration, which would be shared equally. The first and required effort at resolution would be informal mediation, in which a professional mediator would seek to resolve the dispute directly and reconcile the disputants.

If mediation failed, the grievance would move to arbitration. Each side could choose either to represent itself or be represented by any chosen agent, including a labor-relations expert, a co-worker, personnel official, union representative (whether or not the grievant was a union member), or lawyer. The arbitrator would be chosen by the parties themselves from lists of certified arbitrators or from rosters maintained by, for example, the American Arbitration Association. As is now sometimes the case in private arbitration, each party would have the right to strike potential arbitrators from the list.[5] Alternately, each side could be granted an unlimited number of strikes, with an arbitrator being assigned by default by a labor board if all the names were struck.

The arbitrator would hear the grievance, the employer's response, and any other information either party thought relevant. Hearings would proceed under informal rules similar to those currently used in the arbitration of collective-bargaining agreements. The burden of proof would be on the employee to establish the validity of the claim. The arbitrator would, after consideration, issue a binding judgment.

The system could give deference to private or company-based settlement mechanisms, providing only that they met minimal standards for acceptable arbitration. Thus, for example, where employers (like National Can, Polaroid, and Northrop) have already established or wished to establish their own arbitration mechanisms, they could do so. Indeed, one of the most wholesome consequences might be the incentive for employers to establish private arbitration and mediation systems, either on an internal, company-based model or on an external, extra-firm basis, much like what has happened in California and elsewhere with respect to the court system.[6] These mechanisms would simply need to provide a significant role for employees comparable to their role in the national system and ensure the reasonable independence of the arbitrator.

Many elements of such an arbitration system remain to be specified, and necessarily some important issues would need to be addressed, including the types of remedies that the arbitrators could fashion, the method of enforcing arbitrators' awards, the relation of this arbitration system to the unionized sector, connections to other statutes, and appeal rights. Nonetheless, none of these issues appears insurmountable, should the overall benefits of the system seem compelling.[7]

Arbitration offers a middle ground between management-dominated review and court litigation for nonunionized employees, a middle ground serving the same function as arbitration in collective-bargaining situations. As a middle ground, arbitration offers some of the advantages of both review and litigation: expeditious, relatively informal, inexpensive, and predictable dispute resolution that would nonetheless possess legitimacy because of its independence. Its aim would be remediation and "making whole" rather than assessing and assigning liability as in the courts. This system would be similar to the labor courts used in several European countries. Such courts focus exclusively on labor issues, so they can build up an expertise and establish predictability in their decisions. They work to assist in the function of industrial governance, seeking to permit reasonably quick and informal resolutions of workplace disputes.[8]

American employers might be concerned that such a system would produce an avalanche of grievances, many frivolous or patently ill-based but nonetheless requiring arbitration. Although it is difficult to predict the number of grievances that would be filed, and even harder to know what proportion would be frivolous, there are reasons to believe that this fear is misplaced. First, only grievances relevant to statutory rights or handbook enterprise rights could be filed. For statutory rights, having an arbitration system as a substitute for litigation might cause more cases to be filed, but each case would be resolved more quickly, predictably, and inexpensively. Dispute resolution could be routinized, as it should be. For enterprise rights, arbitration would add nothing new substantively: employers would decide what enterprise rights to grant, and nothing in this proposal would prevent an employer, if it discovered that a burdensome level of grievances was being filed relative to a certain enterprise right, from rewriting, altering, or even abolishing that right. All the arbitration system would do is ensure that employers' adherence to their promises would become predictable and routine.

Second, the requirement that each side pay half of the costs of arbitration would serve to filter out frivolous cases because employees would know that such claims would be costly. As a middle ground between company complaint systems and the courts, an arbitration system ought to have a price of entry that is also middling—that is, between the zero price (in dollars, at least) of the company review and the hundreds or thousands of dollars it costs to press a lawsuit. (There could in fact be several prices, depending on the nature of the complaint or extent of arbitration required.) This price would still permit easier access and quicker disposition than the courts, yet it would inhibit frivolous or mischievous complaints. Placing the burden of proof on the employee would likewise discourage frivolous cases.

Third, the experience elsewhere, although admittedly sparse and gained under various circumstances, suggests that a mass of frivolous cases is not likely to appear.[9]

Another employer concern is that there is not a sufficient number of trained arbitrators available to handle the expected caseload. Although the success of such a system would clearly depend upon the general quality of the arbitrators, there is no reason to believe that the current rosters of arbitrators cannot be expanded sufficiently over time to staff such a system. For one thing, as the authors of "To Strike a New Balance" point out, there are many trained arbitrators currently available who are not chosen only because they lack experience and therefore are not known.[10] At most, this objection would seem to require a careful phasing-in of the arbitration system, to keep the level of grievances consistent with the (presumably increasing) number of available arbitrators and therefore maintaining speedy disposition of cases. For example, the phase-in could begin with arbitration available only to employees in the largest enterprises, and then gradually extended to smaller firms.

A final employer concern is what has been termed the "narcotic effect"—that parties to a dispute, and especially employees, will come to depend on arbitration to settle their differences and therefore will be less willing to settle or reconcile their disputes before arbitration. Evidence from both field and experimental studies casts doubt on the existence of such an effect.[11] But this concern seems especially misplaced in the current proposal, because significant costs are imposed upon the employee to undertake a grievance. Indeed, this proposal moves some distance from the current mechanism (litigation) toward encouraging mediation, conciliation, and settlement even before arbitration.

On the other side, workers'-rights advocates may fear that arbitration is intrinsically too biased in favor of management to offer significant relief to workers. This concern exists on several levels. Most immediately, as noted by the authors of "To Strike a New Balance," this type of arbitration system places the arbitrator in a fundamentally different position from that of an arbitrator in the collective-bargaining context. In collective bargaining, arbitrators face two permanent institutions (firm and union) and know that if they are to be selected for arbitration again, they must to some extent satisfy both sides. Here, however, the arbitrator would face only one permanent institution (the firm), because a firm, especially a large firm, is likely to be involved in many future grievances, while the individual employee grievant is not. Hence the structural incentives toward balance in arbitral decisions would be greatly altered in management's favor. This is undoubtedly true, although offset to some extent by the employee's right to strike arbitrators' names; presumably arbitrators who gained a reputation for being consistently biased would also find themselves consistently struck from the rolls.

More penetrating criticisms have been leveled at the arbitration process by scholars who claim that arbitrators consistently, often unknowingly, or at least in an unexamined fashion, accept the presumptions and perspectives of management when making decisions.[12] (These studies all examine arbitration in the context of union contract disputes.) For example, James Gross and Patricia Greenfield studied arbitral judgments in health and safety disputes and concluded that

> the analysis of these published decisions . . . reveals that the management rights value judgment is dominant and that this value judgment clearly controls the appearance and use of another value judgment: the notion that a worker has a right to a safe and healthful workplace. [These] decisions

> read together constitute a classic illustration of how the acceptance of a certain value judgment determines a decision-maker's whole orientation when deciding an issue. . . . Where . . . a worker health and safety value judgment comes into conflict with management rights concepts of profit, property, authority, efficiency, cost-benefit analysis, technology or "progress," worker health and safety is relegated, at most, to a range of secondary considerations.[13]

James Atleson, who has provided perhaps the most comprehensive and profound analysis, notes, "Arbitrators have tended to confirm rather than challenge the assumption that employees have an obligation of fealty and deference to their supervisors and employers."[14]

Yet the question remains: arbitration is too biased toward management, *compared to what*? Is the legal system—with its vast deference to the laws of supply and demand and its high entry cost that effectively bars all workers but those most seriously aggrieved—less biased? Is having *no* external system, and therefore relying solely on thoroughly tame in-house complaint systems, better? The authors of "To Strike a New Balance" blandly appeal to the "integrity of most arbitrators who we believe will act in an impartial and unbiased manner."[15] The integrity of arbitrators would be an important ingredient, but other, more structural elements—rules for arbitrators, the growth of a case law, judicial oversight and review, and exposure of arbitrators' decisions to public scrutiny—would be needed as well.

An external, independent arbitration system for the limited class of rights disputes outlined above would greatly contribute to making these rights effective in practice. It would create a separate forum, removed from the intensities and conflicting interests of everyday work relations, in which to have grievances aired and speedily and inexpensively resolved. Undoubtedly access to the system would be highly unequal, with vulnerable workers fearing retaliation and poor workers inhibited by the cost; it is hard to envision any system that would not be susceptible to some of these defects. Moreover, many disputes, especially over wages and benefits, would remain outside this system's jurisdiction. Nonetheless, for many unorganized workers who today must rely on employers' promises backed up only by expensive and highly uncertain litigation, an arbitration system would be a big step forward.

Choosing Rights: The Employee's Handbook as Workers' Bill of Rights

The proposals discussed so far constitute important and reasonable lines of advance for a new workers'-rights regime. They are as much needed for more efficient *market* determination of workers' rights as they would be prerequisites for effective legal intervention to establish rights. However, these proposals do not address one crucial aspect of workers' rights, and therefore they do not incorporate all the desiderata for a new rights regime. As argued in chapter 3, workers' rights cannot be efficiently contracted for by individual workers because of the unequal bargaining status of most individual workers and their employers, the public-goods characteristics of workers' rights, and economies of scale in the provision of workers' rights. Thus, measures that simply enhance the efficiency of individual bargaining, though helpful in themselves, are inadequate to address the full problem of market failure with respect to workers' rights.

That workers' rights are an inappropriate topic for individual bargaining makes for an awkward impasse. The difficulty is that it is almost impossible to disentangle this issue of market efficiency from the political question of whether workers should have fewer or more rights. On one side, workers' advocates would simply add the inappropriateness of individual bargaining to other equity or political rationales as reasons for them to advance their rights agenda through unionism, collective bargaining, political action, and legislation. On the other side, conservatives, suspicious that any legal intervention will turn out to be simply a sub rosa method of advancing workers' distributive claims, tend to refuse to recognize that any market failure concerning workers' rights exists at all. Yet a market failure remains in both theory and practice; the following proposals are intended to address it.

The schema proposed herein, termed *Choosing Rights*, would provide a framework for incorporating all the desired elements (discussed in the last chapter) of a new workers'-rights regime. It would build upon the original premises, though not the institutions, of the National Labor Relations Act and its predecessors. Recall that a principal concern of legislators and the courts in setting or interpreting labor law was and remains the fundamental bargaining inequality between an employer and the individual worker. This concern led Congress in the 1930s to declare that encouraging collective bargaining was national policy. It led the courts, when collective bargaining withered in the 1980s, to reinterpret labor law and intervene to protect workers' rights. This effort included, most dramatically, the curbing of employers' prerogatives under the at-will doctrine (a process that continues today). *Choosing Rights* would address the problem of imbalance in a direct way. It would permit maximum scope for private-sector, voluntary action and for diverse local arrangements, yet it would also stimulate progress on rights.

The basic idea of *Choosing Rights* is simple. Every firm over a certain size would be required by law to promulgate and distribute to its workers an employee handbook. The handbook would state the work rights possessed by workers employed by that employer. The handbook would be recognized in law as a binding and enforceable employment contract. Employers could promulgate handbooks in one of two ways:

1. *The employer chooses and implements a standard handbook.* A specially chartered public-private employee rights commission would be charged with developing a set—ten or more—of standard handbooks. Each standard handbook would define a minimal level for workers' rights but contain a different mix of specific rights. For example, in the area of job security, one standard handbook might permit dismissal only for just cause, another maintain the employment-at-will doctrine but with substantial severance pay rights, and a third provide less job security but enhanced workers' rights to notification and "say" within the company. The employer would have the prerogative simply to elect whichever standard handbook it wished to have prevail in its workplace. It would certify its choice by registering it with the labor board designated to administer *Choosing Rights* (the National Labor Relations Board or a state labor commission).

2. *The employer writes its own handbook, which is promulgated when employees ratify it.* An employer could develop its own handbook, tailored to the specific circumstances of its industry, work-

force, location, and method of operations, and reflecting its own entrepreneurial preferences and decisions. There would be no restrictions placed upon the content of this handbook, and it could incorporate whatever rights, rules, variations, entrepreneurial preferences, provisions maintaining unique company personnel policies, or idiosyncracies the employer thought important. The handbook would be promulgated when it was ratified by the firm's workers as follows. The specially tailored handbook would be entered in an election alongside one of the standard handbooks, chosen by the employer. The firm's workers would then vote to adopt either the tailored handbook or the standard handbook. The election could be supervised by the NLRB, as is now the case with certification elections.

The employer's handbook would thus become the workers' bill of rights. *Choosing Rights* captures the principal virtues of collective bargaining and statutory mandate without suffering the limitations of either, and in so doing it embodies all the desiderata discussed in the last chapter. On the one hand, like collective bargaining, it would allow for virtually infinite variation in workers' rights, accommodating the vast diversity of the American workplace resulting from factors such as different management philosophies, industry types, markets, regional company customs, and levels of labor availability. It would foster creative local, private-sector solutions to specifically parochial circumstances. It would encourage each employer to develop and implement any set of workers' rights that fits its interests, so long as it could convince a majority of its workers that its system, in the firm's specific circumstances, was better than at least one of the standard handbooks.

On the other hand, *Choosing Rights* builds on the best in statutory mandating, because it is both permissive and stimulative. It permits wide variation and does not require employers (or workers) to adhere to unwieldy uniform national standards. It breaks with the assumption that national regulations can be written with sufficient wisdom and detail so as to apply appropriately to all work situations. But it is nonetheless stimulative, because it requires employers to do something, and guarantees workers a rights minimum. It uses the force of law to create processes whereby workers can obtain rights, as does the National Labor Relations Act, but it does not narrowly circumscribe the choices of either employers or workers.

This model would permit the development of workers' rights to draw most closely on actual practice in today's workplaces, as codified in employers' current handbooks. One can imagine employers strengthening the workers'-rights provisions in their current handbooks to prepare for an election; is it too utopian to suggest that an employer might work cooperatively with its workers to develop a set of rules with which each can live? The employer always has the "out" of unilaterally imposing a standard handbook; the workers are empowered by knowing that the employer must choose something.

The standard handbooks would aim, not at comprehensiveness or at mandating ideal work conditions, but rather at providing an acceptable minimum of workplace rights and protections for workers. In this manner the standard handbooks would serve as the mechanism for resolving the market failure based on the inappropriateness of individual bargaining over workers' rights, and so appropriately they are aimed at implementing minimal standards. Nothing in the law should restrain employers from offering, and presumably market competition among employers would encourage them to offer, more expansive rights than contained in the standard handbooks. Indeed, the review of enterprise rights in chapter 6 indicates that many already do so.

An essential element in constructing the standard handbooks would be creating diversity in the mix of rights across different handbooks. Handbooks would need to cover perhaps five major areas of workers' rights, clearly stating within each category what rights, if any, were provided: (a) complaint and grievance rights; (b) rights involving the procedures and nature of discipline; (c) job security, including procedures and permissible reasons for dismissal; (d) rights concerning promotion, career advancement, training, and growth; and (e) rights concerning eligibility for insurance, pensions, leave, and other benefits. Within each of these categories, substantial variation is possible not only in the "amount" of rights but, more relevant here, in the types and content of the rights. The standard handbooks would aim at providing a package of rights such that the "total amount" of rights would be equal across standard handbooks, while the composition or mix of rights within each would vary greatly. It is not necessary nor even desirable that the rights *within* each category be equal between standard handbooks; indeed, they should be unequal to provide greater diversity. However, each total package would offer a comparable level of rights or degree of protection across standard handbooks. It is this diversity in the mix of rights that would permit employers to choose a rights package best suited to the particular circumstances of the firm.

Thus for example in the category of complaint and grievance rights, the variation currently existing in employers' handbooks could be used to construct standard handbooks with comparable diversity. As was shown in chapter 6, this variation included the right to appeal to several higher levels of the supervisory staff, the right to outside arbitration, the right to review by a special management grievance committee, and the right to a hearing and a binding decision by a joint employee-management grievance committee. Similarly, the standard handbooks could provide great diversity by building upon the provisions currently existing in employer handbooks on disciplinary procedures, job security, promotion and training, and benefits.

The standard handbooks might themselves be attractive to many employers. Employers would find that the provisions were similar to ones now in common use by many employers. Employers would incur no costs of developing the new personnel policies, and if the standard handbooks were printed at public expense, employers would not even have to pay for printing or distributing them. Moreover, because standard handbooks in use elsewhere would be the basis for a growing arbitral case law, an employer could benefit from their relatively routinized interpretation and enforcement by achieving a certain predictability and stability in labor relations based on them.[16]

Nonetheless, many employers presumably would choose to develop their own tailored handbooks, and their efforts should be facilitated, not discouraged. Current handbooks already offer models, and these could be revised to make them as attractive as possible to workers while still retaining features employers consider crucial to effective operations. Indeed, even if an employer failed to convince its employees of the merits of its tailored handbook and thus lost the ratification election, the worst it would suffer would be imposition of that handbook which, of all the standard handbooks, it would otherwise have chosen anyway.

Thus, it might be presumed that many, perhaps most, employers would seek to have their own handbooks ratified. This is a great strength of *Choosing Rights*, because it means that employers who found that in their own particular circumstances a standard handbook would be overly burdensome would have the incentive to develop an innovative way to accommodate workers' rights to these firms' special circumstances. The employer would be stimulated to develop a set of rights superior in the workers' eyes to a standard handbook yet less costly or disruptive to the firm's operations, as judged by management. Such innovative voluntary activity is exactly what is needed to reduce the regulatory deadweight loss often associated with the imposition of uniform national standards or similar regulations.

The very smallest firms (perhaps those with fewer than twenty employees) should be exempted entirely from the requirements of *Choosing Rights*. (They could of course participate voluntarily.) Although a significant proportion—perhaps as many as a quarter—of all private-sector employees work in such firms, and often such workers are in great need of rights protection, so also the real burden of regulation on such employers is often very great.[17] Moreover, the difficulty and costs (political and moral as well as financial) of enforcement also grow large in very small firms. In such enterprises, family members often constitute a significant segment of the staff, and externally guaranteed rights may be both infeasible in practice and inappropriate. Finally, if rights are guaranteed in the remaining three-quarters of private-sector jobs, market competition will give workers in small enterprises improved opportunities to exit their current jobs and take up positions in firms covered by *Choosing Rights*. Indeed, many smaller employers would undoubtedly elect to participate in *Choosing Rights* as a recruiting strategy.

One of the standard handbooks would be designated as the default option: its provisions would automatically become effective for recalcitrant employers who, after an ample period for selecting handbooks under the two methods described earlier, nonetheless failed or refused to do so.

There would need to be provision in *Choosing Rights* for changing or revising handbooks already established or in force. An employer might wish to change the provisions of a tailored handbook, switch to a standard handbook, or switch from one standard handbook to another. There seems to be little reason to prevent such changes, the main objection being that workers employed by the firm may have taken up or continued employment with it because it offered the particular package of rights they preferred. (Under present laws, the employee has almost no protection from unilateral employer-imposed changes.) This objection could be met, first, by requiring that alterations in tailored handbooks be submitted to the worker-ratification process; and second, by restricting the number of times an employer could switch to or among standard handbooks to, perhaps, once every three years.

Disputes concerning handbook-derived rights would be settled through currently existing mechanisms supplemented by an arbitration-based system like that outlined in the previous section of this chapter. First, all employers would have an incentive to augment and improve their own internal complaint or grievance mechanisms to forestall formal disputes and resolve conflicts at the informal, internal level. Employers would have a further incentive to establish formal arbitration mechanisms that would meet the standards (outlined in the previous section) for employer systems to which the national arbitration system would defer. Thus the first element in conflict resolution would be the reform and strengthening of those local, diverse, and voluntary company-based processes.

Second, conflicts could be resolved through mediation. The proposed arbitration system, like arbitration in collective bargaining, is aimed at preventive or, more accurately, *in medias res* remediation, rather than post hoc identification of blame and award of damages. A sensible support for this goal would be to require mediation before arbitration. This is a substitute, albeit a poor one but the best available, for the extensive and continuous informal mediation carried on by local union officials to resolve routine conflicts at the lowest, most informal levels—efforts to represent workers' complaints to managers through discussion, implicit bargaining, worker counseling, and other informal conflict resolution. (This same activity is carried on in a watered-down form in non-union firms by employer complaint systems.)

Finally, disputes over rights might be resolved through arbitration or, as a last resort, through litigation. As proposed, arbitration would not be without cost to the worker, and therefore presumably only the most important disputes, and those for which the worker felt there was a good evidentiary base, would go to arbitration. However, the availability of external arbitration would immediately offer workers a forum to air grievances and obtain redress of serious violations of their rights. Moreover, by its example arbitration would undoubtedly deter other egregious violations of rights by employers.

These four proposals, if implemented, would begin to move industrial relations toward a new common ground where the legitimate aspirations of workers for fair dealing and rights at their workplaces need not interfere with, and indeed can contribute positively to, employers' competitive needs for flexibility and responsiveness. In this new place, unions would likely find new roles for themselves and fertile new opportunities for representing the interests of workers. Also, employers might find new possibilities for mobilizing and unleashing the talents and enthusiasms of their workers in pursuit of shared goals. Most important, workers themselves would find new ways of ensuring that their work lives could proceed with fairness and dignity.

Notes to Chapter 9

1. This proposal may be measured against the three criteria that I derived earlier for the effective use of statutory mandate. The first criterion (explicit statement) seems satisfied, so long as an acceptable definition of a handbook, such as that given above, can be adduced; the employer's obligations under the law can be clearly stated. The second criterion (an effective system for detecting violations) also seems easily satisfied: either an employer files a handbook and is certified as being in compliance, or not; a definite identifiable employer action is required. The third criterion (an available mechanism for enforcement) is also apparently satisfied directly: any employer who failed to file a handbook for certification would be presumed to have elected a standard handbook by default. Thus the new requirement itself would readily meet my three criteria.
2. Montana Code Ann. @ 39-2-504(3) (1987).
3. James N. Dertouzos, Elaine Holland, and Patricia Ebener (1988), table 16.
4. This section depends heavily on the arbitration system proposed in William R. Gould and others (1984). See also John R. Allison (1990); David W. Ewing (1989). See also Joseph Herman, "Arbitrate, Don't Litigate, at Work," *New York Times*, April 14, 1991, p. F11.
5. For example, a system could be used whereby first a list with an odd number (n) of arbitrators would be supplied, and then each side would be able, alternately, to strike one name from the list until only one was left. Only as a last resort would an arbitrator be supplied by the labor board.

6. See D. Keith Denton and Charles Boyd (1990); David W. Ewing (1989), especially case studies of Polaroid and Northrop.

7. William B. Gould and others (1984, p. 22) specify these conditions for "significant employee involvement" as:

> (1) employees should be permitted to be represented at any stage of the procedure by anyone they choose, including non-employees, union representatives, or lawyers in a hearing procedure which permits full examination and cross examination of witnesses and presentation of testimony including exhibits and other relevant materials;
>
> (2) employees, as well as the employer, must determine the selection of arbitrators through procedures such as those provided for by the American Arbitration Association or other panels normally utilized by unions and employers in labor arbitration cases;
>
> (3) all costs of the procedures, insofar as arbitration itself is concerned, should be shared equally by the employee and employer;
>
> (4) the arbitrator must be authorized to fashion remedies at least as beneficial to employees as those provided by statute.

See also the discussion in Joseph Herman, "Arbitrate, Don't Litigate, at Work," *New York Times*, April 14, 1991, p. F11.

7. Many of these issues are addressed, though in a slightly different context, in William B. Gould and others (1984).

8. Werner Blenk (1989). This volume is a collection of papers from the Second Meeting of European Labour Court Judges, and the papers cover both the internal organization and functioning of labor courts and the handling of disputes concerning termination of employment.

9. See William B. Gould and others (1984), p. 10 and note 18; G. England (1982).

10. William B. Gould and others (1984), p. 10.

11. See, for instance, Janet Currie and Henry S. Farber (1992), and the literature cited therein.

12. James A. Gross (1967), for example, examined arbitrators' decisions involving subcontracting and out-of-unit transfers of work; he found that the arbitrators assume that efficiency is one of the most important and fundamental rights of management and that pursuit of efficiency creates a presumptive right to subcontract. Katherine Van Wezel Stone (1981), p. 1565, writing in the *Yale Law Review*, is even harsher: "Arbitration [is not] a judicial process of law application. It becomes an element in the existing conflicts between management and the union. . . . By intervening to preserve order, arbitrators are not only nonneutral, they are acting consistently on the side of management." James A. Gross and Patricia A. Greenfield (1986, p. 688) simply note that "arbitration has become part of an industrial relations system that has as its aim the maintenance of managerial control over all aspects of an enterprise." For other discussions of arbitration, see Paul Weiler (1984), pp. 377–80; and the essays in Joseph M. Weiler (1981).

13. James A. Gross and Patricia A. Greenfield (1986), pp. 684–85.

14. James B. Atleson (1983), p. 213, note 34.

15. William B. Gould and others (1984), p. 10.

16. An analogy may be helpful: when the teachers' insurance program (TIAA) was created, it was possible for prospective professors to learn much about a possible position simply by inquiring if the employing college or university belonged to the TIAA. Soon it became virtually a prerequisite for such institutions, especially private-sector ones, to belong to TIAA, because of their inability otherwise to attract the best candidates and because of internal pressure from their own teachers.

17. In 1988, 23,582,752 persons, or 26.8 percent of nongovernment, nonrailroad employees (of whom there were 87,881,632) were employed in establishments with fewer than twenty employees; calculated from U.S. Bureau of the Census (1990), table 1b. "Establishment" is defined as a single location at which business is conducted. An enterprise (firm, company, corporation) may operate many establishments, so 26.8 percent is an upper bound on the proportion of employees in enterprises of fewer than twenty employees; the true figure may be considerably less than the "one-quarter" cited in the text.

Appendix: State Recognition of Implied Contracts[a]

State	Implied contract? (with controlling case)	Further case that extends, follows or reverses
Alabama	Yes	Extend
	Hoffman-LaRoche Inc. v. *Campbell*, 512 So. 2d 725 (Ala. 1987)	*Atkinson* v. *Long*, 559 So. 2d. 55 (Ala. Civ. App. 1990)
Alaska	Yes	Follow
	Eales v. *Tanana Valley Medical-Surgical Group, Inc.*, 663 P.2d 958 (Alaska 1983)	*Rutledge* v. *Aleyeska Pipeline*, 727 P.2d. 1050 (Alaska 1986)
Arizona	Yes	Follow
	Leikvold v. *Valley View Community Hosp.*, 141 Ariz. 544, 688 P.2d 170 (1984)	*Loffa* v. *Intel Corp.*, 738 P.2d. 1150 (Ariz. App. 1987)
Arkansas	Yes	Follow
	Gladden v. *Arkansas Children's Hosp.*, 292 Ark. 130, 728 S.W. 2d 501 (1987)	*Brewer* v. *Parkman*, 918 F.2d. 1336 (8th Cir. 1990)

State	Implied contract? (with controlling case)	Further case that extends, follows, or reverses
California	Yes	Follow
	Pugh v. *See's Candies Inc.*, 116 Cal. App.3d 311, 171 Cal. Rptr. 917 (Cal. 1981)	*Kern* v. *Levolor Lorentzen, Inc.* (9th Cir.) 899 F.2d 772
Colorado	Yes	Extend
	Continental Air Lines v. *Keenan*, 731 P. 2d 708 (Colo. 1987)	*Tuttle* v. *A & R Freight System, Inc.*, 797 P.2d. 1336 (Colo. 1990)
Connecticut	Yes	Follow
	Finley v. *Aetna Life Cas. Co.*, 202 Conn. 190, 520 A.2d 208 (1987)	*Heller* v. *Champion International Corp.*, 891 F.2d. 432 (2nd. Cir. 1989)
Delaware	No	Narrow Exception
	Heideck v. *Kent Gen. Hosp.*, 446 A.2d 1095 (Del. 1982)	*Heller* v. *Dover Warehouse Market, Inc.*, 515 A.2d. 178 (Del. Super. 1986)
Florida	No	Narrow Exception
	Muller v. *Stromberg Carlson Corp.*, 427 So.266 (Fla. Dist. Ct. App. (1983)	*Vienneau* v. *Metropolitan Life Ins. Co.*, 548 S. 2d 856 (Fla. App. 4 Dist. 1989)
Georgia	No	Follow
	Garmon v. *Health Group of Atlanta, Inc.*, 183 Ga. App. 587, 359 S.E.2d 450 (1987)	*Wofford* v. *Glynn Brunswick Memorial Hosp.*, 864 F.2d. 117 (11th Cir. 1989)
Hawaii	Yes	Follow
	Kinoshita v. *Canadian Pac. Airlines*, 724 p.2d 110 (Hawaii 1986)	*Leong* v. *Hilton Hotels Corp.*, 698 F.S. 1496 (D. Hawaii 1988)

State	Implied contract? (with controlling case)	Further case that extends, follows, or reverses
Idaho	Yes	Extended
	Harkness v. *City of Burley*, 110 Idaho 353, 715 P.2d 1283 (1986)	*Metcalf* v. *Intermountain Gas Co.*, 764 P.2d. 744 (1989)
Illinois	Yes	Extended
	Duldulao v. *Saint Mary of Nazareth Hosp. Center*, 505 N.E.2d 314 (Ill. 1987)	*Perman* v. *Arcventures*, 196 Ill. App. 3d 758, 554 N.E. 2d 982 (1990).
Indiana	Yes	Partial Follow
	Romack v. *Public Service Co.*, 511 N.E.2d 1024 (Ind. 1987)	*Gries* v. *Zimer, Inc.*, 709 F.S. 1374 (W.D. N.C. 1989)
Iowa	Yes	Significant Retrenchment
	Cannon v. *National By-Prods., Inc.*, 422 N.W.2d 638 (Iowa 1988)	*Fogel* v. *Trustees of Iowa College*, 446 N.W. 2d. 541 (Iowa 1989)
Kansas	Yes	Follow
	Morriss v. *Coleman*, 241 Kan. 501, 738 P.2d 841 (1987)	*Greenlee* v. *Board of Co., County Commissioners of Clay County*, 740 P.2d. 606 (Kan. 1987)
Kentucky	No	Previous Controlling Case
	Nork v. *Fetter Printing Co.*, 738 S.W. 2d. 824 (Ky. App. 1987)	*Shah* v. *American Synthetic Rubber Corp.*, 655 S.W.2d. 489 (Ky. 1983)
Louisiana	Unresolved	. . .
Maine	Yes	Follow
	Larrabee v. *Penobscott Frozen Foods, Inc.*, 486 A.2d 97 (Me. 1984)	*DeSalle* v. *Key Bank of So. Maine*, 685 F.S. 282 (D. Me. 1988)

State	Implied contract? (with controlling case)	Further case that extends, follows, or reverses
Maryland	Yes	Follow
	Staggs v. *Blue Cross*, 61 Md., App. 381, 486 A.2d 798 (1985)	*MacGill* v. *Blue Cross*, 77 Md. App. 613, 551 A.2d 501 (1989)
Massachusetts	Yes	Follow
	Garrity v. *Valley View Nuring Homes, Inc.*, 10 Mass. App. Ct. 423 406 N.E.2d 423 (1980)	*Hobson* v. *Mclean Hosp.*, 522 N.E. 2d 975 (Mass. 1988)
Michigan	Yes	Follow
	Toussaint v. *Blue Cross & Blue Shield*, 408 Mich. 579, 292 N.W.2d 880 (1980)	*Schippers* v. *SPX Corp.*, 465 N.W. 2d 34 (Mich. App. 1990)
Minnesota	Yes	Follow
	Pine River State Bank v. *Mettille*, 333 N.W.2d 622 (Minn. 1983)	*Piekarski* v. *Home Owners Savings Bank*, FSB, 752 F.S. 1451 (D. Minn. 1990)
Mississippi	Yes	Follow
	Robinson v. *Board of Trustees of E. Cent. Junior College*, 447 So.2d 1352 (Miss. 1985)	*Hoffman* v. *Board of Trustees of Eastern Mississippi Junior College*, 567 So.2d 838 (Miss. 1990)
Missouri	No	Follow
	Johnson v. *McDonnell Douglas Corp.*, 745 S.W.2d 661 (Mo. 1988)	*Duncan* v. *Creve Coeur Fire Protection Dept.*, 802 S.W. 2d 205 (Mo. App. 1991)
Montana	Yes	. . .
	Montana Code Ann. @ 39-2-504(3) (1987)	. . .

State	Implied contract? (with controlling case)	Further case that extends, follows, or reverses
Nebraska	Yes	Follow
	Johnston v. *Panhandle Coop. Ass'n.*, 225 Neb. 732, 408 N.W.2d 261 (1987)	*Goodlett* v. *Blue Cross and Blue Shield*, 449 N.W. 2d 9 (Neb. 1989)
Nevada	Yes	Follow
	Southwest Gas Corp. v. *Ahmad*, 99 Nev. 594, 668 P.2d 261 (1983)	*Cordova* v. *Harrah's Reno Hotel-Casino*, 707 F.S. 443 (D. Nev. 1988)
New Hampshire	Unresolved	. . .
New Jersey	Yes	Follow
	Woolley v. *Hoffman-La Roche, Inc.*, 99 N.J. 284, 491 A.2d 1257 (1985)	*Preston* v. *Claridge Hotel and Casino, LTD.*, 231 N.J. Super. 81, 555 A.2d 12 (App. Div. 1989)
New Mexico	Yes	Follow
	Forrester v. *Parker*, 93 N.M. 781, 606 P.2d 191 (1980)	*Newberry* v. *Allied Stores, Inc.*, 773 P.2d 1231 (N.M. 1989)
New York	Yes	Follow
	Weiner v. *McGraw-Hill, Inc.*, 57 N.Y.2d 458, 443 N.E.2d 441, 457 N.Y.S.2d 193 (1982)	*DiCocco* v. *Capital Area Community Health Plan, Inc.*, 559 N.Y.S. 2d 395 (A.D. 3 Dept. 1990)
North Carolina	No	Follow
	Harris v. *Duke Power Co.*, 319 N.C. 627, 356 S.E.2d 357 (1987)	*Rucker* v. *First Union National Bank*, 98 N.C. App. 100, 389 S.E.2d 622 (1990)

State	Implied contract? (with controlling case)	Further case that extends, follows, or reverses
North Dakota	Yes	Extend
	Hammond v. *North Dakota State Personnel Bd.*, 345 N.W.2d 359 (N.D. 1984)	*Sadler* v. *Basin Electric*, 409 N.W. 2d. 87 (N.D. 1987)
Ohio	Yes	Follow
	Mers v. *Dispatch Printing Co.*, 19 Ohio St.3d 150, 483 N.E.2d 150 (1985)	*Helmick* v. *Cincinnatı Word Processing, Inc.*, 45 Ohio St. 3rd 131 (1989)
Oklahoma	Yes	Follow
	Langdon v. *Saga Corp.*, 569 P.2d 524 (Okla. Ct.App. 1976)	*Grayson* v. *American Airlines, Inc.*, 803 F.2d 1097 (10th Cir. 1986)
Oregon	Yes	Follow
	Yartzoff v. *Democratic-Herald Publishing Co.*, 281 Or.651, 576 P.2d 356 (1978)	*Fox* v. *Bear Creek Corp.*, 99 Or. App. 328, 781 P.2d 378 (1989)
Pennsylvania	Yes	Follow
	DiBonaventura v. *Consolidated Rail Corp.*, 372 Pa.Super. 420, 539 A.2d 865 (1988)	*Ramsbottom* v. *First Pennsylvania Bank, NA*, 718 F.S. 405 (D. N.J. 1989)
Rhode Island	Unresolved	. . .
	Roy v. *Woonsocket Inst. for Sav.*, 525 A.2d 915 (R.I. 1987)	. . .
South Carolina	Yes	Follow
	Small v. *Spring Indus. Inc.*, 292 S.C. 481, 357 S.E.2d 452 (1987)	*Toth* v. *Square D Co.*, 712 F. Supp. 1231 (D.S.C. 1989)

State	Implied contract? (with controlling case)	Further case that extends, follows, or reverses
South Dakota	Yes	Extend
	Osterkamp v. *Alkota Mfg., Inc.*, 332 N.W.2d 275 (S.D. 1983)	*Larson* v. *Kreisers, Inc.*, 427 N.W.2d 833 (S.D. 1988)
Tennessee	Yes	Follow
	Hanby v. *Genesco, Inc.*, 627 S.W.2d 373 (Tenn. Ct. App. 1981)	*William* v. *Maremont Corp.*, 776 S.W. 2d 78 (Tenn. App. 1988)
Texas	Yes	Follow
	Aiello v. *United Air Lines*, 818 F.2d 1196 (Cir. 1987)	*Hicks* v. *Baylor University Medical Center*, 789 S.W. 2d 299 (Tex. App.-Dallas 1990)
Utah	Yes	Follow
	Piacitelli v. *Southern Utah State College*, 636 P.2d 1063 (Utah 1981)	*Brown* v. *Ford, Bacon & Davis, Utah, Inc.*, 850 F.2d 631 (10th Cir. 1988)
Vermont	Yes	Follow
	Sherman v. *Rutland Hosp., Inc.*, 146 Vt. 204, 500 A.2d 230 (1985)	*Benoir* v. *Ethan Allen, Inc.*, 147 Vt. 268, 514 A.2d 716 (1986)
Virginia	Yes	Follow
	Thompson v. *American Motor Inns, Inc.*, 623 F.Supp. 409 (W.D. Va. 1985)	*Seabolt* v. *Westmoreland Coal Co.*, 730 F.S. 1235 (1989)
Washington	Yes	Follow
	Thompson v. *St. Regis Co.*, 102 Wash. 2d 219, 685 P.2d 1081 (1984)	*Stewart* v. *Chevron Paper Chemical Co.*, 111 Wn. 2d 609, 762 P.2d 1143 (1988)

State	Implied contract? (with controlling case)	Further case that extends, follows, or reverses
West Virginia	Yes	Follow
	Cook v. *Heck's Inc.*, 342 S.E.2d 453 (W. Va. 1986)	*Twigg* v. *Hercules Corp.*, Supreme Court no. 19501
Wisconsin	Yes	Follow
	Ferraro v. *Koelsch*, 124 Wis. 2d 154, 368 N.W. 2d 666 (1985)	*Shaver* v. *F. W. Woolworth Co.*, 84 F.2d 1361 (7th Cir. 1988)
Wyoming	Yes	Follow
	Mobil Coal Producing, Inc. v. *Parks*, 704 P.2d 702 (Wyo. 1985)	*Griess* v. *Consolidated Freightways*, 776 P.2d. 752
Totals Yes	41	
No	6	
Unresolved	3	

Sources: Constructed by author based on William B. Gould IV (1986b), Michael Chagares (1989), and substantial assistance from counsel for the listed cases in each state. See also James Dertouzos and Lynn Karoly (1992), table A.1.

a. "Extends" means the cited case adopts the basic argument of the controlling case but carries it further, for example applying it to novel circumstances. "Follows" means the cited case accepts the logic of the controlling case. "Reverses" means the cited case rejects the argument of the controlling case. "Narrow exception" means the cited case rejects some particular element of the controlling case's argument but accepts the overall argumentation.

References

Abowd, John, and Henry S. Farber. 1990. "Product Market Competition, Union Organizing Activity, and Employer Resistance." National Bureau of Economic Research paper 3353.

Adler, Mortimer J., ed. 1952. *The Great Ideas: A Synopticon of Great Books of the Western World*, vol. I. Chicago: Encyclopaedia Britannica.

Aghion, Philippe, and Benjamin Hermalin. 1990. "Legal Restrictions on Private Contracts Can Enhance Efficiency." *Journal of Law, Economics, and Organization*, vol. 6 (Fall), pp. 381–409.

Akerlof, George A., and Janet L. Yellen, eds. 1986. *Efficiency Wage Models of the Labor Market*. Cambridge University Press.

Allen, Beth, and Costas Azariadis. 1988. "Informational Theories of Employment." *American Economic Review*, vol. 78 (May, *Papers and Proceedings, 1987)*, pp. 104–09.

Allison, John R. 1990. "Five Ways to Keep Disputes Out of Court." *Harvard Business Review*, vol. 68 (January–February), pp. 166–77.

American Federation of Labor–Congress of Industrial Organizations (AFL-CIO). 1987. "Executive Council Statement on the Employment-at-Will Doctrine." February 20. Bal Harbour, Florida.

———. 1985. "The Changing Situation of Workers and their Unions." AFL-CIO Committee on the Evolution of Work. February. Washington, D.C.

Argyris, Chris. 1965. *Organization and Innovation*. Homewood, Ill. R. D. Irwin.

Arrow, Kenneth J. 1973. "Social Responsibility and Economic Efficiency." *Public Policy*, vol. 21 (Summer), pp. 303–17.

Atleson, James B. 1983. *Values and Assumptions in American Labor Law*. University of Massachusetts Press.

Bacow, Lawrence S. 1980. *Bargaining for Job Safety and Health*. MIT Press.

Barkin, Solomon. 1961. *The Decline of the Labor Movement, and What Can Be Done about It*. Santa Barbara, Calif.: Center for the Study of Democratic Institutions.

Barnett, George E. 1933. "American Trade Unionism and Social Insurance." *American Economic Review*, vol. 23 (March), p. 6.

Berenbeim, Ronald. 1980. "Non-Union Complaint Systems: A Corporate Appraisal," report 770. The Conference Board.

Bergstrom, T. 1971. "On the Existence and Optimality of Competitive Equilibrium for a Slave Economy." *Review of Economic Studies*, vol. 38 (no. 113), pp. 23–36.

Black, Dan A., and Mark A. Loewenstein. 1991. "Self-Enforcing Labor Contracts with Costly Mobility." In Ronald Ehrenberg, ed., *Research in Labor Economics*, vol. 12, pp. 63–83.

Blades, Lawrence E. 1967. "Employment at Will vs. Individual Freedom: On Limiting the Abusive Exercise of Employer Power." *Columbia Law Review*, vol. 67, no. 8, pp. 1404–35.

Blenk, Werner, ed. 1989. *European Labour Courts: Current Issues*. Geneva, Switzerland: International Labour Office.

Bowles, Samuel. 1985. "The Production Process in a Competitive Economy: Walrasian, Neo-Hobbesian, and Marxian Models." *American Economic Review*, vol. 75 (March), pp. 16–36.

Bowles, Samuel, and Richard Edwards. 1985. *Understanding Capitalism*. Harper and Row. (revised edition, 1992.)

Bowles, Samuel, and Herbert Gintis. 1993. "Post-Walrasian Political Economy." In Samuel Bowles, Herbert Gintis, and Bo Gustafsson, eds., *The Microfoundations of Political Economy*. Cambridge University Press.

———. 1990. "Contested Exchange: New Microfoundations of the Political Economy of Capitalism." *Politics and Society*, vol. 18 (no. 2), pp. 165–222.

———. 1986. *Democracy and Capitalism: Property, Community, and the Contradictions of Modern Social Thought*. Basic Books.

Bowles, Samuel, Herbert Gintis, and Bo Gustafsson, eds. 1993. *The Microfoundations of Political Economy: Participation, Accountability, and Efficiency*. Cambridge University Press.

Bowles, Samuel, David M. Gordon, and Thomas E. Weisskopf. 1990. *After the Waste Land: A Democratic Economics for the Year 2000*. Armonk, N.Y.: M. E. Sharpe.

———. 1989. "Business Ascendancy and Economic Impasse: A Structural Retrospective on Conservative Economics, 1979–1987." *Journal of Economic Perspectives*, vol. 3 (Winter), pp. 107–34.

———. 1983. *Beyond the Waste Land: An Economic Alternative to Economic Decline*. Anchor Press/Doubleday.

Brown, Clair, and Michael Reich. 1989. "When Does Union-Management Cooperation Work? A Look at NUMMI and GM-Van Nuys." University of California, Berkeley, Institute of Industrial Relations.

Brubaker, William Rogers, ed. 1989. *Immigration and the Politics of Citizenship in Europe and North America*. Lanham, Md.: University Press of America.

Buchanan, James M., and Charles J. Goetz. 1972. "Efficiency Limits of Fiscal Mobility: An Assessment of the Tiebout Model." *Journal of Public Economics*, vol. 1, pp. 25–43.

Bureau of National Affairs. 1988a. "California Statistics for 1987 Suggest Stabilization in Plaintiff Awards." *Daily Labor Reporter*, no. 25 (February 8). In Ira Michael Shepard, Paul Heylman, and Robert L. Duston. 1989. *Without Just Cause: An Employer's Practical and Legal Guide on Wrongful Discharge*. Washington, D.C.: BNA.

———. 1988b. "Employee Handbooks Important Tool Despite Some Problems, Experts Say." *Employee Relations Weekly*, vol. 6, pp. 771–72.

Burtless, Gary, ed. 1990. *A Future of Lousy Jobs? The Changing Structure of U.S. Wages*. Brookings.

Calabresi, Guido. 1968. "Transaction Costs, Resource Allocation, and Liability Rules—A Comment." *Journal of Law and Economics*, vol. 11 (April), pp. 67–73.

Calamari, J., and J. Perillo. 1977. *The Law of Contracts*, 2d ed. St. Paul, Minn.: West Publishing.

Carolina Alliance for Fair Employment. 1987. *Basic Guide to Workers' Rights in South Carolina*. Greenville, S.C.

Chagares, Michael A. 1989. "Utilization of the Disclaimer as an Effective Means to Define the Employment Relationship." *Hofstra Law Review*, vol. 17 (Winter), pp. 365–405.

———. 1986. "Limiting the Employment-at-Will Rule: Enforcing Policy Manual Promises through Unilateral Contract Analysis." *Seton Hall Law Review*, vol. 16, no. 2, pp. 465–90.

Chelius, James Robert. 1977. *Workplace Safety and Health: The Role of Workers' Compensation*, AEI studies 174. Washington, D.C.: American Enterprise Institute.

Clark, John Maurice. 1939. *Social Control of Business*. McGraw-Hill.

Coase, Ronald. 1960. "The Problem of Social Cost." *Journal of Law and Economics*, pp. 1–44.

Coles, J. L., and Peter J. Hammond. 1986. "Walrasian Equilibrium without Survival: Existence, Efficiency, and Remedial Policy," Economics technical report 483. Stanford University Institute for Mathematical Studies in the Social Sciences.

Commerce Clearing House. 1985. *Employment at Will*. Commerce Clearing House.

Connerton, Marguerite, Richard B. Freeman, and James L. Medoff. 1983. "Industrial Relations and Productivity: A Study of the U.S. Bituminous Coal Industry." Harvard University.

Connolly, Walter B., Gary E. Murg, and Clifford Scharman. 1983. "Abrogating the Employment-at-Will Doctrine: Implications for Personnel Policies and Handbooks." *Preventive Law Reporter*, vol. 2 (December), pp. 53–60.

Cooke, William N., and Frederick H. Gautschi III. 1981. "OSHA, Plant Safety Programs, and Injury Reduction." *Industrial Relations*, vol. 20 (Fall), pp. 245–57.

Cooper, Lyle W. 1932. "The American Labor Movement in Prosperity and Depression." *American Economic Review*, vol. 22 (December), pp. 641–59.

Cooter, Robert. 1984. "Prices and Sanctions." *Columbia Law Review*, vol. 84, pp. 1523–60.

Currie, Janet, and Henry S. Farber. 1992. "Is Arbitration Addictive? Evidence from the Laboratory and the Field." Paper prepared for the meeting of the Industrial Relations Research Association, January.

Dahl, Robert Alan. 1985. *A Preface to Economic Democracy*. University of California Press.

Davis, Mike. 1980a. "Why the US Working Class is Different." *New Left Review*, no. 123, pp. 3–44.

———. 1980b. "The Barren Marriage of American Labour and the Democratic Party." *New Left Review*, no. 124, pp. 43–84.

Decker, Kurt H. 1983. "At-Will Employment in Pennsylvania—A Proposal for Its Abolition and Statutory Regulation." *Dickinson Law Review*, vol. 87 (Spring), pp. 477–506.

Denton, D. Keith, and Charles Boyd. 1990. *Employee Complaint Handling*. Quorum Books.

Dertouzos, James N., Elaine Holland, and Patricia Ebener. 1988. *The Legal and Economic Consequences of Wrongful Termination*. Santa Monica, Calif.: RAND.

Dertouzos, James N., and Lynn A. Karoly. 1992. *Labor-Market Responses to Employer Liability*. Santa Monica, Calif.: RAND.

Dertouzos, Michael L., Richard K. Lester, and Robert M. Solow. 1989. *Made in America: Regaining the Productive Edge*. MIT Press.

Dickens, William T., and Jonathan S. Leonard. 1985. "Accounting for the Decline in Union Membership, 1950–1980." *Industrial and Labor Relations Review*, vol. 38, no. 3 (April), pp. 323–34.

Doeringer, Peter B., and Michael J. Piore. 1971. *Internal Labor Markets and Manpower Analysis*. Lexington, Mass.: D.C. Heath.

Drucker, Peter F. 1990. "The Emerging Theory of Manufacturing." *Harvard Business Review*, vol. 68 (May–June), pp. 94–102.

Duncan, Greg J., and Frank P. Stafford. 1980. "Do Union Members Receive Compensating Wage Differentials?" *American Economic Review*, vol. 70 (June), pp. 355–79.

Dunlop, John Thomas. 1982. "Are the Unions Dead, or Just Sleeping?" *Fortune*, September 20, pp. 99–112.

———. 1958. *Industrial Relations Systems*. Holt.

Dworkin, Ronald. 1977. *Taking Rights Seriously*. Harvard University Press.

Edel, Matthew, and Elliott Sclar. 1974. "Taxes, Spending, and Property Values: Supply Adjustment in a Tiebout-Oates Model." *Journal of Political Economy*, vol. 82 (September–October), pp. 941–54.

Edwards, Richard. 1979. *Contested Terrain: The Transformation of the Workplace in the Twentieth Century*. Basic Books.

Edwards, Richard, and Paolo Garonna. 1991. *The Forgotten Link: Labor's Stake in International Economic Cooperation*. Savage, Md.: Rowman and Littlefield.

Edwards, Richard, and Michael Podgursky. 1986. "The Unraveling Accord: American Unions in Crisis." In Richard Edwards, Paolo Garonna, and Franz Tödtling, *Unions in Crisis and Beyond: Perspectives from Six Countries*. Dover, Mass.: Auburn House.

Ehrenberg, Ronald G. 1986. "Workers' Rights: Rethinking Protective Labor Legislation." In Ronald Ehrenberg, ed., *Research in Labor Economics*, vol. 8, pt. B. Greenwich, Conn.: JAI Press.

Ehrenberg, Ronald G., and George Jakubson. 1990. "Why WARN? Plant Closing Legislation." *Regulation* (Summer), pp. 39–46.

Ehrenberg, Ronald G., and Paul L. Schumann. 1984. "Compensating Wage Differentials for Mandatory Overtime?" *Economic Inquiry*, vol. 22 (October), pp. 460–77.

———. 1982. *Longer Hours or More Jobs? An Investigation of Amending Hours Legislation to Create Employment*. Ithaca, N.Y.: ILR Press.

Ehrenberg, Ronald G., and Robert S. Smith. 1985. *Modern Labor Economics: Theory and Public Policy*, 2d ed. Glenview, Ill.: Scott, Foresman.

England, G. 1982. "Unjust Dismissal in the Federal Jurisdiction: The First Three Years." *Manitoba Law Journal*, vol. 12, pp. 9–30.

Engler, Rick. 1984. *A Job Safety and Health Bill of Rights*. Philadelphia: Philaposh.

Epstein, Richard A. 1984. "In Defense of the Contract at Will." *University of Chicago Law Review*, vol. 51, no. 4, pp. 947–82.

Ewing, David W. 1989. *Justice on the Job: Resolving Grievances in the Nonunion Workplace*. Harvard Business School Press.

Farber, Henry S. 1990. "The Decline of Unionization in the United States: What Can Be Learned from Recent Experience?" *Journal of Labor Economics*, vol. 8, no. 1, pt. 2, pp. S75–S105.

———. 1985. "The Extent of Unionization in the United States." In T. A. Kochan, ed., *Challenges and Choices Facing American Labor*. MIT Press.

Farley, Reynolds. 1984. *Blacks and Whites: Narrowing the Gap?* Harvard University Press.

Farrell, Joseph. 1987. "Information and the Coase Theorem." *Journal of Economic Perspectives*, vol. 1 (Fall), pp. 113–29.

Feldman, Allan. 1980. *Welfare Economics and Social Choice Theory*. Boston: Martinus Nijhoff Publishing.

Flanagan, Robert J. 1987. *Labor Relations and the Litigation Explosion*. Brookings.

Foner, Philip S. 1947. *History of the Labor Movement in the United States from Colonial Times to the Founding of the American Federation of Labor*, vol. 1. International Publishers.

Freeman, Richard B. 1988. "Contraction and Expansion: The Divergence of Private Sector and Public Sector Unionism in the U.S." *Journal of Economic Perspectives*, vol. 2 (Spring), pp. 63–88.

Freeman, Richard B., and James L. Medoff. 1984. *What Do Unions Do?* Basic Books.

Friedman, Milton. 1962. *Capitalism and Freedom*. University of Chicago Press.

Galbraith, John Kenneth. 1973. *Economics and the Public Purpose*. Houghton Mifflin.

———. 1958. *The Affluent Society*. Houghton Mifflin.

Glendon, Mary Ann. 1991. *Rights Talk: The Impoverishment of Political Discourse*. Free Press.

Goldfield, Michael. 1987. *The Decline of Organized Labor in the United States*. University of Chicago Press.

Gould, William B. IV. 1986a. "The Idea of the Job as Property in Contemporary America: The Legal and Collective Bargaining Framework." *Brigham Young University Law Review*, vol. 1986, no. 4, pp. 885–918.

———. 1986b. *A Primer on American Labor Law*, 2d ed. MIT Press.

Gould, William B., and others. 1984. "To Strike a New Balance" (report of the Ad Hoc Committee on Termination at Will and Wrongful Discharge, the State Bar of California). *Labor and Employment Law News*. February 8.

Green, James R. 1978. *Grass-roots Socialism: Radical Movements in the Southwest, 1895–1943*. Louisiana State University Press.

Greenwald, Bruce C. 1986. "Adverse Selection in the Labour Market." *Review of Economic Studies*, vol. 53, pp.325–47.

Gross, James A. 1967. "Value Judgments in the Decisions of Labor Arbitrators." *Industrial and Labor Relations Review*, vol. 21 (October), pp. 55–72.

Gross, James A., and Patricia A. Greenfield. 1986. "Arbitral Value Judgments in Health and Safety Disputes: Management Rights over Workers' Rights." *Buffalo Law Review*, vol. 34, no. 3, pp. 645–91.

Guasch, J. Louis, and Andrew Weiss. 1981. "Self-Selection in the Labor Market." *American Economic Review*, vol. 71 (June), pp. 275–84.

Gutman, Herbert. 1973. "Work, Culture, and Society in Industrializing America, 1815–1919." *American Historical Review*, vol. 78 (June), pp. 531–88.

Hall, Robert E. 1982. "The Importance of Lifetime Jobs in the U.S. Economy." *American Economic Review*, vol. 72 (September), pp. 716–24.

Hammond, Peter J. 1990. "Theoretical Progress in Public Economics: A Provocative Assessment." *Oxford Economic Papers*, vol. 42, pp. 6–33.

Harris, Louis. 1989. "The Harris Poll (July 9)." Louis Harris and Associates, Inc., Information Services.

Hart, H. L. A. 1961. *The Concept of Law*. Oxford University Press.

Harvard Law Review, 1980. Vol. 93, p. 1816, note 93.

Head, John G. 1974. *Public Goods and Public Welfare*. Duke University Press.

Hill, Herbert. 1989. "Black Labor and Affirmative Action: An Historical Perspective." In Steven Shulman and William Darity, Jr., *The Question of Discrimination: Racial Inequality in the U.S. Labor Market*. Wesleyan University Press.

Hirschman, Albert. 1981. *Essays in Trespassing*. Cambridge University Press.

———. 1970. *Exit, Voice, and Loyalty: Responses to Decline in Firms, Organizations, and States*. Harvard University Press.

Jensen, Howard. n.d. *Unions and the Decline of Individual Rights*. New York: National Association of Manufacturers.

Kantor, Rosabeth. 1990. "How to Compete." *Harvard Business Review*, vol. 68 (July–August), pp. 7–8.

Kennedy, Duncan. 1982. "Distributive and Paternalist Motives in Contract and Tort Law, with Special Reference to Compulsory Terms and Unequal Bargaining Power." *Maryland Law Review*, vol. 41, no. 4, pp. 563–658.

———. 1981. "Cost-Benefit Analysis of Entitlement Problems: A Critique." *Stanford Law Review*, vol. 33 (February), pp. 387–445.

Kirkland, Lane. 1986. "It's All Been Said Before. . . ." In Seymour Lipset, *Unions in Transition*. San Francisco: Institute for Contemporary Studies Press.

Klein, Benjamin, and Keith B. Leffler. 1981. "The Role of Market Forces in Assuring Contractual Performance." *Journal of Political Economy*, vol. 89, no. 4, pp. 615–41.

Kochan, Thomas A. 1979. "How American Workers View Labor Unions." *Monthly Labor Review* (April), pp. 23–31.

———, ed. 1985. *Challenges and Choices Facing American Labor*. MIT Press.

Kochan, Thomas A., Harry C. Katz, and Robert B. McKersie. 1986. *The Transformation of American Industrial Relations*. Basic Books.

Laffont, Jean-Jacques. 1990. *The Economics of Uncertainty and Information*. MIT Press.

Lazear, Edward P. 1988. "Employment-at-Will, Job Security, and Work Incentives." In Robert A. Hart, ed., *Employment, Unemployment, and Labor Utilization*. Boston: Unwin Hyman.

Levine, David I. 1992. "Public Policy Implications of Imperfections in the Market for Worker Participation." *Economic and Industrial Democracy* (May).

———. 1991. "Just Cause Employment Policies in the Presence of Worker Adverse Selection." *Journal of Labor Economics*, vol. 9, no. 3, pp. 294–305.

———. 1989. "Just-Cause Employment Policies When Unemployment Is a Worker Discipline Device." *American Economic Review*, vol. 79 (September), pp. 902–05.

Levitan, Sar A., Peter E. Carlson, and Isaac Shapiro. 1986. *Protecting American Workers*. Washington, D.C.: Bureau of National Affairs.

Lipset, Seymour Martin, ed. 1986. *Unions in Transition: Entering the Second Century*. San Francisco: Institute for Contemporary Studies Press.

Logothetis, Sorrell. 1985. "An Analysis of Significant Recent Decisions of the National Labor Relations Board: An Organized Labor Perspective." *Capital University Law Review*, vol. 14 (Spring), pp. 327–63.

Lynd, Staughton. 1978. "Company Constitutionalism?" *Yale Law Journal*, vol. 87 (March), pp. 885–95.

MacCormick, Neil. 1982. *Legal Right and Social Democracy*. Oxford University Press.

Machan, Tibor R. 1987. "Human Rights, Workers' Rights, and the 'Right' to Occupational Safety." In Gertrude Ezorsky, *Moral Rights in the Workplace*. State University of New York Press.

MacLeod, W. Bentley, and James M. Malcomson. 1988. "Reputation and Hierarchy in Dynamic Models of Employment." *Journal of Political Economy*, vol. 96, no. 4, pp. 832–54.

MacNeil, Ian R. 1982. "Efficient Breach of Contract: Circles in the Sky." *Virginia Law Review*, vol. 68, p. 947.

McGregor, Douglas. 1960. *The Human Side of Enterprise*. McGraw-Hill.

McKersie, Robert, and Werner Sengenberger. 1983. *Job Losses in Major Industries: Manpower Strategy Responses*. Paris: OECD.

McWilliams, Kelly. 1986. "The Employment Handbook as a Contractual Limitation on the Employment At Will Doctrine." *Villanova Law Review*, vol. 31, pp. 335–75.

Magaziner, Ira C., and Robert B. Reich. 1982. *Minding America's Business: The Decline and Rise of the American Economy*. Harcourt Brace Jovanovich.

Marmor, Theodore R. 1973. *The Politics of Medicare*. Chicago: Aldine Publishing.

Marrinan, Susan. 1984. "Employment at-Will: Pandora's Box May Have an Attractive Cover." *Hamline Law Review*, vol. 7, no. 2, pp. 155–201.

Medoff, James L. 1987. "The Public's Image of Labor and Labor's Response." *Detroit College of Law Review*, vol. 1987 (Fall), pp. 609–36.

Mendeloff, John M. 1988. *The Dilemma of Toxic Substance Regulation: How Overregulation Causes Underregulation*. MIT Press.

———. 1979. *Regulating Safety: An Economic and Political Analysis of Occupational Safety and Health Policy*. MIT Press.

———. 1976. *An Evaluation of the OSHA Program's Effect on Workplace Injury Rates: Evidence from California through 1974*, report prepared for the U.S. Department of Labor. July.

Mitchell, Olivia S. 1990. "The Effects of Mandating Benefits Packages." In Ronald Ehrenberg, ed., *Research in Labor Economics*, vol. 11, pp. 297–320.

Montana Code. 1987. State of Montana Code Ann. @ 39-2-504(3), 7-1-1987.

Montgomery, David. 1979. *Workers' Control in America*. Cambridge University Press.

Morris, Richard B. 1965. *Government and Labor in Early America*. Harper and Row.

Musgrave, Richard, and Peggy B. Musgrave. 1973. *Public Finance in Theory and Practice*. McGraw-Hill.

National Conference of Catholic Bishops. 1986. *Economic Justice for All: Pastoral Letter on Catholic Social Teaching and the U.S. Economy*. Washington, D.C.: United States Catholic Conference.

National Labor Relations Board. Various dates. *Annual Report*. Washington, D.C.

National Safe Workplace Institute. 1990. "Beyond Neglect: The Problem of Occupational Disease in the U.S." Chicago.

———. 1987. "The Rising Wave: Death and Injury among High Risk Workers in the 1980s." Chicago.

Nelson, Daniel. 1975. *Managers and Workers: Origins of the New Factory System in the US, 1880–1920*. University of Wisconsin Press.

Nelson, Richard R. 1991. "State Labor Legislation Enacted in 1990." *Monthly Labor Review*, vol. 114 (January), pp. 41–56.

———. 1986. "Labor Legislation: 1984–85." *The Book of the States, 1986–87*. Lexington, Ky.: Council of State Governments.

Newman, Winn. 1976. "The Policy Issues: Presentation III." In Martha Blaxall and Barbara Reagan, eds., *Women and the Workplace*. University of Chicago Press.

Nichols, Albert L., and Richard Zeckhauser. 1977. "Government Comes to the Workplace: An Assessment of OSHA." *Public Interest*, no. 49 (Fall), pp. 39–69.

Nozick, Robert. 1974. *Anarchy, State, and Utopia*. Basic Books.

Okun, Arthur. 1975. *Equality and Efficiency: The Big Tradeoff*. Brookings.

Parker, Mike, and Jane Slaughter. 1988. *Choosing Sides: Unions and the Team Concept. A Labor Notes Book*. Boston: South End Press.

Parsons, Donald O. 1986. "The Employment Relationship: Job Attachment, Work Effort, and the Nature of Contracts." In Orley Ashenfelter and Richard Layard, eds., *Handbook of Labor Economics*. North-Holland Publishing.

Phlips, Louis. 1988. *The Economics of Imperfect Information*. Cambridge University Press.

Plato. 1952. *The Dialogues of Plato*. Translated by Benjamin Jowett in Robert Maynard Hutchins, ed., *Great Books of the Western World*, vol. 7. Chicago: Encyclopaedia Britannica.

Posner, Richard A. 1977. *Economic Analysis of Law*, 2d ed. Boston: Little Brown.

Prescott, Edward C., and Robert M. Townsend. 1984. "General Competitive Analysis in an Economy with Private Information." *International Economic Review*, vol. 25 (February), pp. 1–20.

Rawls, John. 1971. *A Theory of Justice*. Harvard University Press.

Rebitzer, James B. 1987. "Unemployment, Long-Term Employment Relations, and Productivity Growth." *Review of Economics and Statistics*, vol. 69 (November), pp. 627–35.

Reich, Michael. 1981. *Racial Inequality: A Political-Economic Analysis*. Princeton University Press.

Reich, Robert B. 1991. *The Work of Nations*. Random House.

Reid, Joseph D. ed. 1983. *New Approaches to Labor Unions*. Greenwich, Conn.: JAI Press.

Republican Platform. 1988. "An American Vision: For Our Children and Our Future." Committee on Resolutions to the Republican National Convention.

Republican Platform. 1992. "The Vision Shared: Uniting Our Family, Our Country, Our World." Republican National Committee.

Restatement of the Law Second Contracts 2d. 1981. Vol. 1, sec. 90, p. 242.

Reynolds, Morgan O. 1987. *Making America Poorer: The Cost of Labor Law*. Washington, D.C.: Cato Institute.

———. 1982. "Are the Unions Dead, or Just Sleeping?" *Fortune*, September 20, pp. 99–112.

Rosen, Sherwin, ed. 1981. *Studies in Labor Markets*. University of Chicago Press.

Samuelson, Paul A. 1954. "The Pure Theory of Public Expenditure." *Review of Economics and Statistics*, vol. 36 (November), pp. 387–89.

Samuelson, William. 1985. "Comments on the Coase Theorem." In Alvin E. Roth, ed., *Game Theoretic Models of Bargaining*. Cambridge University Press.

Schlossberg, Stephen I., and Steven M. Fetter. 1987. "U.S. Labor Law and the Future of Labor-Management Cooperation." *Labor Lawyer*, vol. 3 (Winter).

Schor, Juliet B. 1991. *The Overworked American*. Basic Books.

Schor, Juliet B., and Samuel Bowles. 1987. "Employment Rents and the Incidence of Strikes." *Review of Economics and Statistics*, vol. 69 (November), pp. 584–92.

Schumpeter, Joseph A. 1954. *History of Economic Analysis*. Oxford University Press.

Sellekaerts, Brigitte, and Stephen Welch. 1981. "Minimum Wage Non-compliance for Fully Subject Workers: 1973–1980." Report of the Minimum

Wage Study Commission, vol. 3, *Non-Compliance with the FLSA*. Government Printing Office.

Sexton, Patricia Cayo. 1982. *The New Nightingales: Hospital Workers, Unions, New Women's Issues*. Enquiry Press.

Shapiro, Carl, and Joseph E. Stiglitz. 1984. "Equilibrium Unemployment as a Worker Discipline Device." *American Economic Review*, vol. 74 (June), pp. 433–44.

Shepard, Ira Michael, Paul Heylman, and Robert L. Duston. 1989. *Without Just Cause: An Employer's Practical and Legal Guide on Wrongful Discharge*. Washington, D.C.: Bureau of National Affairs.

Simmons, John, and William Mares. 1983. *Working Together*. Alfred A. Knopf.

Smith, Adam. 1937. *The Wealth of Nations*. Modern Library. Originally published 1776.

Smith, Robert Stewart. 1976. *The Occupational Safety and Health Act: Its Goals and Achievements*. Washington, D.C.: AEI Publications.

———. 1979. "The Impact of OSHA Inspections on Manufacturing Injury Rates." *Journal of Human Resources*, vol. 14, no. 2, pp. 145–70.

Solow, Robert M. 1980. "On Theories of Unemployment." *American Economic Review*, vol. 70 (March), pp. 1–11.

Stiglitz, Joseph E. 1977. "The Theory of Local Public Goods." In Martin S. Feldstein and Robert P. Inman, eds., *The Economics of Public Services*. Halsted Press.

Stone, Katherine Van Wezel. 1981. "The Post-War Paradigm in American Labor Law." *Yale Law Journal*, vol. 90 (June), pp. 1509–80.

Summers, Lawrence H. 1989. "Some Simple Economics of Mandated Benefits." *American Economic Review*, vol. 79 (May 1988 *Papers and Proceedings*), pp. 177–83.

Sutton, John. 1986. "Non-Cooperative Bargaining Theory: An Introduction." *Review of Economic Studies*, vol. 53, pp. 709–24.

Taguchi, Genichi, and Don Clausing. 1990. "Robust Quality." *Harvard Business Review*, vol. 68 (January–February), pp. 65–69.

Thomas, Jonathan, and Tim Worrall. 1988. "Self-Enforcing Wage Contracts." *Review of Economic Studies*, vol. 55 (October), pp. 541–54.

Tiebout, Charles M. 1956. "A Pure Theory of Local Expenditures." *Journal of Political Economy*, vol. 64 (October), pp. 416–24.

de Tocqueville, Alexis. 1841. *Democracy in America*, 2 vols. New York: J. and H. G. Langley.

Treiman, Donald I., and Heidi I. Hartmann. 1981. *Women, Work, and Wages: Equal Pay for Jobs of Equal Value*. Washington, D.C.: National Academy Press.

Troy, Leo. 1986. "The Rise and Fall of American Trade Unions: The Labor Movement from FDR to RR." In Seymour Martin Lipset, *Unions in Transition*. San Francisco: ICS Press.

Troy, Leo, and Neil Sheflin. 1985. Union Sourcebook. West Orange, N.J.: Industrial Relations Data Information Services.

Tyler, Tom R. 1990. *Why People Obey the Law*. Yale University Press.

U.S. Bureau of the Census. 1990. *County Business Patterns, 1988*, CPB-88-01. Department of Commerce.

U.S. Commission on Civil Rights. 1982. *Nonreferral Unions and Equal Employment Opportunity*.

———. 1976. *The Challenge Ahead: Equal Opportunity in Referral Unions*, A Report of the United States Commission on Civil Rights.

U.S. Congress. House Committee on Education and Labor. 1986. *Oversight Hearings on Employee Benefit Plans*, Hearings before the Committee on Education and Labor. Government Printing Office.

U.S. Department of Labor. Various dates. *Employment and Earnings* (January issue).

U.S. Employment Standards Administration. Annual. *Minimum Wage and Maximum Hours Standards under the Fair Labor Standards Act*. Department of Labor.

U.S. General Accounting Office. 1993. *Dislocated Workers: Worker Adjustment, Retraining, and Notification Act Not Meeting Its Goals*, GAO/HRD-93-18.

———. Office. 1990. *Occupational Safety and Health: Options for Improving Safety and Health in the Workplace*, GAO/HRD-90-66BR.

———. 1985. *The Department of Labor's Enforcement of the Fair Labor Standards Act*, GAO/HRD-85-77.

———. 1981. *Changes Needed to Deter Violations of Fair Labor Standards Act*, HRD-81-60.

U.S. Minimum Wage Study Commission. 1981. *Report of the Minimum Wage Study Commission*, vol. 1: *Commission Findings and Recommendations*.

U.S. Statutes at Large. 1932. Norris-LaGuardia Act, vol. 47, pt. 1, p. 70.

Utgoff, Kathleeen P. 1990. "The Proliferation of Pension Regulation." *Regulation* (Summer), pp. 29–38.

Vanderbilt Law Review. 1988. "Special Project: Labor-Management Cooperation." Vol. 41 (April), pp. 537–666.

Viscusi, W. Kip. 1986a. "The Impact of Occupational Safety and Health Regulation, 1973–1983." *Rand Journal of Economics*, vol. 17 (Winter), pp. 567–80.

———. 1986b. "Reforming OSHA Regulation of Workplace Risks." In Leonard W. Weiss and Michael W. Klass, eds., *Regulatory Reform: What Actually Happened*. Boston: Little, Brown.

———. 1979. "The Impact of Occupational Safety and Health Regulation." *Bell Journal of Economics*, vol. 10 (Spring), pp. 117–40.

Voos, Paula B. 1984. "Trends in Union Organizing Expenditures, 1953–1977." *Industrial and Labor Relations Review*, vol. 38 (October), pp. 52–63.

———. 1983. "Union Organizing Costs and Benefits."*Industrial and Labor Relations Review*, vol. 36 (July), pp. 576–91.

Wald, Martin, and David W. Wolf. 1985. "Recent Developments in the Law of Employment at Will." *Labor Lawyer*, vol. 1 (Summer), pp. 533–54.

Ware, Norman. 1924. *The Industrial Worker, 1840–1860*. Boston: Houghton Mifflin.

Weiler, Joseph M., ed. 1981. *Interest Arbitration: Measuring Justice in Employment*. Toronto: Carswell.

Weiler, Paul. 1984. "Striking a New Balance: Freedom of Contract and the Prospects for Union Representation." *Harvard Law Review*, vol. 98, pp. 351–420.

Weitzman, Martin L. 1990. "Capitalism and Democracy: A Summing Up of the Arguments." In Samuel Bowles, Herbert Gintis, and B. Gustafsson, eds., *The Microfoundations of Political Economy*. Cambridge University Press.

Welch, Stephen. 1981. "FLSA Enforcement Policy Issues." *Report of the Minimum Wage Study Commission*, vol. 3: *Non-Compliance with the FLSA*. Government Printing Office.

Wicksell, Knut. 1958. "A New Principle of Just Taxation." In R. A. Musgrave and A. T. Peacock, eds., *Classics in the Theory of Public Finance*. Macmillan.

Winters, Richard Harrison. 1985. "Employee Handbooks and Employment-at-Will Contracts." *Duke Law Journal*, vol. 1985, pp. 196–220.

Wood, H. G. 1887. *A Treatise on the Law of Master and Servant: Covering the Relation, Duties, and Liabilities of Employers and Employees*. Albany, N.Y.: J. D. Parsons.

Cases Cited

Aiello v. *United Air Lines, Inc.*, 818 F.2d 1196 (5th Cir. 1987)
Allabashi v. *Lincoln National Sales Corp.* Case no. 89-CA-1346 (decided January 31, 1991)
American Shipbuilding Co. v. *NLRB*, 380 U.S. 300 (1965)
American Steel Foundries v. *Tri-City Central Trades Council et al.*, 257 U.S. 184 (1921)
American Textile Manufacturers Institute v. *Donovan*, 452 U.S. 490 (1981)
Banas v. *Matthews International Corp.*, 502 A.2d 637 (Pa. Super. 1985)
Cain v. *Allen Electric & Equipment Co.*, 78 N.W.2d 296 (Mich. 1956)
Cannon v. *National By-Products, Inc.*, 422 N.W.2d 638 (Iowa, 1988)
Carter v. *Kaskaskia Community Action Agency*, 24 Ill. App.3d 1056, 322 N.E.2d 574 (Ill. 1974)
Castiglione v. *Johns Hopkins Hospital*, 69 Md. App. 325, 517 A.2d 786 (Md. 1986)
Chambers v. *Valley National Bank*, 3 IER Cases, No. CIV 88-472 PCT RGS, (D.Ariz., 1988)
Continental Air Lines, Inc. v. *Keenan*, 731 P.2d 708 (Colo. 1987)
Cook v. *Heck's, Inc.*, 342 S.E.2d 453 (W.Va. 1986)
Courtney v. *Canyon Television and Appliance Rental*, 899 F.2d 845 (9th Cir. 1990)
Cronk v. *Intermountain Rural Electric Association*, 765 AP.2d 619 (Colo. App. 1988)
Dolak v. *Sullivan*, 144 A.2d 312 (Conn. 1958)

Duldulao v. *Saint Mary of Nazareth Hospital Center*, 505 N.E.2d 314 (Ill. 1987)
Ferrera v. *Nielsen*, 799 P.2d 458 (Colo. App. 1990)
Finley v. *Aetna Life and Casualty Company*, 520 A.2d 208 (Conn. 1987) at 213.
Fortune v. *National Cash Register Co.*, 364 N.E.2d 1251 (Mass. 1977)
Fournier v. *United States Fidelity and Guaranty Company*, 82 Md. App. 31, 569 A.2d 1299 (Md. 1990)
Gladden v. *Arkansas Children's Hospital*, 728 S.W.2d 501 (Ark. 1987)
Greene v. *Oliver Realty Co.*, 526 A.2d 1192 (Pa. 1987) at 1200.
Hall v. *Farmers Ins. Exchange*, 713 P.2d 1027 (Okla. 1986)
Henningsen v. *Bloomfield Motors, Inc.*, 32 N.J. 358 (1960) at 389, 161 A.2d 69 (N.J. 1960)
Hoffman-La Roche, Inc., v. *Hugh Campbell*, 512 So.2d 725 (Ala. 1987)
Hunt v. *IBM Mid America Employees Federal*, 384 N.W.2d 853 (Minn. 1986)
Industrial Union Department, AFL-CIO, v. *American Petroleum Institute*, 448 U.S. 607 (1980)
Johnston v. *Panhandle Cooperative Association*, 408 N.W.2d 261 (Neb. 1987)
Libby v. *Calais Regional Hospital*, 554 A.2d 1181 (Me. 1989)
Low v. *Rees Printing Co.*, 41 Neb. 127, 59 N.W. 362 (Neb. 1984)
McClelland v. *Northern Ireland General Health Services Board*, 1 W.L.R. 594 (1957)
McDonald v. *Mobil Coal Producing, Inc.* 789 P.2d 866 (Wyo. 1990)
Morriss v. *Coleman Company, Inc.*, 738 P.2d 841 (Kan. 1987)
National Labor Relations Board v. *Yeshiva University*, 444 U.S. 672 (1980)
Nees v. *Hock*, 536 P.2d 512 (Or. 1975)
Novosel v. *Nationwide Insurance Co.*, 721 F.2d 894 (1983)
Oil, Chemical, and Atomic Workers v. *American Cyanamid Co.*, 741 F.2d 444 (1984)
Palmateer v. *International Harvester Co.*, 421 N.E.2d 876 (Ill. 1981)
Payne v. *Western & Atlantic Railroad*, 81 Tenn. 507 (Tenn. 1884)
Perman v. *Arcventures, Inc.*, 196 Ill. App. 3d 758, 554 N.E.2d 982 (Ill. 1990)
Petermann v. *International Brotherhood of Teamsters*, 344 P.2d 25 (D.Ct. App. CA. 1959)
Pine River State Bank v. *Mettille*, 333 N.W.2d 622 (Minn. 1983)
Pugh v. *See's Candies, Inc.*, 116 Cal.App. 3d 311, App., 171 Cal.Rptr. 917 (Cal. 1981)
Richardson v. *Cole Memorial Hospital*, 466 A.2d 1084 (Pa. 1983)
Sala & Ruthe Realty, Inc. v. *Campbell*, 89 Nev 483, 515 P.2d 394 (Nev. 1973)
San Antonio Ind. School Dist. v. *Rodriguez*, 411 U.S. 1 (1973)
Small v. *Springs Industries, Inc.*, 357 S.E.2d 452 (S.C. 1987)
Sullivan v. *Snap-On Tools Corp.*, 4 IER Cases 439 (E.D. Va. March 8, 1989)
Tilbert v. *Eagle Lock Co.*, 165 A. 205 (Conn. 1933)
Toussaint v. *Blue Cross & Blue Shield of Michigan*, 292 N.W.2d 880 (Mich. 1980)

United States v. *Bethlehem Steel Corporation*, 315 U.S. 289, 326 (1942)
Weiner v. *McGraw-Hill, Inc.*, 57 N.Y.2d 458, 443 N.E.2d 441, 457 N.Y.S.2d 193 (N.Y. 1982)
Woolley v. *Hoffman-La Roche, Inc.*, 491 A.2d 1257 (1985), modified 499 A.2d 515 (N.J. Super. A.D. 1985)
Yartzoff v. *Democrat-Herald Publishing Co., Inc.*, 281 Or. 651, 576 P.2d 356 (Or. 1978)
Zaccardi v. *Zale Corp.*, 856 F.2d 1473 (10th Cir. 1988)

Index